Playing in a BIGGER *Space*

Transformational Relationships for Powerful Results

Eric de Nijs

GRACE Press

Library of Congress Control Number: 2011929648

ISBN: 978-0-9833403-0-0

First Edition

Published by:

GRACE Press

Richmond, Virginia

www.graceatwork.com

Printed in the United States of America

Dedication

This book, and the whole of G.R.A.C.E. at Work,
is dedicated to my wife,
Nancy,
who is the sunshine of my life.

She is the consummate wife, mom, friend, and all around
great person. Her love, selflessness, encouragement, humor,
and yes, grace, has made it possible for me, Paul, Melissa and Danny
to play in our bigger space.

Thank you so very much for
all your love and support.

Table of Contents

Foreword

TODAY'S world, business or life in general, means living with uncertainty and complexity in the midst of diverse, unending and often confusing issues. Sustaining and growing organizations requires leaders who draw from deeper wells than technical and business knowledge. We often define organizations in terms of size, structure, product or markets served. But Walter Truet Anderson's insightful definition discloses the clue for effective leadership:

> *"Organisations are linguistic structures built out of words*
> *and maintained by conversations."*

So what does this mean? Organizations are ultimately the outcome of human interactions, and those interactions—relationships—determine its strength, growth and longevity.

Healthy Companies International's research of CEOs who lead highly successful companies reveals that the way to adaptive, innovative and sustainable organizations is *leaders who shape an environment where people work together toward greater purpose, have freedom to develop their own capabilities, and collaborate with trust and confidence in each other.* Isn't it illuminating that the challenges in being part of a company today are answered by the base elements and roots of our humanity? Leadership success is built – above all else – on the ability to nurture powerful and productive relationships. These relationships are built through caring and purposeful dialogue, the conversations and "linguistic structures" of Anderson's statement.

The more difficult the challenge, the more important the relationship is to successfully resolving the issue. Today's leaders must communicate with diverse stakeholders to show how they listen, respond and follow-through so that the interests of all parties are understood and addressed. An executive of a large industrial company arrived as the new CEO at a time when performance issues were emerging. As these problems became more evident, he drew on his ability to listen deeply to front line workers, which built rapport so they could be candid in a workplace where openness was previously grounds for punishment. As a result of extending goodwill and building trust through deliberate and authentic ways, he helped his team focus on roadblocks to success—and effectively remove them. This leader built an environment where people knew that he cared deeply about them. They built relationships.

Nurturing those relationships takes real work. Leaders who seek to lead others on a path through creating and sustaining success for multiple, demanding stakeholders know both the difficulty—and the power—of human relationships. The leaders we work with take on the personal and professional challenge of what my colleague Eric de Nijs calls becoming "G.R.A.C.E.-full" leaders, leaders who choose to begin with Goodwill, seek Results, model Authenticity, achieve Connectivity, and enable Empowerment to achieve desired outcomes.

As you read *"Playing in a Bigger Space: Transformational Relationships for Powerful Results"* my wish is that you will find an approach that gives you the courage and genuine support to take the leadership path often less traveled in today's world, one that begins with goodwill and ultimately yields powerful results. In other words, I hope you may establish relationships, based on Eric's ideas, that resonate in your heart and soul – where the goodwill resides that is required for you to build powerful transformational relationships. The world is ready. Are you?

Leigh Shields
President, Consulting Services
HEALTHY COMPANIES INTERNATIONAL

Preface

Talking Turkey

IN 1936 Bill DeWitt and his brother Marvin saw a potential business opportunity by growing turkeys. They started with five toms and 12 hens. Three years later they processed 1200 birds for Thanksgiving. That was the year Bil-Mar Foods was officially incorporated. About 20 years later they built their first USDA inspected turkey plant and continued processing turkeys. In 1977 Bil-Mar Foods expanded into Iowa. In 1987 this company that began and thrived on dogged determination was a $200 million dollar enterprise, and was eventually sold to Sara Lee Foods.

A short time after the Sara Lee purchase of Bil-Mar Foods, I had the opportunity to interview one of the DeWitt brothers. He lived way out in the country, and it was a long dusty ride to get there. This man was, in my thinking, a "gazillionaire" and could afford to live just about anywhere he wanted. Instead of living among the elite, he chose a modest ranch where his front door overlooked the back of their processing plant, the place where the turkeys come into the building. It was a very hot day in July, with me coughing dust balls inside a diesel Rabbit with no air conditioning. In the 98 degree heat, the stench of this plant was overwhelming. I remember thinking how thankful I was that I could get an education and not have to work in a place like that. Little did I know that six months later I would be doing just that.

Sara Lee Foods brought the recently acquired DeWitt plant into their organization and had taken a "hands off" approach, watching from afar for about 18 months. After this observation period the Sara Lee leadership suggested that the "turkey plant" bring in someone from the outside for continued improvement, cost savings, and management development. That someone was me, and there I was, inside the plant where I marveled that anyone would work.

Initially I was hired as a training coordinator, working for another fellow who had responsibility for three such meat (beef, pork and poultry) processing plants in Ohio, Michigan and Iowa. My ultimate task was to get all three plants to participate in decision making at the lowest levels of the company. This would not be easy, as historically Bil-Mar Foods had operated under a typical paternalistic, and somewhat "command and control" manner. Leadership made all the decisions. They took care of you, but you worked for them. Employer-Supervisor elationships were highly transactional, and a formal process for participative decision making was not available to hourly employees, limiting the potential for any collaborative process.

I began working with middle managers and salaried professionals, mixing up the teams so there was the beginning of cross-functionality. I trained around process management and improvement, attempting to get everyone at the middle level on teams so they would understand the process, improve the process, and make it better, faster and easier for everyone. At this point, however, I did not have the trust or goodwill of the folks I was working with. I was working in the manufacturing division, down at the nitty gritty level, and this kind of out of the box thinking didn't sit well after years and years of a "just do your job" enforced attitude.

One of the senior leaders there observed that I was struggling. He made a seemingly simple suggestion, but one that changed everything. He recommended that I get to actually know the guys I was working with. Go down on the floor, see what they were doing, take them to lunch, help them understand me and each other. Slowly we turned a corner as we began to know each other, and they understood I wasn't there to make them miserable. A relationship was forming.

One of my less enjoyable functions was to serve as liaison between these floor workers and the accounting department. If they wanted to change something, they had to provide me with the documentation and explanations I would need to take to Accounting to validate the improvements. This was always a complicated process, and as I was getting more acquainted with the various systems another senior leader took me under his wing and gave me an opportunity to learn and grow. He taught me everything I needed to know, and then some, spending an inordinate amount of time with me. He didn't have a reputation of being that benevolent with others, but for some reason, we just "clicked." We learned a lot from each other, and to this day, I still call him from time to time. It amazed me to think that this guy was from corporate, and I was a dinky training coordinator, and he afforded me the time to grow. He asked me insightful questions and essentially acted as my coach. I ended up reporting to this leader a short time later. I was truly grateful for his investment in me.

I seriously thought about what went into our relationship and why it worked. I realized, more than anything else, it was based on goodwill and trust. He was truly interested in helping me. He found ways to seriously connect with me on various levels, and was interested in not only my job, but me personally.

At a certain point I wanted to challenge him on something he wanted to do, and I remember thinking that this guy had the power to either put me out for good, or help me advance. I decided to go ahead, based on what I experienced of his goodwill and trust toward me. That first time I was scared to death. I couldn't stop my left leg from shaking! As we sat on the couch in his office my hands were cold and my mouth dry, but I told him that he shouldn't really do what he wanted to do. I waited for the ax to fall.

He was amazed I would challenge him, but he agreed to talk about it. He gave me an opportunity to prove my point. I wasn't entirely successful, but he appreciated the fact I would stand up to him and give him something else to think about. That was a turning point for me, thinking about how to challenge more senior people, and to trust that these people are really on your side. They will appreciate what you are trying to do, and they will process through it. And, if they don't, it's probably not the place you want to work anyway.

I knew I always had to be real with this guy and have my ducks — *or turkeys* — in a row, and connect with him and his understanding of what he wanted to do. But after that day I knew where I was standing in conversations with him. He was quite a character and had a number of sayings that I learned to translate. For example, one of his favorites was *"Hey, I got this great idea."* The actual interpretation of this meant that he had something he wanted me to try and make work for him. Many of these I would attempt, but some would fail. On those occasions I'd report back later and he would ask me where in the world I got that idea! Another such remark was *"What else you got for me?"* after I'd ask him about an idea I had. This is code for *"Listen moron, you haven't thought this through!"*

I had a number of similar relationships and responsibilities with various other leaders in this company. The people behind the leaders, once known, were real. The work I did with and for these people was enhanced by the relationships we established and maintained over the years. Some time later I found myself reflecting on the work I did here, and the people I worked with. The many relationships I made here caused me to spend some dedicated time to identify what was special about them, and what really made them work, both for the individuals and for the organization.

People don't really care about how much you know, until they know how much you care.

The first thing on the list of things that made these relationships productive was what I called generosity, or a willingness to give, as well as trust. I didn't call it goodwill until a bit later. In those moments I just thought they were being gracious. I realized that our best work came when we were clear on the desired outcomes, and that the best work was done by creating a safe place for me and others to grow, to develop different perspectives and experience the unselfish support of a team working toward mutual shared purposes. "Me" and "you" became a united "us" – a bigger and better entity that yielded bigger and better results. As the various elements and components of these working relationships became clear to me, I ultimately did my dissertation based on my work in this place.

People don't really care about how much you know, until they know how much you care. That's the way it was in this situation. It wasn't really about process improvement, but change management from a leader's perspective to bring all-around improvement to benefit everyone. Over the years I continued to think about those working experiences and relationships. The actual model of *G.R.A.C.E. at Work* went through a number of renditions and changes until I believe I was given this ultimate working model. I am now an executive coach serving clients through this reliable, tried-and-true model that encourages coaching others, developing trust, extending goodwill and transparency and growing a safe space for everyone to grow and experience success.

Whoever said you can't soar with the eagles when you live (and work) among the turkeys didn't know about G.R.A.C.E. at Work. Working with turkeys taught me quite a lot. It is the place my relationships learned how to fly, and the place where G.R.A.C.E. was born.

Welcome to G.R.A.C.E. at Work,
Dr. Eric de Nijs

Chapter 1

The Quest for Balance

Balancing Strategy and Relationships

It is the harmony of the diverse parts, their symmetry, their happy balance; in a word it is all that introduces order, all that gives unity, that permits us to see clearly and to comprehend at once both the ensemble and the details.

— Henri Poincare

The Great Quest for Balance

BALANCE is literally defined as stability that is produced by even distribution or equality of generally opposing or interacting things or forces. It is a condition that affords maximum stability or steadiness, whether speaking of our planet, business, or life in general. It is the realized state of equilibrium, where everything works together to sustain optimum conditions for growth, whatever kind of growth we want to realize.

In our universe, precise balance holds everything together. Consider these amazing facts and figures concerning the perfect equilibrium of our universe:

- If the **rotation period** of the earth was longer, the day and night temperature differences would be too great. It if was shorter, the atmospheric wind velocities would be too high.

- If earth's **surface gravity** was stronger, the planet's atmosphere would retain huge amounts of ammonia and methane, making it toxic to life. If it was weaker, the earth's atmosphere would lose too much water to sustain life.

- **Matter and energy** exist in specific, and finite, amounts and cannot be created or destroyed. It is in perfect balance.

- If our **gravitation interaction with the moon** was greater, tidal effects on the oceans, atmosphere and rotational period would be too severe. If it was less, the earth's orbital obliquity would change too much, causing climatic instabilities.

- We have just enough **seismic activity**. If there were more earthquakes, we would have greater destruction of too many life-forms. If we had less, the nutrients on the ocean floors would not be uplifted and available for intake.

These are just a few of the literally hundreds of balanced physical conditions on this planet and within this universe that allow us to live here. But we know about the importance of balance for many other reasons. Most of us have come to understand that when we do not balance our checkbooks, we will be unpleasantly surprised eventually, usually having to pay for such folly. We also learned about balance in a memorable way the first time we plopped down on the high end of a teeter-totter, or when we eat too much, don't sleep enough, or neglect any other of a number of life issues that must be balanced for optimal growth and well-being. It is no different in business. Stability, and ultimately growth–in business, or in life–cannot be achieved without balance.

The People Factor

Organizational health, the bottom line, depends on balance, in many areas, and of many things. But it seems that we are just now getting back to understanding the importance of relationships in business and balancing the loudly lauded strategy with those relationships. For too many years we have placed all our eggs in the strategy or tactical basket, focusing heavily on what we do, instead of who we do it with. We have lost sight of the people factor while concentrating only on the bottom line. We seem to have forgotten that nothing is achieved, nothing is gained, without doing it in partnership with others. We might have achieved some level of success, for some limited period of time with these tactics, but it won't last, and it won't yield sustainable growth. It is time to return to the understanding, and the practice, that our business results rely on the people who do the work of that business. Without people, there *is* no bottom line.

Merely understanding that fact is only part of the equation for achieving better business results. Along the way, we have also apparently forgotten the lessons

> BALANCE =
> sustained
> equilibrium
> of interacting
> forces
> to afford
> optimum
> dynamic
> conditions
> for growth.

about dynamics of human interaction, and how to build and maintain the relationships necessary to achieve optimal results, whether referencing the bottom line, or individual and community well-being. Studies have shown that in our race to achieve, to gain more stuff, we have not at all bettered our level of happiness or contentment. We have fostered an environment of achievement alone, leaving relationships and wellness (in body, mind and spirit) in the dust. This condition has found its way into the business world as well. Building relationships should not be about targeting a better annual report, or achieving a bigger bonus, while trying to milk people for all they're worth. Motives are highly transparent and cannot be faked or produced for the sole purpose of padding already fat wallets. Short term relationships built with these motives may succeed for a short time, but will ultimately backfire. Relationship building must be approached with sincerity and a genuine desire to honor one another and build meaningful partnerships for shared purposes.

> Without people, there is no bottom line.

Balancing Strategy and Relationships

STRATEGY	RELATIONSHIPS

THERE is a long-standing and proven basic formula for business success that yields solid results. Results are always the product of two powerful and balanced components: Strategy, a strong, comprehensive set of competencies that deal with the tactical and strategic operations of any business, and powerful relationships that ensure these operations are successfully executed. Many organizations lose sight of the fact that both are required for desired results. Solid strategy cannot deliver results, unless driven by powerful, productive relationships within and without the organization. It is vital to have both. One cannot deliver strong results without the other. They must be inseparable.

Strategy + Relationships = Results

Transforming Balance

Successful leadership requires balance, on many points. The first point of balance is between STRATEGY and RELATIONSHIPS. **STRATEGY and tactical behavior** can be based on any number of leadership models, organizational direction and vision, leadership styles, etc. The Baldrige National Quality Program Criteria for Performance Excellence is used as a standard to represent the strategic side of business, when it is portrayed in relationship with the *G.R.A.C.E. at Work* model family. All organizations make their own suitable choice for strategy. *G.R.A.C.E. at Work* does not address strategy, except as it relates to the relationship side of successful leadership.

RELATIONSHIPS in business should be based on sound human dynamics, or what is proven to yield productive relationships. **G.R.A.C.E. at Work** provides a simple yet profound model for such relationships—anywhere, with anyone. It is based on the balance of five components: **Goodwill, Results, Authenticity, Connectivity and Empowerment.**

The Dynamic Dartboard

To facilitate understanding of this organizational success model, let's picture a dartboard of sorts. The center of the board represents the relationships. The next "ring" is the strategic or operational component of business results. The outer ring represents the results themselves. The center of this model representing relationships is so placed because relationships must drive and empower strategy. This can be pictured with an arrow flowing from the center outward toward the results ring. It is also important to visualize this model as dynamic, not static. Each aspect of powerful relationships, which we will investigate a little later, dramatically influences each aspect of strategic operations. This can be pictured as "wheels within wheels" on this model.

Strategy

It is not the purpose of this book to thoroughly discuss business strategy. However, in order to illustrate a strong organizational success model, the Baldrige National Quality Program Criteria for Performance Excellence is used to highlight the strategy portion of this model. There are literally hundreds of organizational leadership competency models and strategies to choose from, but if an organization designs its strategy around these Criteria, it is significantly increasing its chances of success. It is not our purpose to dictate or highlight the strategic operations of any organization, but to couple a powerful relationship model with a powerful strategic model to show how results are achieved. The Baldrige Criteria is developed by the National Institute of Standards and Technology, based on what is considered the highest standards for business strategies and integrity. Each year this partnership between government and private organizations bestows its coveted "Malcom Baldrige National Quality Award" on organizations who exhibit these high standards in leadership and business results. There are seven basic core criteria contained in the Baldrige National Quality Program.

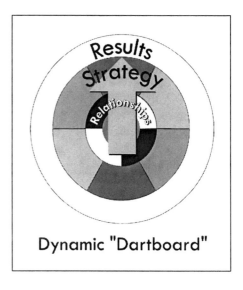

Dynamic "Dartboard"

- **LEADERSHIP**
- **STRATEGIC PLANNING**
- **CUSTOMER AND MARKET FOCUS**
- **MEASUREMENT ANALYSIS AND KNOWLEDGE MANAGEMENT**
- **HUMAN RESOURCES FOCUS**
- **PROCESS MANAGEMENT**
- **RESULTS**

In the Baldrige model, each core criteria includes a number of elements and processes necessary to make each criteria complete. These are specified in great detail by Baldrige as their Program Criteria for Performance Excellence. Again, it is not the purpose of this book to detail strategic excellence, but merely to use a model

Given by the President of the United States, The Malcolm Baldrige National Quality Award recognizes both public and private U.S. organizations in the business, health care, education, and nonprofit sectors for performance excellence. This award program is administered by the Baldrige Performance Excellence Program, based at and managed by the National Institute of Standards and Technology, part of the U.S. Department of Commerce. This program was established by the Malcolm Baldrige National Quality Improvement Act of 1987 (Public Law 100–107), and is named for Malcolm Baldrige, United States Secretary of Commerce from 1981 until 1987.

"The Baldrige Criteria for Performance Excellence are about winning! They are about winning business success with a high-performing, high integrity, ethical organization…. The Criteria help organizations respond to current challenges and address all the complexities of delivering today's results while preparing effectively for the future."

Harry S. Hertz,
Director
Baldrige National
Quality Program

of excellence to highlight the importance of balanced strategy and relationships. Anyone interested in the Baldrige Criteria may obtain abundant information at their website.

For purposes of our illustration, we have placed the first six core criteria into the strategy portion of our model. The last Baldrige core criteria is called Results, so we will separate that from the other six. Results are the bottom line. They are what we are all seeking to achieve. They are the direct result of the performance of the other six criteria. We have fashioned a "wheel" containing the first six Baldrige criteria as the "Strategy (inner) Wheel" with the Results criteria forming the "outer wheel."

The seventh Baldrige criteria is Business Results, which, for purposes of this model, is shown as the sum of the relationship plus strategy, or the outer ring of the dynamic dartboard. The overall "Results" wheel will typically include:

- **Product and Service Results**
- **Customer Results**
- **Financial Market Results**
- **Human Resources Results**
- **Operational Performance Results**
- **Leadership and Social Responsibility Results**

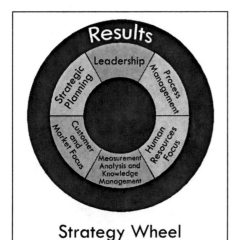

Strategy Wheel
Baldrige Criteria

Relationships

As our "dartboard" shows, powerful relationships are at the heart of strong business results. Before all the strategies can be implemented, they must be built on a foundation of cohesive, dynamic, and strong relationships. While organizations may incorporate independent strategic models to govern their operations, they cannot avoid the fact that powerful relationships are the heart, the bull's-eye, of successful business results. Without these powerful and productive relationships no strategy can provide the kind of results every business desires, and needs, for ultimate survival.

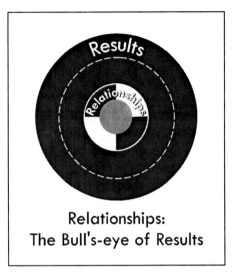

Relationships:
The Bull's-eye of Results

G.R.A.C.E. at Work: An Overview

G.R.A.C.E. at Work is an elegantly simple model to ensure these powerful relationships. It is composed of five elements that address all the facets of productive relationships, which in turn will empower operations to yield results.

- **Goodwill**
- **Results** *(Reasons for Relationship)*
- **Authenticity**
- **Connectivity**
- **Empowerment**

G.R.A.C.E. at Work is typically represented with a diamond shaped graphic, and will be seen this way throughout this book. To fit our "dartboard" illustration, however, we are going to show it as a circle in this introductory material — the bull's-eye of Results.

G.R.A.C.E. at Work
The 5 Components

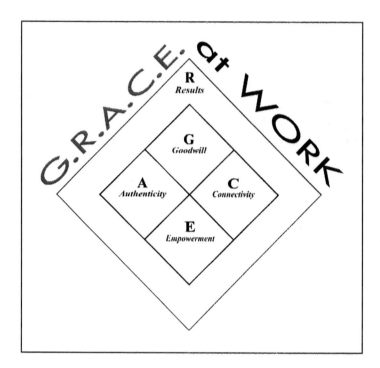

> It is the creation of a safe place for people to perform....

An interaction model that facilitates trust and transparency is needed to guide performance and productivity in the workplace. Powerful relationships can form the basis for achieving breakthrough performance and building the capacity for future growth. Whether you are an executive, manager, coach, or colleague, *G.R.A.C.E. at Work* can provide greater opportunities to build relationships and facilitate performance. Employees and leaders are authentic, achieve a special kind of chemistry for growth, empower each other and extend good will.

The Safe Space of G.R.A.C.E.

The practice of *G.R.A.C.E. at Work* is the creation of a safe place for people to perform—within stated boundaries—without fear of failure. Without G.R.A.C.E., business (and other) relationships are reduced to a series of transactional interactions that neither satisfy nor inspire, and generally will not produce desired results.

The diagram on the next page depicts the two kinds of relationships possible, and their expected results. A relationship, whether business, professional or personal, will either be **transactional,** or **transformational.** The *transactional* relationship is shown to the "northwest" of the dotted line, and the *transformational* relationship to the "southeast." The transactional relationship does not contain any of what we can call a "click" factor *(more on this in Chapter 2),* or what seems to make relationships work. It is all about compliance *(following the rules),* as opposed to the transformational relationship which relies on the solid commitment of the partners to yield results. A transformational relationship changes people by enabling them to dream, comfort, explore, heal, grow and celebrate together through the five components of *G.R.A.C.E. at Work.*

...an interactive, interrelational model that is dynamic... not static.

It all begins with **Goodwill**. Goodwill, in fact, drives all the other elements of *G.R.A.C.E. at Work,* and all the other components of any tactical model. Goodwill involves assuming positive intent, suspending judgment, looking out for the other person's best interest, giving without condition, offering forgiveness, being at peace with what is, providing support and safety in times of risk and failure. It's about making things all right, regardless of what is happening in the relationship.

The **Results** component actually contains three "R"'s: Reason, Relationship and Results. It is the reason for being in a relationship, which ultimately yields results. It focuses on the ability of all parties to mutually create meaning and value. It is a shared sense of purpose. A key enabler for this attribute is self-knowledge and an ability to empathize with others.

A glue that holds this model together is **Authenticity**—being real with yourself and others. Being real means choosing how you wish to relate to others, declaring what your stand is, holding yourself accountable for your

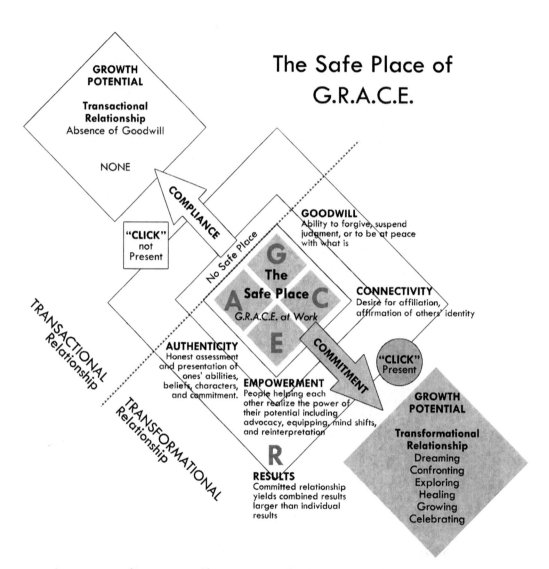

actions, rewarding yourself appropriately, being open and vulnerable, openly communicating needs, desires, moods, attitudes, values and feelings —even about the other person.

Connectivity means finding ways to identify with, affirm and encourage the other person, understanding how the other person feels, what is important to them, sharing assumptions and beliefs, identifying and realizing differences in intention and impact on others, and the genuine desire to associate with and relate to others.

Empowerment is helping others overcome obstacles, develop new skills, establishing a safe environment to succeed (for self and others), creating catalysts for change, helping others see potential and possibilities, being open to possibilities, allowing time for testing and learning, seeing the larger whole but being aware of smaller components.

When these five components are combined in the right order and the right context, they will yield a powerful, purposeful and productive relationship which advances the goals of both the organization and the professional. This model is explored in greater detail in the next chapter.

The Dynamics

Now let's reassemble our dartboard. Remember that this is an interactive, inter-relational model that is dynamic in nature, not static. Business moves quickly, and at any given moment, a different issue will need attention. The more consistently both models (relationships and strategy) are practiced in tandem, the more natural will be the right response to any given business need. To get a feel for how this model works interactively, we'll try lining up various aspects of both models.

Let's spin the wheels and line up the **RESULTS** element of the *G.R.A.C.E. at Work* model for powerful relationships with one of the Baldrige Criteria, #1, Leadership, and choose one of their criteria to illustrate how these models work together.

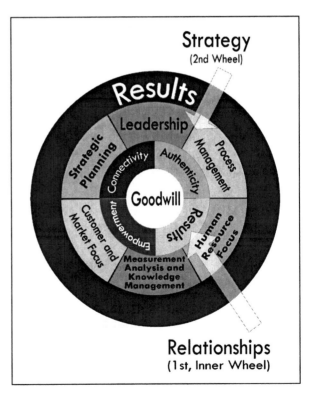

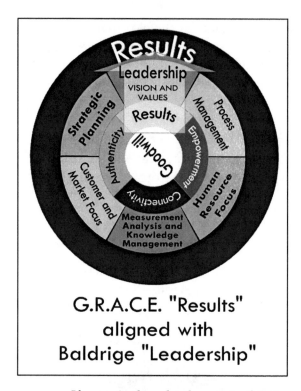

G.R.A.C.E. "Results" aligned with Baldrige "Leadership"

Vision and Values is at the top of the Baldrige Leadership Criteria list. To achieve results, all actions are relationship-based, and performed through the lens of the **RESULTS** component of the *G.R.A.C.E. at Work* model. Leadership clearly understands the reasons for organizational being, employee and/or customer relationships, and expected **RESULTS**, which drive all operations, and impart a sense of shared purpose and mutual value. This understanding is incorporated into stated vision and values that clearly define the reason for organizational relationships, and how the organization does business to achieve the results.

If we spin the wheel again to this time align the **CONNECTIVITY** component of the *G.R.A.C.E. at Work* model with the Baldrige Vision and Values criteria (under the main criteria of Leadership), we can further identify how strategy and relationships work together in balance. Under the influence of the **CONNECTIVITY** component, leadership has a genuine desire to connect with employees, customers, stakeholders, etc., and finds ways to identify with and affirm others. Vision and Values and associated strategies are created to have connection points and appropriate engagement methods for all parties.

And so, on it goes. For every point in the Baldrige Criteria, or any other organizational strategy or process, the elements of powerful relationships as contained within the *G.R.A.C.E. at Work* model will drive these strategic operations with foundational relationship attitudes, behaviors and competencies. This model can also serve as a powerful tool in reverse, to pinpoint breakdowns, and highlight where repairs and corrections need to occur.

This book, and the *G.R.A.C.E. at Work* model, are about building powerful relationships, that when coupled with sound strategy, will produce strong results. This is success from the inside out.

In order for *G.R.A.C.E. at Work* to really be effective, however, it requires developing an internal sense of open doors and opportunities to make a choice to extend Goodwill. The *G.R.A.C.E. at Work* model will anchor your efforts, giving the needed framework for relationships that are committed, not just compliant. But all the advance plans on paper *(or in a book)* mean nothing until someone breathes life into them. There will be many opportunities in this book to plan, but I hope you actually embody and embrace *G.R.A.C.E. at Work* to give your relationships life, to play in a bigger space, and to realize more powerful results.

G.R.A.C.E. "Connectivity" aligned with Baldrige "Leadership"

G.R.A.C.E. at Work yields a powerful, purposeful and productive relationship which advances the goals of both the organization and the professional.

Chapter 2

G.R.A.C.E. at Work

*The Model for
Transformational Relationships*

"Gettin' good players is easy.
Gettin' 'em to play together is the hard part."

--*Casey Stengel*

New Social Contract

JUST a short generation ago an implied mutual contract existed between organizations and their employees. The company would provide long-term secure employment in return for employee loyalty. It wasn't uncommon for someone to begin a career in his or her early 20's, and years later retire from the same company, taking home the coveted gold watch and good wishes. As business and economic conditions changed, however, so did this unspoken agreement of lasting relationship. The "effective career lifetime" of employees during the late 1970s and early 1980s was found to average about 25 years. In the 1990s that number dropped to just a little over five years. Today, some have estimated that time to be as little as 18 months. Job security, fulfillment, safety and lasting relationships have been swept out onto the street with the rest of the workplace turnover statistics. The workplace today has morphed into something less friendly and more intimidating. It is characterized by outsourcing, reorganization, streamlining, exploding technology and the need for speed. The old implied social work contract is forever broken. The notion of the old social contract whereby employers and employees would grow old together is now a fond memory, a romantic relic of the workplace.

> The notion of the old social contract whereby employers and employees would grow old together is now a fond memory, a romantic relic of the workplace.

We can't go back to those days either, even if we wanted to. The swift corporate current will drown you if you stop paddling. But we have traveled, too quickly, from a place of win-win working relationships to a sorry state of survival of the fittest. Is there a way to return to mutual benefit for employer and employee? A safe place that fosters productivity and powerful results for both the organization and the professional? Yes, there is. This book will introduce a simple but proven model for turning the business battlefield into a winning playing field—a model that involves a fundamental change in attitude and approach to leadership. It isn't about a checklist of competencies and behaviors. It's about building a new kind of powerful relationship between an employer and an employee that creates mutually satisfying results for today, and sets up the players for success in the future.

RELATIONSHIP:

"a state of affairs existing between those having relations or dealings."

Reviving Relationships: Leadership Key

Webster's Dictionary defines relationship as *"a state of affairs existing between those having relations or dealings."* What we need to know, however, is not the definition, but the condition of the relationship. A vital leadership model for today's business environment would be one based on trust and transparency between leaders and employees that can weather the storms of outsourcing, downsizing and the "unpredictables"—good and bad—of business as usual. It would create a compelling vision that captures the hearts and souls of those engaged in the pursuit of the organization's goals, and generate mutual benefit for employer and employee.

And this approach is precisely what is missing in today's corporate culture. These relationships are what died during the transition from a social contract for lifetime work to a frantic, distrustful and self-advocating work survival culture. Webster's definition above assumes a relationship between those "having relations or dealings." But what we've done is remove the relationship from the relations. The organization, employer and employee may have dealings together, but the relationship has been abandoned.

Developing relationships is the single-most critical success element for any leadership model. Leaders who develop powerful, purposeful, productive relationships with their employees *(for mutual benefit—we can't repeat that too often!)* are more likely to inspire greater productivity, career growth, innovation and overall employee performance. Studies have shown that managers and leaders who excel at employee development—building a relationship—realize a full 25% improvement in performance and productivity. The facts are clear: an employer-employee relationship based on mutual benefit and commitment will impact the bottom line—in no small way.

> Developing relationships is the single most critical success element for any leadership model.

Powerful and Productive Relationships

The "Click" of Powerful Relationships

Can you recall a powerful relationship in your life where you just seemed to "click" with the other person or group? You can't really put your finger on it, but for some reason you just felt right, comfortable and accepted, and the relationship was productive. You simply and profoundly, "clicked." "Click" seems to defy definition, and is an elusive quality, but in reality it is the meshing and balancing of several components. Bring to mind one of your relationships where it could be said "we just clicked." What adjectives would you use to describe this relationship? Chances are very good that you could define, characterize and diagram this relationship's "click factor" into five categories: Goodwill, Results, Authenticity, Connectivity and Empowerment—the five components of the G.R.A.C.E. model. "Click" is not coincidental or accidental. It is the result of practicing G.R.A.C.E. And, it is what makes relationships powerful and productive.

We know we're in a powerful relationship when we can trust the other person implicitly and help each other

click!

achieve our goals. A powerful relationship is a relationship based on a mutual commitment to a shared purpose that provides affirmation, inspiration, and personal transformation. Powerful relationships, relationships that "click," are transformational in that they facilitate change and the ability to do things that require a great amount of trust.

The Continuum of Relationships

Relationships exist on a continuum with transactional relationships on one end and transformational relationships on the other. **Transactional** relationships are, as the name implies, those where a transaction occurs on the basis of one party requesting the help of the other. These transactions can be formal

or informal, simple or complex. They are at the heart of how we get things done everyday in every organization across the world. Listed below are a few examples:

- Your team involves IT specialists and they're asked to provide some highly specialized expertise

- Your finance team produces quarterly business updates for the organization

- You're asked to critique a proposal for a new business venture

These kinds of interactions are very results-focused and can be positioned to minimize the time spent on people's moods, attitudes, and feelings.

Transformational relationships, at the opposite end of the continuum, involve a deeper level of interaction between the people in the relationship. These interactions necessitate a greater measure of trust and facilitate a greater awareness of the risks and opportunities that the relationship can offer. Transformation in the relationship may be greater for one person than the other but change does occur either in the way people in the relationship view themselves, the other person, or their ability to perform a given competency. Some examples may include:

- A results-oriented leader is confronted by his dictatorial approach and realizes that his behavior is driving a wedge between himself and his people. He works hard at creating a more participative style of leadership.

- A soft spoken leader realizes the need to create a stronger, more visible presence in the organization. She creates and articulates her purpose and her passion for her work in such a way that people are motivated by her leadership.

- An analytically-oriented leader can't understand why his team didn't seem to be motivated by the data he presented. In fact, his team was put off by his presentation and now he senses a deeper rift between him and his team. He gets a coach and learns how to leverage his emotional intelligence.

The negative aspect of the transactions above forced individuals to look deeper in themselves and their relationships. It is possible, although not probable, that you could develop transformational relationships with all the people with whom you interact. However, time and priorities will limit the number of transformational relationships you can have. But you can create the conditions for others to grow and develop. In this way, the relationship sits more heavily on the transformational end of the continuum, rather than transactional.

Building Blocks of Powerful Relationships

A foundation of trust is one of the most important measures to determine the strength of a relationship.

THE CASE FOR *Powerful Relationships*

- Create an environment where people can maximize their talents.

- Help organizations and individuals develop greater trust with co-workers.

- Do a better job of taking "politics" out of the work place.

- Help people resolve conflict more effectively and efficiently.

- Foster better decision making aligned with values.

- Be more effective and efficient with fewer resources.

- Create more powerful conversations.

- Make work a more meaningful and fulfilling part of workers' lives.

Trust is the act of placing confidence or belief in someone or something. It also implies creating an environment that is conducive to trust for all parties involved. It has the connotation of extending credit, or assuming good rather than bad of people, and of situations. It is about placing trust, and encouraging trust. Trust is confident reliance on the character, ability, strength, or truth of someone or something. Trust must have a dynamic, back-and-forth, environment to thrive. People in strong relationships recognize the need for and contribution of trust, but also for shared purpose. For example, I can trust someone to fulfill their commitments but if we don't create a shared sense of purpose, we really don't have the basis for engaging ourselves in building something bigger than either one of us could do individually. People in powerful relationships utilize trust as the fuel for creating momentum. Relationships start with trust, and build on trust. For every fulfilled commitment, every achieved result, trust grows, and the relationship grows. Relationships are always dynamic, or they are not really a relationship. They are either growing or dying; there is no such thing as a static relationship.

However, powerful relationships rely on more than trust and purpose. People in powerful relationships extend to each other unconditional acceptance and unmerited favor — *the fundamental building blocks of the most powerful relationships*. Unconditional acceptance means acknowledging and accepting people for who they are, with strengths and weaknesses. Unmerited favor means giving time, opportunity, or resources *disproportionate* to what is deserved or expected. It means going the extra mile even when the circumstances would not require it. It can be said to define the word "grace."

> People in powerful relationships utilize trust as the fuel for creating momentum.

Powerful relationships are transformational in that they facilitate change and the ability to do things that require a great amount of trust. We've all had those relationships where we "clicked" with people — when everything about the relationship was right. It's that special connection felt with certain people that allows us to be who we are. We share a common purpose. We tend to be more trusting in these relationships and have a greater tendency to forgive and forget. We also tend to find that we are more readily able to give and receive. These people are most likely practicing certain attributes that can be understood through an acronym called "G.R.A.C.E."

> Trust must have a dynamic, back-and-forth, environment to survive.

G.R.A.C.E. at Work

G.R.A.C.E. AT WORK is an interactive relationship model that yields the trust and transparency necessary to guide performance and productivity in the workplace, and is essential for achieving results. Powerful relationships can form the basis for achieving breakthrough performance and building the capacity for future growth.

Powerful relationships emerge only through the presence and practice of *five key components:* Goodwill, Results, Authenticity, Connectivity and Empowerment. These five components are the basis and foundation for the *G.R.A.C.E. at Work* model. When all elements are present, and functioning together as a finely tuned and diligently maintained vehicle for relationships, true grace is present.

G.R.A.C.E. at Work creates a safe space for people to share their deepest feelings, their vulnerabilities, and their aspirations, and gives them the opportunity to learn new things in a safe environment. The space of *G.R.A.C.E. at Work* enables transformational relationships.

G.

Goodwill provides support and safety in times of risk and failure. Its about making things all right regardless of what's going on in the relationship.

R.

Results are about the goals of the relationship, the reason for being together. It creates a shared sense of purpose and answers "for the sake of what" are we coming together.

A.

Authenticity declares that people in the relationship need to be able to express themselves openly, communicating their needs, desires, moods, attitudes, and feelings. And they also need to be able to share how they feel about the other person.

C.

Connectivity is the desire for affiliation and affirmation with a significant other. Connectivity relies heavily on empathy but also on a desire and intention to associate with someone.

E.

Empowerment is the process of helping people overcome obstacles or develop new skills, providing resources to meet goals and generally pave the way to growth and results achievement. Helping others create a catalyst for change means helping people help themselves.

Whether you are an executive, manager, coach, or colleague, *G.R.A.C.E. at Work* can provide greater opportunities to build relationships and facilitate performance. Employees and leaders are authentic, achieve a special kind of chemistry for growth, empower each other and extend goodwill. It is the creation of a safe place for people to perform—*within stated boundaries*—without fear of failure.

The generally understood concepts behind the word "grace" lend themselves to this model well. Grace usually brings to mind two ideas. One, simply put, is unmerited favor. In other words, we are treated much better than we deserve. The other is a certain poise or elegance in movement. Both of these ideas contribute to leading with grace. G.R.A.C.E. leadership assumes goodwill, which will many times translate into undeserved favor. In a leadership state of G.R.A.C.E., energy is abundant and performance effortless. Obstacles are anticipated, but with the expectation that they will be overcome. Failure is seen as an opportunity to learn. This does not imply that this kind of relationship is pain free or even easy. It requires effort, commitment and yes, grace. But the anticipation and realization of success supersedes pain and difficulty.

> **Without G.R.A.C.E., what remains is a series of transactional interactions that neither satisfy nor inspire.**

Leading with G.R.A.C.E. encourages people to learn new things and express themselves authentically in a safe environment. G.R.A.C.E. encourages commitment, not compliance, because G.R.A.C.E. assumes that development and high performance occur most effectively in the context of a purposeful relationship. Without G.R.A.C.E., what remains is a series of transactional interactions that neither satisfy nor inspire.

The graphic representation of the model of *G.R.A.C.E. at Work* is presented on the following page. We will begin with the *basic* model, which consists of five diamonds, four inside one. We will then take it apart one component at a time, one attribute at time, to reveal its detailed content and power. After the components are presented, we will assemble the *master* model, with the detail of each component indicated visually.

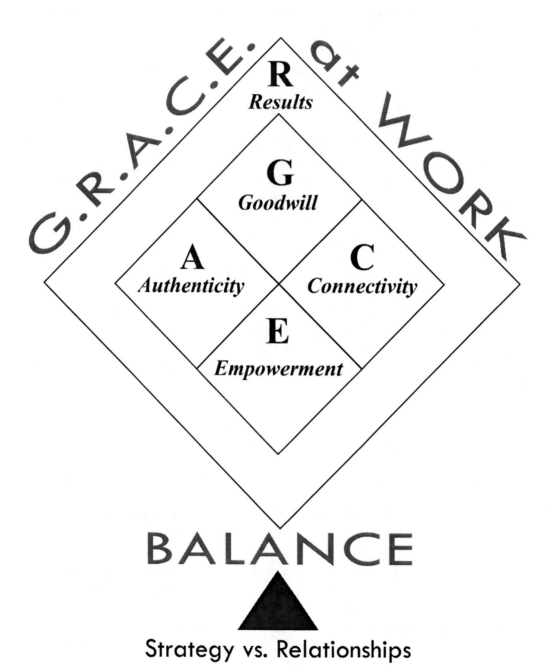

We have already discussed the critical element of balance. In business, and really in any venue, it is the balance between strategy and relationship. The entire G.R.A.C.E. model rests on this delicate balance. This balance also involves something we have not yet introduced - *Dynamic Tensions*. We will discuss those later in this book, but keep in mind that they will affect the balance of the entire model.

Notice that the model is represented by a large diamond, which is balanced "on point." *(You will be seeing a lot of diamonds throughout this book.)* Within the larger diamond are several smaller diamonds. The larger diamond is labeled "Results." This is the "R" component in G.R.A.C.E. and literally holds the other components within. The ultimate size of this outer diamond (the extent of the results achieved) is directly proportional to the size of each of the inner diamond components. In other words, the results achieved in any relationship are dependent upon the size and balance of the other inner components.

For every one of the five acronym components (G, R, A, C, E) there are seven attributes which contain and define the behaviors typical for each component. In the outer diamond, the Results component, those attributes are shown in the dark gray diamond. The attributes of the other components are also seen surrounding the diamonds of the remaining four components (G, A, C, E). Just as the these four components are the "heart" of Results, so also each other component has a "heart" or core which helps define this part of the G.R.A.C.E. model.

Have you ever seen the famous brightly painted Russian nesting dolls? There are several wooden dolls of varying sizes that fit inside one another, beginning with the larger "outer" doll. If you keep unpacking and opening the dolls, another one is revealed inside. In some respects it is the same with the *G.R.A.C.E. at Work* model. We will begin unpacking the model one piece at a time. Instead of the outer diamond, however, we will begin where the entire model begins: with Goodwill.

Chapter 3

The Components of G.R.A.C.E.

Ralph Waldo Emerson said:

"Beauty without grace is the hook without the bait."

I'd like to rephrase that to

"ANYTHING without grace is a hook without the bait."

GOODWILL: *It All Begins Here*

THE basis for G.R.A.C.E., both from the start and all the way to the finish, is Goodwill. According to Webster's Dictionary, Goodwill can be defined as:

1) a kindly feeling of approval and support; benevolent interest or concern, the favor or prestige that a business has acquired beyond the mere value of what it sells; and

2) cheerful consent, willing effort.

Any of these definitions requires effort and intention, and must demonstrate in tangible, or intangible, ways achievement of some standard or expectation that means something to the organization and the people it serves.

Goodwill: The fuel of high performance relationships.

Attributes of Goodwill become success criteria for every interaction the organization has with its various constituents, including employees, customers, partners, regulators, and community neighbors. They are manifest in behaviors such as assuming positive intent, suspending judgment, looking out for the other person's best interest, giving without condition, offering forgiveness, being at peace with what is, providing support and safety in times of risk and failure, and being grateful. This component is expressed by sincerely desiring to benefit others, and to work for their benefit. In a successful cycle of high performance, on an individual or organizational level, the fuel is always Goodwill.

Goodwill is the ultimate basis for a trusting relationship. Without it, the relationship will be reduced to mere tactics and stressed strategic actions in order to achieve some shared goal. In the absence of Goodwill, trust starves and ultimately dies completely, and you will not be able to align purposes or goals for the relationship. In an employee-manager or boss relationship, the employee's behavior resorts to compliance, following the rules to avoid confrontation, rather than true collaboration and initiation of new ideas or growth. The employee who does not experience, or exhibit, Goodwill in a dynamic (give and get) relationship, will "fear the stick" and will not offer more than he or she is expected to give.

We can make basic observations about being human, which require various measures of Goodwill:

- We all make mistakes; none of us is perfect
- We could all do things better
- We all desire relationship
- We all desire to make a contribution
- We all desire to be recognized for who we are, or what we bring to the relationship

Ultimately, it's about making things right, regardless of what is happening in the relationship. Powerful relationships begin with Goodwill. The leader creates a "safe space" for working relationships to flourish, where people work together to achieve similar and collaborative goals. Goodwill doesn't mean ignoring the effects of poor decisions. It means creating the conditions, the safe space, so both parties know the other is looking out for his or her best interests. Sometimes that might involve giving without condition or extending forgiveness. Sometimes it might mean simply being at peace with what is.

Risk plays a big role in setting the value of the results and the nature of the relationship and can be mitigated by the presence of trust and goodwill in the relationship. Goodwill is closely linked to trust and creates the psychological safety net that encourages people to take the risks often associated with

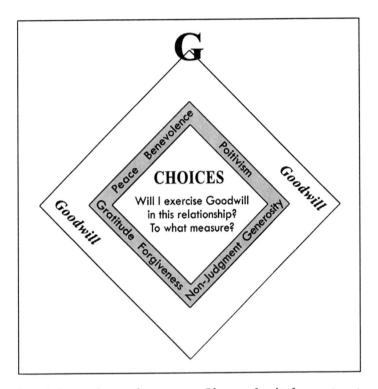

breakthrough performance. If we don't have trust built into a relationship, it is likely we will experience the "fight or flight" response when the inevitable breakdown occurs. At this point, the best we can hope for is a transactional interaction that does not inspire or affirm. If trust is present when a breakdown occurs, we are more likely to give the other person the benefit of the doubt, and a second chance.

Like every other attitude or behavior we exhibit, the core of Goodwill involves a choice. We are the only ones who can decide whether or not we will have an attitude of Goodwill, and whether or not we will then exhibit that Goodwill, and how often or how much. The beginning of a powerful relationship begins with the *choice* to exercise Goodwill.

The leader creates a "safe space" for working relationships to flourish, where people work together to achieve similar collaborative goals.

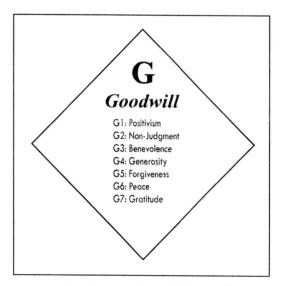

The 7 Attributes of GOODWILL

In order to further understand how the Goodwill component of G.R.A.C.E. operates, we have assigned seven attributes that help define its function in relationships. Keep in mind those relationships you've experienced where you just "clicked." Consider how these attributes, not only for Goodwill, but for all of the five G.R.A.C.E. components, contributed to that clicked relationship. Each component has its associated "cluster" of attributes, all of which must work together to enable that component to empower the relationship. Carefully consider how each attribute works with the others.

G1: Positivism

This literally means the quality or attitude of being and thinking in a positive (not negative) manner. In this model, it means that all thoughts and actions are approached with positive intent. It is keeping a positive attitude in all situations, being driven by positive rather than negative outlooks, attitudes and actions towards people, situations and ideas. Thinking positively is an open door to forward progress. Negative thinking is a door slammed shut.

G2: Non-Judgment

This is the ability to refrain from making judgments of people and situations, based on personal values, expectations, preconceptions, misconceptions, or any other personal bias. This attribute seeks solutions and answers rather than fault and blame, and does not hinder openness and trust. We all carry preconceptions, misconceptions and stereotypical thinking into relationships. These can serve to shut down communication, collaboration and end any hope of growth, both in the relationship as well as in the bottom line. We must consider wiping clean the cluttered blackboard of pre-judgment. In our justice system we presume a person innocent until proven guilty. This is a good practice in relationships as well. Since it is our natural human tendency to judge, we may have to put a little more effort and work into shaping pre-judgment into non-judgment so that it becomes our normal response.

G3: Benevolence

This implies a disposition to do good, mostly for others, to give especially when it may not be earned. Benevolence often has tangible evidence, such as gifts, provisions, mercy or other acts of kindness. It is an attitude of altruism that will manifest itself in a long-term sincerity to advance others. Benevolence may involve only one-time acts of kindness, but benevolence in this model means the person has an ongoing attitude of kindness, and often giving without condition. Benevolence is an indispensable attribute of goodwill. In involves the heart, rather than the hands and feet. It is a foundational attitude that directs actions towards others. In benevolence, we approach others with the desire to assist them, better them, advance them, and lift them. It is looking out for each other's best interest.

G4: Generosity

Quite simply, this means giving in a big way. It is being magnanimous, open-handed, giving beyond normal, and beyond expectation. One can be generous in the latitude offered others, or in actual giving of things to others. It is an attitude that what one has to give, should be given, not withheld. It is also a generosity of spirit, which gives freely to others. In all relationships, it is a general feeling that willingly desires to share whatever one has with others in relationship. This can be information, resources, assistance, words...anything and everything, as appropriate.

GOODWILL In Brief...

G1. Positivism
Positive attitude and manner. All actions are driven by positive intent.

G2. Non-Judgment
Refrain from judgments of people, or situations, based on preconceptions, misconceptions or any other personal bias.

G3. Benevolence
Attitude of kindness, doing good for others, often in tangible ways, and often without condition.

G4. Generosity
A generosity of spirit, freely giving to others, beyond normal and beyond expectation.

G5. Forgiveness
Able to excuse an offence without extracting payment; not harboring hard feelings.

G6. Peace
At peace with "what is" and in harmony in relationship.

G7. Gratitude
An attitude of thankfulness, able to express gratitude for others.

G5: Forgiveness

Forgiveness is the act of giving up resentment, blame or the need for restitution. It is the excusing of an offence, without extracting a payment. Forgiveness implies more than mere lip service. It is the genuine surrender, emotionally, of the need for restitution, vengeance, or personal acknowledgement of a wrong. No hard feelings are harbored, and forward progress and growth are more important than backward wallowing. Forgiveness gives up the need to hold a grudge, and future interactions are not colored by past offences. As with many other attributes of these G.R.A.C.E. components, this is not a normal or natural human response. Forgiveness is a deliberate choice, one that quite often is in opposition to our natural choices.

G6: Peace

Peace is defined as an attitude of tranquility, a peaceful spirit, and freedom from anything that disturbs this quiet. Peace can be experienced in the environment, the world at large, but also within the individual. In the case of the model, it implies the person is "at peace" with whatever "is," and not struggling against something. It is a harmony in relationship.

G7: Gratitude

Gratitude is an attitude of thankfulness. It is the ability to feel and express thanks for something, to someone, understanding and appreciating the benefits derived. This attitude of thankfulness also generally has an action of expression appropriately given. Gratitude is often a cultivated attitude whereby we approach everything and everyone, thankful for opportunities, for relationships, for potential.

ALL of these attributes and definitions, in order to be fully understood and fully discharged, happen in association with other people. In general, it is an attitude that thinks of and serves others always, quite often before self. Consider your current relationships. Are there any that exhibit signals of a lack of goodwill? Here are some indicators of the Goodwill component missing from a relationship:

- Feeling like I can't trust the other person
- Micro-managing
- Second-guessing
- A laundry list of written expectations, parameters
- Propensity for bad-mouthing the other person
- Negative attitude
- Not willing to risk much
- Compliance, not cooperation or collaboration
- Seeking approval
- Avoidance
- Lack of initiation
- Fearing "the stick"
- Follow the rules, but no further
- Self-interests first
- Irritation over even small things

We could include pages of missing Goodwill indicators, especially since Goodwill is the foundational basis for the entire *G.R.A.C.E. at Work* model. There may be many other indicators to signal a lack of Goodwill in a relationship which may not immediately appear to be related to this component. Upon careful consideration, honest evaluation and thoughtful dialogue, however, almost every red flag within any relationship can be traced back to missing Goodwill. When a relationship is solidly based in this component, all the other pieces will function much more smoothly.

The best for Karl was, after all, the best for Jim, and the organization as well.

Jim revealed many years later that he believes all people are part of a bigger picture, and that we all share responsibility for helping others achieve their fullest potential.

As their relationship developed, Karl said he began to feel valued for his contributions, but more importantly, he developed a strong sense of security that allowed him to admit to Jim that he didn't always have the answers and often needed help in dealing more effectively with people. This successful relationship embodied a leadership approach that focused not only on improving the business, but also on unleashing the power of a person's potential.

> **Almost every red flag within any relationship can be traced back to missing Goodwill.**

RESULTS: *Formula for Purpose*

THERE are actually three "R"s in this component: Reason, Relationship and Results. Anticipated *results* represent the tangible *reason* for the *relationship*. The "R" factor focuses on creating a shared sense of purpose and value that is commensurate with the mutual investments of both parties. This component has *two objectives*: the achievement of the intended results, and the achievement of the betterment of those in the relationship. This is a mutual intended result, or desired outcome. In this model, the reason for being in relationship has these two intentions firmly in mind. When both objectives are approached as one unified outcome, the results achieved for either are multiplied.

Results:
A dual factor component concerned not only with tangible bottom line results, but also desired outcomes for the people in relationship.

◇

G.R.A.C.E. at Work is a relationship model. In this component, we are not as concerned with the strategy for achieving results, as we are with the *human dynamic involved in realizing those results*. Our primary concern, and our primary goal in this component, is the interaction of the human players and their hopes and desired outcomes for one another — as much a desired outcome as the actual products and services.

Effective leaders help their employees identify their purpose and passion. G.R.A.C.E. helps answer the questions, *"What is my reason for being here?"* and *"Why are we in this relationship?"* Long after leaving an organization or exiting a relationship, people realize that success isn't just about the numbers. It's about making a contribution by doing the things they love to do—things that are meaningful. Research conducted by the CLC Learning and Development Roundtable found that "by changing the way employees think about themselves, their jobs, and their organizations, managers have another means of obtaining dramatic improvements in the performance of their employees." Effective leaders recognize this desire as a powerful motivator for people, and they leverage it to create commitment to the vision and purpose of the organization.

You are also more likely to be G.R.A.C.E.–full, and ultimately achieve the desired results, when you have a clear understanding of, and commitment to, your own purpose and passion, and that of others in the relationship. G.R.A.C.E. provides an opportunity to build reputations and legacies that impact individuals and organizations long after they are gone. Success, therefore, involves developing the next generation of leaders by helping people develop their gifts and talents, in the process of achieving results.

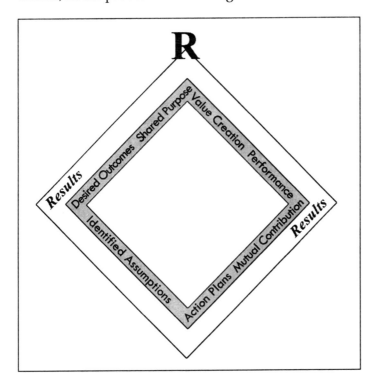

The Results diamond and 7 attributes.
This component "houses" all the others, hence it is depicted a larger size than the others.

The 7 Attributes of RESULTS

As you consider each of these attributes, remember to keep in mind the "click factor" you have may have experienced in relationships. The RESULTS component of the *G.R.A.C.E. at Work* model may seem

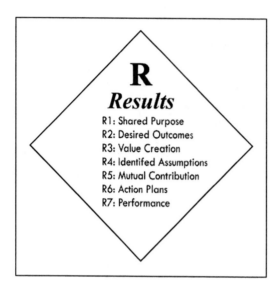

R
Results

R1: Shared Purpose
R2: Desired Outcomes
R3: Value Creation
R4: Identifed Assumptions
R5: Mutual Contribution
R6: Action Plans
R7: Performance

to be a bit "dry," at least as it relates to the human aspects of relationship. However, when these attributes are present, a relationship will not only click faster and better, it will also more readily produce the results desired for that relationship. Keep in mind also that this component has a "dual" nature. On one side are the tangible results desired for the relationship, while on the other hand are the less tangible, but just as critical, human results desired. We'll deal with that issue in a moment.

R:1 Shared Purpose

Shared purpose goes well beyond the statement and knowledge of intended or desired outcomes. It implies that people in a relationship believe in what they are doing together. It is a sense of why they are doing what they are doing. Shared purpose gives relationships a deeper purpose for their goals, and allows people to relate well to the intended outcomes. Shared purpose suggests an inspirational quality, one people can believe in, rather than a dry set of goals. All parties within a relationship must share this sense of purpose in order achieve these goals. Shared purpose creates commitment to the vision and the goals.

R:2 Desired Outcomes

These are essentially the purpose, or reason, for the relationship. They are the intended results all parties hope to achieve, and should be observable (by those inside the relationship and those outside), able to be measured and stated in specific terms. Desired outcomes are expressed in terms of vision, mission, goals and intended results. In essence, they are what the relationship has been formed to achieve. Once stated, all parties in the relationship should understand them, be able to repeat them, and keep them foremost in all activities within the relationship.

R3: Value Creation

This is a term that today has many meanings for many different people. Essentially it means what it says, the process of creating value for any or all of several stakeholders, including customers, employees and investors. All three of these groups are linked, however, and the value created for one affects the others. In any business, the customers are the first focus of value creation. This means making products or providing services that meet the needs of the customer on a consistent basis. Value creation consistently strives to improve value for customers in offered products and services. Such value is not achieved, however, if it is not also created for the employees who must produce the product or service. And any value created for employees and customers directly affects investors. In a relationship there must always be an "attitude" of value creation, whereby all parties are constantly seeking ways to improve value for all involved. This may include better products for the customer, better compensation, training and respect for employees, and better returns for investors. There is a known cycle within value creation that places customer value first, but understands that customers cannot benefit without value created for employees, and employees cannot realize improved value creation without the continued value added for investors who continue to invest in the organization making any value creation possible. In relationships, value creation must be at the heart of all processes, the commitment to consistently create value for all parties involved.

> ...value creation must be at the heart of all processes, the commitment to consistently create value for all parties involved.

R4: Identified Assumptions

Assumptions are things that we believe to be true, accepted as truth, sometimes without proof. When we "assume" things, we literally take them for granted. We may or may not be able to establish them as true, but hold that they are likely to be true. In relationships, often times there is a great degree of unknown. We must make certain assumptions in order to proceed together. Everyone in a relationship brings certain assumptions, and those must be identified, communicated, investigated and evaluated, and perhaps

RESULTS
In Brief...

R1. Shared Purpose
A shared sense of why
we are doing what we
are doing.

R2. Desired Outcomes
Purpose or reason
for the relationship.
Intended results.

R3. Value Creation
A commitment to
consistently create
and improve the value
for all parties in the
relationship.

**R4. Identified
Assumptions**
Known beliefs of what
parties in relationship
believe to be true.

**R5. Mutual
Contribution**
All parties contribute
to the relationship in
mutual or equal parts.

R6. Action Plans
Tactical methodology
to accomplish desired
outcomes.

R7. Performance
Execution and
measurement of action
plans, the work of the
relationship.

revised. All parties in relationship must explore and examine individual assumptions to be sure they align with those of other parties in the relationship, or known truths regarding the desired outcomes and shared purpose. Assumptions are not always truths, and can change in the term of a relationship, which may require revisiting.

R5: Mutual Contribution

This is the contribution of all parties in the relationship in mutual or equal levels and measure. It carries the idea that all members of the relationship are contributing, performing, in equal manner, with equal effort, in measurable ways. Mutual contribution is a term to describe the agreement that everyone in the relationship will do his or her part, to the best of his or her ability. It is generally part of the understanding of shared purpose through shared effort.

R6: Action Plans

Action plans are a part of strategies and tactical methodology to accomplish the desired outcomes. Action plans include specifics regarding tasks and actions, responsibilities and accountabilities, time frames, and resources needed. Actual actions performed in action plans are governed by action principles. In relationship, action plans are known and shared, generally not created in isolation. Action plans are necessary for both strategy and relationships in order to deliver results.

R7: Performance

Performance is the accomplishment and implementation of action plans and strategies. It is the execution of an action, a given task or plan. Performance is often measured, based on previously accepted standards and expectations. Performance is the work of the relationship, the accomplishing of the intended results through action plans, governed by action principles, in agreement with shared purpose. Performance includes both execution and measurement. To measure something is to determine the dimensions, quantity, quality or capacity of whatever we are measuring. In the Results component, this measurement process is applied to everything and everyone associated with achieving the intended results. Actions and processes are measured periodically to determine if they are producing the desired outcomes. Are the action plans succeeding in moving toward the goals? Is the output on target to meet stated outcomes? Are people working at a level that will yield the results desired, within the boundaries set for shared purpose? Achieving intended goals requires measurement on a periodic basis. And measurement requires standards by which observations can determine meaningful data. Measurement requires pre-established benchmarks, markers for successful outcomes along the way. Measurement also includes a level of accountability for the observed progress, or lack of progress, toward goals. Provision for regular measurement must be established at the very beginning of any relationship for any purpose to determine if the relationship is achieving the desired outcomes. Provision for correction and course alteration, changes and revision of people and processes, are part of the measurement factor.

WHILE all seven attributes of the Results component of the *G.R.A.C.E. at Work* model are focused on delivering the desired outcomes, there is another vital factor assumed in these attributes: *they pertain to the individuals within the relationship, as well as to the outcomes.*

...and RESULTS for the *people.*

For example, desired outcomes are not just the results those in relationship wish to achieve for product or services, or other intended goals. They are not strictly the reason for the relationship, or the means of achieving that reason. They apply to the persons involved as well. The desired outcomes for any member of the relationship should include their individual growth, advancement, satisfaction and excellence during the process of achieving

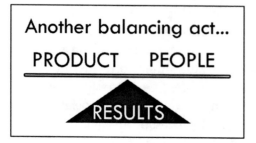

results-based outcomes. In the *G.R.A.C.E. at Work* model, each member in the relationship also keeps in mind, and works to advance, the outcomes desired for every individual, not merely for the purpose of realizing results. Let's take another look at these attributes as they refocus on the people in the relationship.

Shared Purpose

Individuals in a relationship have a shared purpose not only in achieving intended results, but in building the passion and satisfaction of the purpose within each other. The shared purpose is to treat each other with respect, work effectively together, form bonds of camaraderie and generally to improve the well-being of everyone in the relationship. We're not talking about getting mushy, or *touchy-feely* stuff. This is about genuine respect and real desire to improve and edify our fellow "relationship-mates."

Desired Outcomes

This may include the personal growth of the people *(advancement, improvement of skills and competencies, overall satisfaction of being in this relationship)*. When a relationship is formed for the purpose of achieving some desired outcome, the well-being and advancement of the individual members becomes part of those desired outcomes.

Value Creation

The cycle of value creation for customers, employees and investors is only one form of value creation in a relationship. As stated before, those in relationship are constantly seeking to create value for each other. It is a back-and-forth, mutual and dynamic effort to constantly and consistently create improved value for fellow members in any relationship. This involves being aware of potential, opportunities and possibilities, that may enhance value for individuals within the relationship, not just customers, employees and investors. It is a mind-set or attitude that one of the reasons we are in relationship is to create value for those with us in relationship.

Identified Assumptions

Assumptions include what individuals in relationship assume about each other. These are explored, and sometimes corrected or modified, in the course of achieving results together. The goal here is to make sure the assumptions are true, and shared.

Mutual Contribution

While all parties in a relationship may agree to contribute their part in the reach for results, they must also agree to contribute to each other wherever and whenever possible. And again, this is not just about results. Those in relationship understand that each person is looking out for the other, and will contribute mutually to their well-being. Lop-sided contribution to the betterment of others in the relationship will throw obstacles and hurdles into the path, sidelining the ultimate desired outcomes for not only product or service, but fellow growth.

> One of the reasons we are in relationship is to create value for those with us in relationship.

Action Plans

The plans, strategic or tactical, to achieve results are not the only action plans included in this factor. Each individual in relationship also "plans" to achieve the betterment of fellow members, and will conduct him or herself according to these plans. One of the desired outcomes of any relationship is to advance the well-being of those within the relationship. It is sometimes helpful if actual plans are developed to do this.

Performance

Those in relationship approach performance as not only a series of actions executed to achieve the intended results, but as a way of performing those actions that elevates others in the relationship. It is vital, in any of these attributes of this component, to remember that the desired outcomes do not merely include the achievement of results, but the achievement of the advancement of those in the relationship. Advancement does not mean mere status or position advancement. It applies to the entire well-being of individuals. In addition, the measurement of processes and actions to achieve goals also applies to our personal processes and actions in interaction with others. If we are practicing all the other attributes, we have already determined we want the best for our fellow relationship members. Do our own personal set of processes, how we relate to one another, achieve that objective? It may be necessary from time to time to consciously evaluate— to measure—this factor against desired outcomes for one another. And it may also be necessary to revise our approach, to improve our processes and actions, for the betterment of others. This is not possible without honest measurement.

Product and People Results

To fully understand the dual nature of this component, it is helpful to ask yourself a number of questions designed to develop the kind of behaviors that truly allow the Results component to come alive. You might even try making a personal list of new opportunities for you and your teammates to expand the boundaries of your working relationships previously centered around bottom line results. These *product* results may be significantly strengthened by adding the component of *people* results. Many of these questions have probably never even been considered by you, or by others in relationship with you. What new possibilities can you see? Could your fellow "relationship-mates" benefit from these questions?

Consider your answers to these questions carefully, and perhaps even take the time to jot down a few brief responses to serve as "behavior reminders."

1. How can I achieve the well-being and advancement of those in relationship with me? What are the desired outcomes for each person, personally?

2. How can I build passion and provide a sense of shared purpose in working together to build each other up?

3. What do I assume about my "relationship-mates" that should be explored? Are these assumptions true, and shared?

4. What "relationship principles" guide how I work with these people? Have we all committed to these?

5. How can I plan to better my fellow relationship members?

6. How do my actions elevate others in this relationship, and do they contribute to their overall well-being?

7. How can we mutually contribute to each other, and not just to the intended results of this relationship?

8. How will I manage my personal processes, attitudes and motives analysis in this relationship, and how will I know to make changes?

9. How can I create and improve the value for those working with me in relationship?

10. How will I know if the desired outcomes for my team members are being achieved? How will I measure progress, and how will I modify actions and attitudes to achieve them?

AUTHENTICITY: *Essential Reality*

Authenticity:

Knowing and Showing
Your Real Self

AUTHENTICITY is being honest with yourself and others, choosing how you wish to relate to others, declaring what your stand is, holding yourself accountable for your actions, rewarding yourself appropriately, being open and vulnerable, openly communicating needs, desires, moods, attitudes, values and feelings–even about the other person.

Being real—and being all that you can be—is essential to any relationship, but especially to one with expectations for real (authentic) results. Open and uncompromising standards, positive attitudes and the desire to be exactly who you are, are at the heart of a fruitful relationship. Authenticity keeps the relationship balanced and healthy. Each person must first identify, then "own up" to his or her own place of reality. Successful relationships thrive when both parties reveal exactly who they are, say exactly what they mean, and use the same standards for self and others, and do so in the spirit of goodwill. Great leadership begins by knowing and leveraging strengths and weaknesses. Self-awareness (in leaders first and then promoting it in others) represents a huge opportunity to create consistency between the walk and the talk, and provide a measure of transparency to others that fosters trust in a relationship.

When people make assessments about your authenticity, they're making a judgment about how closely you "walk your talk."

Authenticity and Your Stand

We all have a set of values and beliefs that we use as a basis for our identity and to make decisions. Whether we realize it or not, we act in ways that are basically consistent with the values and beliefs we hold. Being authentic means knowing the defining purpose of your life, and what you are willing to take a stand for, and also knowing what kind of reputation you will build if you are truly authentic.

The Harmony of Profession and Practice

Authenticity is about saying what you're going to do, then doing what you said you were going to do. So when people make assessments about your authenticity, they're making a judgment about how closely you "walk your talk." Similarly, the responsibilities afforded to any position come with certain expectations about how the person in that role should perform. When the person fulfills the expectations, observers say that the performer is executing the role appropriately and hence some measure of authenticity is also conferred on that person.

What You See is What You Get

Often we hear this phrase used to describe an individual's authenticity. Authenticity is not just about walking the talk, it's about talking the truth and *walking the truth*—about yourself. Authenticity requires us to first know ourselves well—to know what drives us, moves us, hurts us, peeves us, and pleases us. What are our personal values, guidelines and direction markers? What are our boundaries? Our hopes and goals? Once we understand these things, we are more able to make the choice, and take the risk, to reveal them to others. Real authenticity means talking and behaving in ways not only in a consistent manner, but consistent with our genuine core.

The Internal Champion and the Internal Critic

Authenticity requires a person to know themselves really well and to be comfortable in the knowledge that we're human, with strengths and weaknesses. Given this fact, our authenticity is multifaceted. We have a powerful authentic self that can be referred to as our "Internal Champion." The Internal Champion is the self we experience when we're at the top of our game and we feel confident. We know what levers to pull and not much phases

Internal Champion | Internal Critic

us when we're in this groove. The Internal Champion encourages us along the way with positive messages of self-assuredness. But we also have an authentic self that contradicts our purposes and sabotages our purest desires and intentions. We can call this self our "Internal Critic." This self is revealed in terms of fight or flight. When we feel cornered, this self can be seen in retreat where we refuse to engage in problem solving. The Internal Critic can also show up as a defensive self, disguised as an aggressive self, where we lash out at the people we are working with. The Internal Critic is quick to point out our shortcomings and provides unrelenting criticism about ourselves and our performance.

The key to creating a more authentic self is to create awareness about how to present your Internal Champion rather than your Internal Critic in the moment when you have been asked to present your authentic self. Both the Internal Champion and Internal Critic represent your authentic self *(the "good" and the "dark" side of self)*. The question is how you want to "show up" and be perceived. We need to identify why we sometimes present our Internal Champions, and at other times our Internal Critic. Can you identify within yourself why it is that when you receive the call to authenticity sometimes you feel powerful and ready to accept the challenge while other times your critic answers and reflects all the bad attributes you desperately wanted to avoid?

There is also the important issue of *self* Goodwill. Our Internal Critics put us in the place of self condemnation, with no option to show up differently. Extending Goodwill to self means to grant ourselves a measure of courage and resolve, *allowing* opportunity to show up in this way *(the Internal Champion)* and helping manage any conflict between the critic and champion in internal discussions *(more information on this internal conversation is found in chapter 8).*

Your Internal Critic:

- Thinks it's all or nothing; defines things as purely black and white
- Considers one negative event a pattern of defeat
- Rejects positive events because they "don't count"
- Jumps to negative conclusions with little to no facts
- Exaggerates inappropriately
- Attaches negative labels to individuals or events
- Identifies himself/herself as the cause of negative event

Internal Critic

Your Internal Champion:

- Trusts the facts
- Gives yourself the same advice given to a friend
- Tests the validity of negative ideas
- Thinks in "Shades of Gray"
- Identifies a partial success (not a complete failure)
- Asks others if thoughts are realistic
- Uses language that is less colorful or emotionally loaded
- Focuses on solving the problem rather than placing blame or feeling guilty
- Lists advantages and disadvantages of a feeling before responding

Internal Champion

NOTE: I want to acknowledge Dr. David. D. Burns for his work on "Cognitive Distortions" in his book "Feeling Good - The New Mood Therapy" (ISBN 978-0380810338, Harper Collins, New York, 1999). This book has influenced my development of these concepts.

The Battle for the Authentic Self

When we interact with people we do so on a variety of different levels. We have all learned behaviors that are acceptable in the social setting. Often times what people exhibit socially does not truly reflect what they are feeling or thinking. When we get to know people better and we feel some measure of trust, we tend to share more of the intimate details of our identity both in terms of what we are confident with and what we're not confident with. The

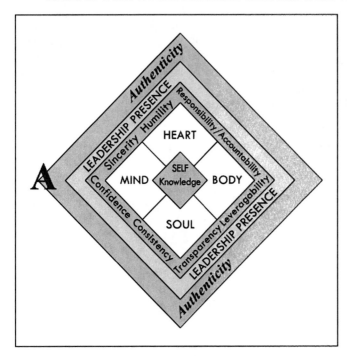

more we can understand about the dynamics of a powerful relationship and learn how to leverage them, the more likely we are able to share what's really going on for us, and who we really are.

The Heart of G.R.A.C.E.

Authenticity is the very center and heart of the G.R.A.C.E. model. All the other components flow from this center. It begins with *Self Knowledge*, which involves the heart, mind, soul and body. The attributes of authenticity flow from this knowledge of self, and together are seen as something we often call *leadership presence*. Because authenticity is so important, *absolutely critical for any powerful relationship*, we will deal more with this concept in coming chapters.

The 7 Attributes of AUTHENTICITY

It will serve you well to bring to mind someone in your life, past or present, who has honestly and openly displayed each of these attributes in relationship with you. It is sometimes difficult for us to evaluate these characteristics of an authentic self, in ourselves. Yet when we see them in others, we can instantly recognize how they have either been honestly present, or lacking, in the relationship. As you consider the other people in your relationships who have been authentic through the presence of these attributes, take a moment for each one and recall what they looked like. How were they manifested? What were the results? This internal exercise is very useful in helping each of us to know how they can be seen

by others in relationship with us. Also keep in mind that we are talking about authenticity, or genuineness. These attributes must be the reality of your observable behavior in relationship. When we try to "fake it" or attempt to *look like* these attributes, without actually owning them internally, we will appear just like the undressed Emperor in Hans Christian Anderson's fairy tale.

A1: Sincerity

This is the ability to be sincere, to speak truthfully about personal feelings, thoughts and desires. It is the lack of deceit or deception, hypocrisy or duplicity. Sincerity involves the intention to communicate with earnestness and honesty. Being sincere is honesty in speech and actions. It comes from a Latin word that meant *clean*, *pure* and *sound*. There is some gamble in sincerity, since typical filters that are commonly found in everyday actions and words are not applied, and this person risks judgment by others. You reveal to others the real "you."

A Case In Point...

Mark was a hard-charging executive who valued analytical prowess in himself and others. He relished challenging others and being challenged. He was extremely passionate about the work required in business analysis, and was honestly disappointed if people wouldn't push back. Mark's passion and approach were often misinterpreted as arrogance. To make matters worse, others could sense that he had contempt for people who wouldn't stand up for their work or themselves. Mark eventually realized his approach compromised his desire to be positioned as a mentor in the field. He had to own up to the fact that his behavior was not serving him well and would prevent him from further promotions.

A2: Humility

Humility, or being humble, addresses intrinsic self-worth. It is the mark of an unpretentious and modest person, not given to pride or arrogance. This person does not think he or she is better or more important than anyone else. It is derived from a Latin word meaning "low," or "from the earth." A humble person is truly "down to earth." Humility is not an act, or pretense of being humble. A "humble" front covering a self-important interior will always be seen through. True humility is consistently observed in words, body language, actions and interactions.

A3: Responsibility/Accountability

This is, quite simply, the ability to be accountable, an obligation or willingness to accept responsibility and give account for actions. It is being answerable, explainable, and able to justify actions and decisions. It may also be considered a "personality trait" which indicates that a person is consistently able and willing to give honest reasons for personal behavior, and does not seek to "duck" this obligation. Accountability does not include excuses, blame, or rationalization. Responsibility is the ability to respond to whatever has been charged to an individual. It implies reliability, trustworthiness, ability to meet obligations and ensure that applied duties are fulfilled. Responsibility generally includes certain tasks and duties, but may be used as an overall indicator of dependability. Different people in relationship may have different responsibilities, but in addition they should all demonstrate responsibility to one another, and to the shared purpose of the relationship.

A4: Transparency

Transparency is one of those metaphorical extensions of a word whose first meaning is in the realm of physical objects. Simply, something that is transparent can be seen through. There is nothing clouding the image. When we apply this word to people, it implies openness, honest communication, being agenda-less (no duplicity, no hidden agendas). It is a freedom from pretense that allows other people to see the real you. You are easily understood, visible, accessible and clear. What you see is what you get, and nothing hidden lurks in the shadows.

A:5 Consistency

Personal consistency means that there is "harmony of parts" in a person. Character consistency means people can count on you to speak and act in the same manner from moment to moment, situation to situation. It is an unchanging and steadfast adherence to the same principles, actions and patterns of behavior. Behavior does not change depending on the situation or the person it impacts. It is the same for everyone, for all situations. It implies no contradiction between what is said and what is done, a harmonious blending of practice and profession.

A6: Confidence

Confidence is a state of being certain, either of self or others, situations, actions or projected ideas. It means knowing self well, certain of your personal values and abilities. Confidence may be placed in others and their values and abilities. It is sometimes thought to be an emotional and subjective state of mind, but real confidence is a steady consciousness of individual powers, and a faith or belief that one

Mark worked on restoring relationships and did so by owning up to his behaviors and seeking to make amends with the people he worked with. Mark declared his intentions to become more balanced in his approach and welcomed others to provide him with feedback, both to recognize his improvements and to point out when he reverted to his old self. Mark became authentic—transparent—and encouraged it in others.

AUTHENTICITY In Brief...

A1. Sincerity
Speaking truthfully about personal feelings, thoughts and desires. Honesty in speech and action.

A2. Humility
Being unpretentious, modest, not given to pride or arrogance.

A3. Responsibility/ Accountability
Ability to respond to whatever has been charged to an individual, and give account for actions. Reliability, trustworthiness, ability to meet obligations, answerable, explainable, able to justify actions and decisions.

A4. Transparency
Freedom from pretense, others see real you– visible, accessible, clear.

A5. Consistency
"Harmony of parts," unchanging adherence to same principles, actions and patterns of behavior

A6. Confidence
Being certain, of self or others, situations, actions or projected ideas. Faith or belief that one will act in a right, proper, or effective manner.

A7. Leveragability
Making most of strengths and managing weaknesses, of self, others.

will act in a right, proper, or effective manner. It is an attitude that is free from uncertainty, diffidence or embarrassment. It does not involve conceit or arrogance. Self-confidence is having confidence in oneself when considering a capability. Overconfidence is having unmerited confidence – believing something or someone is capable when they are not, including self. In relationship, in order to achieve desired outcomes, it necessary to have merited confidence both in self and in others. Unmerited or unproven confidence can be dangerous and disappointing, as well as disastrous.

A7: Leveragability

You won't find this word in any notable dictionary. It's one of those words we have coined in our development of business jargon. In every discipline or industry it will have a slightly different meaning, but in general we all pretty much know what it means. It comes from the word "lever" which is something used to have a mechanical advantage to move something. It means to have greater power, effectiveness, or maneuverability of anything it is applied to. In the case of a relationship, and for this authenticity component, it is applied to strengths and weaknesses of both self and others. It means we know how to get the most out of our strengths, and the strengths of others, and also how to manage weaknesses. In a sense, it is the ability to make the most of the people in the relationship, without "using" them. It affirms and puts to work strengths, and is aware of and minimizes weaknesses.

The Anchor Point

Authenticity, the reality of you, is anchored in your body, mind, heart and soul – in that order. Who you really are shows up first in the body. It is what people notice first. How you take care of yourself, how you express yourself, including your actions and reactions, are a reflection of how you take action in the world, in business or life in general. It will next be seen in your mind, your thought processes, your ideas, and what you pay attention to. It is the next "doorway" to revealing the authentic you. Beyond the mind lies the heart, which reflects your moods and emotions. It shows others how you feel about the world, or the microcosm of any relationship. And then, at the seat of it all, is your soul. The soul represents and reveals what is truly important to you in life, and is where your faith declaration and commitments will be found. It is from this place, your soul, that you commit to a relationship with someone or something that will ignite and feed your life's purpose and passion. The soul's commitments will shape and determine what your body, mind, and heart will pay attention to, what they will react to (and how they will react), and what they will present or manifest to the world.

> Leveragability... exalts and puts to work strengths, and is aware of and minimizes weaknesses.

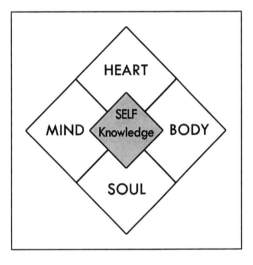

In order to practice this authenticity component of the *G.R.A.C.E. at Work* model, these vital elements of you must be perfectly aligned, focused and known and understood by you. This is *Self Knowledge*. For this reason, we will spend time later helping you understand heart, mind, soul and body more fully, and providing you opportunities to seek and attain that alignment. No relationship, in business or life, can ultimately reach desired outcomes without it.

CONNECTIVITY: *Co-Created Value*

CONNECTIVITY means finding ways to identify with, affirm and encourage other people, understanding how they feel, identifying what is important to them, sharing assumptions and beliefs, and identifying and realizing differences in intention and impact. It is the communication of a genuine desire to associate with and relate to others.

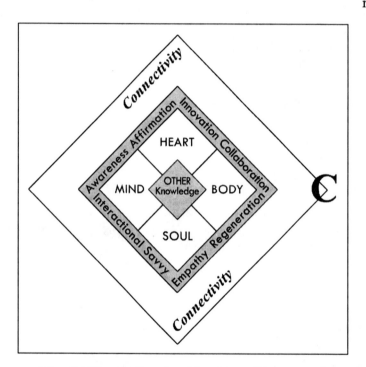

When the components of goodwill, a reason for being in relationship, and authenticity com-bine, they advance the relationship to the place of real connectivity. Connectivity is about empathizing with others, finding ways to engage them in the pursuit of mutual goals, and co-creating value. The Corporate Leadership Council's research on building the high performance workforce found that *"employees perform best when they feel personally connected to their work and their organization."* In fact, they found these connections more important to improving employee performance than almost any other incentives. Leaders connect with others and essentially "team up" for shared results.

We mentioned that the core of the Authenticity component is Self Knowledge. The nucleus of Connectivity then is "Other Knowledge;" that is, the knowledge of others that allows, enables and facilitates connection. In order to truly connect we must not only understand our own heart, mind, soul and body, but also that of others. This means being awake and conscious, paying attention to details beyond ourselves, searching for and finding validity in others, and being sensitive to their feelings, thoughts and experiences. It is much more than a surface attempt that is still focused on self. It is a genuine reaching out with open receptors, and an insightful awareness of how people work best together. We actually *do* that through the employment of this component's seven attributes.

Leaders have their own goals and objectives but must also be sensitive to the goals and objectives of others. Task driven leaders know what they want and they won't hesitate to advocate it. They often perceive the work relationship as an opportunity to negotiate their best deal. If an employee is not up to the task of representing his or her position, he or she loses. Hence both parties lose the opportunity to create a mutually motivating and satisfying experience. When the leader and employee connect, however, through shared motives, values, goals and understanding, the subsequent bond can yield powerful results. The safe space of G.R.A.C.E. easily affords this vital connectivity.

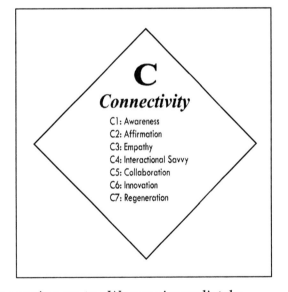

The 7 Attributes of CONNECTIVITY

We connect with people in various ways. We will naturally gravitate toward some, while others take some warming up to. We may immediately open up with some people, while others may cause us to clam up instead. This is a natural dynamic in human relationships, but truly effective leaders have a way of connecting with individuals and audiences of every type, even those that may evoke those initial "turtle" responses. It is true that some people

A Case in Point...

Andrea was a successful IT executive whose expertise was greatly enhanced by a strong conceptual capacity. Andrea also had an exceptional knack for leveraging her intuition in problem solving, and she made no apologies for it. She was good at what she did, and she accomplished a lot. One of her major weaknesses, however, was not taking the time to learn from her co-workers. Andrea didn't allow that free flow of communication with others, because her agenda was focused on selling herself and her solutions. Quite simply, Andrea did not connect with others. Consequently, she lost many opportunities to engage the hearts and minds of her employees. She consistently received low scores on the associate satisfaction survey items related to manager-associate relations.

seem gifted with a unique ability to connect with others. However, this is also an art which can be practiced and polished. The first step begins with taking personal stock of our ability to connect with others. We all know our own personal history of human connection. What are the things you do to connect with people? What do others do to connect with you? What are the kinds of conversations that tend to lend themselves to deepening the relationship? In general, connections begin to form when we find ways to recognize, affirm and empathize with others. There is a definite process where certain attributes can be employed, not just as tools to connect for whatever specified goal or desired outcome, but for the pure sake of connecting, of being a vital part of the human story and plugging into the power of relationships.

C1: *Awareness*

In the *G.R.A.C.E. at Work* model, awareness is not just about perception, knowledge and realization. It is not just about being aware, it is about being watchful. It means knowing your surroundings, knowing the people with whom you are in relationship, and watching for opportunities for connection. It also means being sensitive, awake and conscious of all you do and say (self-awareness), and all others do and say (others-awareness), so connections are optimized. In another sense, it implies that you are aware of the other people in the relationship, including their desired outcomes (beyond the obvious), their authenticity, and their abilities. It is the extent to which you know, and are familiar with, those with whom you are expected to connect, your shared purposes and the possibilities for connection. Awareness in this model carries more of a sense of watchfulness and alertness.

C2: Affirmation

In the legal sense of the word, an affirmation is something that is declared to be true. In the neurosciences, however, it has come to mean positive statements (or actions) that reflect positive beliefs and positive attitudes about things, and about people. Affirmations are intended to express approval, validity and confirmation, which will in turn evoke those attitudes in self or others. Affirmations are not lip service, merely saying nice things in order to obtain something in return. An affirmation, whether for self or others, is a statement that does indeed declare a truth for the speaker. He or she truly believes in the value or truth of something or someone else, and is willing to state it openly, and appropriately. Affirmation follows and confirms acceptance. Affirmations are observable and knowable confirmations of value. Every individual needs affirmation in order to perform at peak levels. Affirmations can be the "grease" of alignment, and the coupling mechanism for connections.

C3: Empathy

Empathy is the ability to recognize, understand and be sensitive to the feelings, thoughts and experiences of other people. This ability goes well beyond typical sympathy, pity or recognition of another's emotions or outlooks. It has often been said that empathy is the ability to "put yourself into another's shoes," to truly feel their emotions and relate to their states of mind. Empathy does not depend on actually having had those experiences, or felt those emotions, or sharing those outlooks, though that will often produce empathy when we share experiences. Perhaps the best definition of empathy is being able to understand how it feels to be someone else. Empathy is necessary to make connections. It is a critical component in

> Through the work of her coach, Andrea came to realize that this behavior limited the innovation needed to succeed in the long run. Andrea needed to learn how to connect with her colleagues so they felt heard, respected, and engaged.

> What are the things you do to connect with people?
>
> What do others do to connect with you?

"hooking up" with others to achieve results. It enables us to anticipate needs, to consider actions and words, and generally to step outside ourselves in order to be "in step with" others. Lack of empathy will be a potent disconnect in relationships.

C4: Interactional Savvy

Interaction is the process of two or more things, or people, having influence (an effect) on one another. Whether in a chemical process, or in relationship, an interaction implies interconnectivity. Interactions may be large scale, or very small. They imply a state of communication and influence. In relationship, the individuals must be in an interactional state in order to achieve results. Savvy is know-how. It means being well-informed, perceptive, shrewd, comprehending. Savvy is a practical understanding in some area. In this attribute it is used to mean the understanding of how human dynamics, human relationships, work. It is a knowledge and insightful awareness of how people work best together, how they influence one another toward desired outcomes. Interactional savvy means individuals know and consider their influence and impact on others, and are also able to identify and manage the intentions and impacts of others.

C5: Collaboration

Collaboration is a hot topic these days. Everywhere you turn, in every industry and in every venue, you will find reference to collaboration. What exactly is it? It sometimes defies definition, though the simplest meaning is people working together to achieve some common goal or mission. Real collaboration goes much deeper than this, however, and its use here as an attribute of Connectivity implies much more. Collaboration is a state of mind, an attitude and willingness to cooperate, a genuine desire to "co-labor" with one another in relationship. Collaboration can exist even in disagreement, because it seeks to identify commonalities that will establish a partner approach in shared pursuit of common objectives. Collaboration assumes the idea that working together in relationship will yield results far larger, wider and more significant than anything that could be achieved individually. It is not just about working together, as the roots of this word imply, it is about wanting to work together, desiring to cooperate, and understanding the richness of jointly achieved results. An attitude and environment of collaboration are required for Connectivity.

C6: Innovation

The literal dictionary meaning of innovation is the process of introducing something new, whether in ideas, processes, products, or services. Innovation generally carries the idea of not only new, but improved, and is often considered to be the goal of collaboration. As an attribute in the Connectivity component, however, innovation is seen as the product of all the other attributes coming together, connecting so to speak. Innovation here is a process of connection, seeking new and improved methods of creating connectivity in order to reach desired outcomes. Members in relationship innovate to connect in new ways, to improve upon the old established methods of connectivity, to strengthen the connection points, sometimes in radically different ways. Innovation in connectivity means being open to potential, being creative, and using fresh thinking to connect with others in new and different ways, improving the strength of those connections, and thereby improving the ultimate results.

C7: Regeneration

Connectivity relies on an unbroken chain of individual connections. In human relationships, disconnects are expected. If these broken connections are left untended, the entire connectivity chain is weakened, and can be more susceptible to further disconnects. In some cases, even one broken link is disastrous. By its very nature, a chain relies on the strength of every link. If a chain is holding something, break one link and the chain fails. For that reason, dedicated, committed attention and vigilance must be given to monitoring the strength of those connected links, with a ready plan to regenerate them. Words that best describe regeneration include *renewal, restoration, revival, rejuvenation, revitalization.* The first two letters of each word, "re-," describe what

---

CONNECTIVITY In Brief...

C1. Awareness
Knowing people and surroundings. Awake, conscious of self, others. Watchfulness, alertness.

C2. Affirmation
Expressing approval, validity and confirmation.

C3. Empathy
Ability to recognize, understand, be sensitive to feelings, thoughts and experiences of others.

C4. Interactional Savvy
Having know-how of human dynamics, relationships. Insightful awareness of how people work best together.

C5. Collaboration
Working together to achieve common goals. An attitude, state of mind, genuine desire to "co-labor."

C6. Innovation
New and improved methods to collaboratively connect to achieve goals.

C7. Regeneration
Repairing, recreating connections. Restoration in case of disconnect.

is necessary. Something must be built again. In this case, we are speaking of rebuilding, renewing, restoring, and regenerating previously established connections that appear to be broken. Regeneration is not about patching something that is broken. It is about recreating it anew, in an improved state.

THERE is an ordered manner in which all the attributes come together in this component of the *G.R.A.C.E. at Work* model. This attribute list is presented in a logical progression, one building upon the other. Connectivity is a process that begins with awareness, is advanced with affirmation, and moves people into empathy. Interactional savvy can create the environment ripe for collaboration (by means of the other attributes), and connections are enhanced and multiplied by innovatively capitalizing on opportunities. Regeneration is the maintenance and repair shop that vigilantly monitors function, and handles breakdowns–inevitable in human relationships. These attributes together form a connected and aligned force that enables movement toward goals.

> Any missing attribute, even just one, from any one of the five G.R.A.C.E. components, will leave a gaping hole, into which will rush dysfunction and disconnects.

While it is a progression, each attribute builds on the strengths of the one before it. Like baking a cake, each ingredient is unique, bringing its own properties into the mix, but leave any one of them out, and you don't really have a cake. It might look like a cake, or smell like a cake, but it sure won't taste like a cake. All seven of these attributes combine to yield the component called Connectivity, vital for achieving results. The same can be said for each of the attributes of all five components of this model. Any missing attribute, even just one, from any one of the five G.R.A.C.E. components, will leave a gaping hole, into which will rush dysfunction and disconnects. The resulting mix of attributes will no long mesh as finely tuned gears, and grace will not be present. The relationship will be something other than is hoped or intended. If you omit the salt from a cake, it doesn't taste like a cake, and will probably be somewhat unpalatable. The same is true for relationships and the balanced blend of all components and their attributes.

EMPOWERMENT: *Enabling Success*

EMPOWERMENT is helping others overcome obstacles and develop new skills, establishing a safe environment to succeed (for self and others), creating catalysts for change, helping others see potential and possibilities, being open to possibilities, allowing time for testing and learning, and seeing the larger whole but being aware of smaller components.

Empowerment is about enabling success. The leader becomes a real coach here through the balanced use of challenge and support, sufficiently motivating others to take risks, to see new things and to do new things. Athletic coaches know how to get their stars to extend further, to excel and eventually shine in their chosen endeavors. A good coach must create a dynamic tension, a balance, which motivates the athlete to advance his or her skills, but still provide that safe space of encouragement and support. It is critical for the leader to create this same balance between challenge and support, advocacy and inquiry, and task and relationship. Successive chapters in this book will deal with this critical balance.

> Trust plays a vital role in empowerment, and begins with a common understanding of expectations and mutual commitments of goals, roles, and consequences.

Leaders and employees need to co-create the boundaries for empowerment, learning and responsibility. Trust also plays a vital role in empowerment, and begins with a common understanding of expectations and mutual commitments of goals, roles, and consequences. Employee development is a fundamental empowerment tool as workers create greater awareness of their abilities and options. Development keeps employees viable and empowered for current and future employers. Failure to develop employees is like benching a star athlete for the season. Given the competition, if you are not moving forward, you are slipping backward.

Self Knowledge is at the core of Authenticity, and the nucleus of Connectivity is "Other Knowledge." The center of successful *Empowerment* is

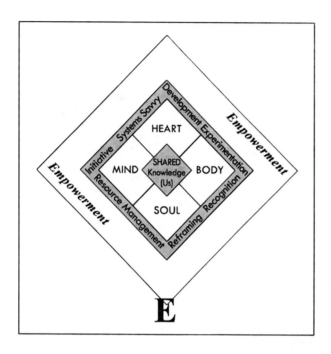

the combined values of both Self and Other Knowledge, yielding what we can term "Us Knowledge." Before empowerment can happen, all parties in the relationship must have a reasonable knowledge of each other—what makes each person "tick" and function best. Self knowledge creates consistent authentic behavior on the part of each individual. Other knowledge allows those individuals to join with others in shared purpose. Together, this knowledge drives the dynamics of interaction, and empowers toward realization of desired outcomes. More information on this knowledge factor is provided in the next chapter.

The 7 Attributes of EMPOWERMENT

Empowerment begins with the desire of people to know each other, beyond the typical workplace "we-have-a-job-to-do" relationship environment. The work may get done that way, but people are not empowered to really achieve jointly as teams with shared purpose. As mentioned earlier, empowerment originates with self knowledge, picks up momentum with knowledge of others, and becomes functional with "us" knowledge. *Who am I?, who are you?, what are we together?, and how can we empower one another to achieve our goals?*, are questions that beg answers in this component of the *G.R.A.C.E. at Work* model. Without this "us" knowledge (and the sincere desire to obtain it), empowerment just flops around with random and often aborted starts and spurts. Each one of these seven attributes of empowerment depend upon this shared knowledge for full implementation.

E1: Initiative

Initiative can be defined as an introductory step, a first action leading to more action. It implies a willingness, readiness and ability to do something first. Empowerment really hinges, is fueled, by initiative. A leader may have the ability, may create innovative ideas and strategies to accomplish something, but without that first step—the initiative—nothing happens. When we depend on others to "get the ball rolling," so to speak, the ball may never roll anywhere. Empowerment enables positive action

toward accomplishing goals, but without personal initiative, empowerment is never, well, empowered. Initiative is the ignition key. Initiative is the personal decision to act, and is not based on someone else's direction or command. It is outside the realm of what is expected by others, except that a good leader will always be counted on to have and show initiative. Initiative is not random, however. Successful initiative first contains the *ability* to act positively, or take the first steps (opening moves) toward making something better. This can be directly related to accomplishing set goals (desired outcomes) or it can be toward making anything better than it was, such as relationships, conditions, opportunities, etc. While initiative implies the beginning of something, it does not end with first steps. Subsequent follow-through is what gives initiative the ability to empower results, and follow-through depends on a plan for achievement of those results.

E2: Systems Savvy

As mentioned earlier, savvy is *know-how*, a practical understanding of something. It implies having knowledge, perception, and comprehension. A system is a group or set of entities that are inter-dependent and interactive, which together form an integrated whole—a system. This integrated whole is generally able to perform functions that would not have been possible as individual parts (or people), but can be completed as a whole system. In

> When we
> depend
> on others
> to "get the
> ball rolling"...
> the ball may
> never roll
> anywhere.

the business environment, there are any number of systems, composed of people and functions. These systems may be departments and teams that interrelate for common goals. They may even be small groups of people, within other systems, who act together to achieve what they could not do alone. Businesses are made of many systems, and entire libraries are filled with academic literature about what is termed *whole systems* – how all the individual systems are, in essence, one bigger system. It is the science of how people and processes work together interdependently to achieve desired outcomes. For this model, and for the G.R.A.C.E.-full leader, Systems Savvy is the thorough knowledge of the entire overall system that defines the actions within relationships (both of people to people, and processes). This systems savvy includes understanding of how all the individual parts (and people) are kept in balance to become and remain "high functioning," and the impact one process, action, or person has on another. This is often called "process management." In this model, however, process management doesn't quite fill the bill. While process management does include knowing how the people work together, it may not include how systems of people work best together, the critical knowledge (savvy) of successful human interaction. That is what is implied with this attribute. To practice the component of empowerment, the leader must comprehend this. The leader must also understand that within systems, one component or function can often sub-optimize the whole by making itself look good at the expense of the others. For example, Purchasing might be able to buy a lesser product, but this impacts the greater whole, and the efficiency of the people who may be putting together the final product. Part of systems savvy is knowing how to leverage the whole *for the better of the whole*, rather than optimize one or more sections at the *cost* of the whole.

Not only will leaders know the systems that reside within the organization and how they are interdependent, he or she will thoroughly understand and utilize the knowledge of *interactive human relationships*. This attribute begins with knowledge and is enhanced with a lot of foresight, born of experience. Systems savvy knows, and predicts, what will occur in human interaction. It thinks, considers and plans... before doing.

E3: Resource Management

Resource management is exactly what it sounds like: the management of resources, of all kinds. It is the careful, thoughtful, tactful and efficient administration and utilization of an organization's assets, for sustainability and accomplishment of desired outcomes. Resources can be tangible, such as goods, equipment, financial assets and labor resources such as employees, vendors, and others. As with all other attributes, there is an implied balance in this one as well. The wise resource manager makes sure there is enough to accomplish the business, but not so much that resources are not used, merely taking up valuable "space." This includes people. People are "managed" so as to make the best use of their skills and backgrounds. Resource management may also include somewhat intangible assets, such as knowledge, experiences, advice and guidance. Reduced to its basics, resources will include people, money, equipment and time. Resource management includes first the recognition of assets, then their implementation, utilization, facilitation, oversight and maximization. Too often those charged with this responsibility think only in terms of dollars

An Artist's Dilemma
A wall mural artist was attempting to save the client some money on a large project. This artist told the client that if they prepped the wall themselves, according to precise instructions, and purchased the paint, the project could be done less expensively. Although exact specifications for everything were provided, when this artist arrived to paint the wall mural, the client had purchased a lesser quality of paint, requiring the artist to spend twice as much time on the actual final painting. There were no cost savings here. In fact, the project cost more due to poor choices that did not consider the overall impact on the whole. **Systems Savvy knows, anticipates, and incorporates all functions into one whole, for the good of the whole.**

and tangibles, finances and equipment. Perhaps the greatest resources for any organization, however, are those who actually do the work – the people. And, the management of these people resources involves much more than merely placing people in the right place based on their experiences and skill sets. It means really knowing the people, knowing how they work, seeing their potential, challenging, supporting and empowering them to do the work charged to them-and sometimes more than what has been officially given them to do. This leader never allows wasteful down time, but always seeks to use the wealth of human resources in productive, and sometimes creative, ways.

E4: Development

The term "development" contains within it certain expectations: growth, the process of improving, expanding, enlarging and refining. It is a process, not a one-time event. In development, something, or someone, passes by degrees from one stage to another—a more advanced or mature stage. It always implies improvement. For this model, development is defined as the consistent enhancement of growth, the maturation of employees to include training, leadership development, or other means to encourage growth. All organizations generally provide some sort of development for its employees, but too often it is in the form of "one-size-fits-all" across the board mandatory trainings. And sometimes even these are provided only because of peer pressure from the business community, government regulations, or HR expectations. Generally, little thought is given to personal, individual development. Successful leaders know the individuals, know what drives them, what interests them, and what they need to grow. Although

...really know people and what will advance their growth....

some "trainings" may be given to all employees, or certain groups, a great leader knows his or her employees well enough to know to build those custom opportunities as well. These will not always take the shape of typical organizational trainings or leadership development. One individual may be ripe, ready and completely able to take on his or her first leadership assignment, which when given by a wise leader, is the most powerful *(and productive)* development tool. Another may be struggling with a certain responsibility, or a certain lack of skills or competencies, and would benefit tremendously by a personalized development opportunity such as being mentored by another employee, or educated formally in a particular area. The G.R.A.C.E.-full leader does not settle for the typical boxed trainings, thinking he or she has satisfied the need for employee development. This leader takes the time to really know the people, and what will advance their growth—then makes those opportunities available.

E5: Experimentation

Experimentation is a search for knowledge and the testing of an idea. An experiment is a controlled test or investigation to verify or falsify a particular idea, concept, process or possibility. It is a searching out by trial, and sometimes error, until a solution (to a problem or potential) is determined. No, we are not talking about the mad scientist or the dedicated researcher with a test tube and Bunsen burner. Experimentation is not confined to the sterile laboratory. It is a vital part of growth and advancement for an organization as well. In order to not only get ahead, but to also stay ahead, an individual and his or her organization will have to employ experimentation, with an attitude of positive gain to be derived from it. It is about doing the testing, research and trials to discover a better means (regarding processes and people) to achieve desired outcomes. It includes the typical collection and analysis of data, an attitude of openness and possibility, and a healthy dose of courage. The experimenting leader has a consistent attitude of betterment, and is always looking for ways to improve, then courageously testing potential paths to that improvement. Experimentation is utilized at every level of business, with both processes and people. The wise leader sees a need, and devises a plausible, sensible plan to meet the need. Experimentation is what determines if that plan will work, or not. Ideas, in themselves, are worth nothing. It is not until they are employed in an experimental attempt toward improvement that they become

EMPOWERMENT In Brief...

E1. Initiative
Readiness and ability to take first steps to make something better. Begin or follow-through energetically with plan for improvement.

E2. Systems Savvy
Thorough knowledge of entire system that defines actions within relationship; understanding impact one process or action or person has on another.

E3. Resource Management
Careful handling of resources to accomplish desired outcomes. Includes recognition, implementation, utilization, facilitation, oversight and maximization.

E4. Development
Consistent enhancement of growth of employees, including training or other means to encourage maturation.

E5. Experimentation
Testing, research, trials to discover better means to achieve desired outcomes (includes processes and people).

powerful. Successful experimentation depends on out-of-the-box thinking, creativity, innovation and positive intent. A cautionary word is advised here, however. Experimentation merely for the sake of something new or different, is not empowering experimentation. It is generally a waste of time and resources, including ideas, and is merely experimentation for the sake of experimentation. Experimentation is only an attribute of empowerment if its intent is toward positive gain.

E6: Reframing

Framing, in a societal or social sciences context, is the method we use to view the world around us. It is the way we interpret things, through our own personal set or collection of perceptions and stereotypes. Framing is what we rely on to understand ourselves, others and the world at large. It is what ultimately will dictate our responses to these inputs and stimuli. RE-framing is the ability to reset these automatic responses by remaining open to other perspectives. Reframing is the practiced ability (it is not an inherent or innate ability) to view things and people from different perspectives, different viewpoints, angles and perceptions, with openness and no hidden agendas. Reframing is free of previously existing stereotypes. We all have those, but reframing sets them aside in order to be completely open to possibilities we may not have considered, due to those stereotypes. Reframing allows us to see things (and people) differently than we normally "see" them, to process them and react to them without first passing them through the filters of personal perceptions and possible misconceptions, where they will tend to be blocked. As an attribute of empowerment, reframing keeps communication channels open, keeps processes moving and ideas flowing, and opens roads to previously blocked potentials.

E7: Recognition

Recognition is a simple word that carries two distinctly different meanings. The initial meaning is merely the ability to observe and be aware of something. It is having knowledge that is discerned through the senses, or perceived with the mind. The additional meaning implies acceptance, acknowledgement and appreciation for something. Both of these meanings are vital to both understanding and doing this element of empowerment. As an attribute of the empowerment component, recognition is the observation, appreciation and acknowledgement of good work, including appropriate affirmation, reward or celebration. We must first have knowledge of exactly what constitutes "good work" and then possess the ability to recognize it when we see it. But this awareness is only one part of this attribute. Leaders may often be cognizant of good work, but fail to take the next step of recognition—acknowledgement. This acknowledgement may either be formal or informal, but is always appropriate, timely and affirming. Acknowledgement is recognition of good work that validates, approves, appreciates and encourages more good work. Rewards and celebrations may be appropriate, but are not completely necessary to fully accomplish this attribute (although there are definitely times and work that calls for this). Recognition may often merely take the form of encouraging words to the "good worker." This simple recognition is like a tonic to the soul of the one receiving it. It means someone took notice, someone was impressed and pleased. The human creature yearns for recognition. Without it, work becomes rote, unexciting, uninspired, and eventually unproductive. It is un-empowered. Exceptional work is generally the product first of the personal passion, inspiration, drive and standards of

EMPOWERMENT In Brief...

E6. Reframing
Viewing things and people from different perspectives, with openness and no hidden agendas.

E7. Recognition
Observation, appreciation and acknowledgement of good work, with appropriate affirmation or reward.

Empowerment enables the success we seek.

the worker, and less about the "have-to's" of that person's job description. Words of acknowledgement for such work are the gold stars that fuel more work just like it.

AT the beginning of this component we stated that empowerment is about enabling success. People may be able to perform their functions, and may even be able to meet expectations for production, but without empowerment, success is really not achievable, let alone sustainable. The human body requires food, nourishment that acts as the fuel for the engine. All of us are able to exist and even function for awhile without it. As time ticks by, however, we find our systems slow down as the former energy reserves melt away. Eventually production ceases, and the body's entire work effort goes into merely surviving, rather than thriving. And, at a certain point if our tanks are still empty, the entire engine dies. This analogy is quite appropriate in relationships as well. We have certain tasks to perform, certain expectations to meet, and for awhile, even without the enabling fuel of empowerment, we can function and perhaps even excel. Continued lack of this fuel will cause first slow down, and then the inevitable shut down. People in relationship, whether business or personal, will merely "go through the motions" without empowerment. And at some point all motion and all production will cease. And so will the relationship.

People in relationship, whether business or personal, will merely "go through the motions" without empowerment. And at some point all motion and all production will cease. And so will the relationship.

Empowerment is the all important commodity that enables the forward motion of any person, or organization. You can have the engines, wings, navigation equipment and even the experienced pilot, but if you don't fill the fuel tank, you won't fly anywhere. Consider each of the attributes that build empowerment. Each one is necessary to fully inspire, develop and enable people to work in ways that not just meet expectations, but far exceed them. Again, empowerment enables the success we seek.

Putting it All Together

NOW that we have explored the *G.R.A.C.E. at Work* model, let's put it all back together to understand how all the pieces work together.

There are five basic components to this model:

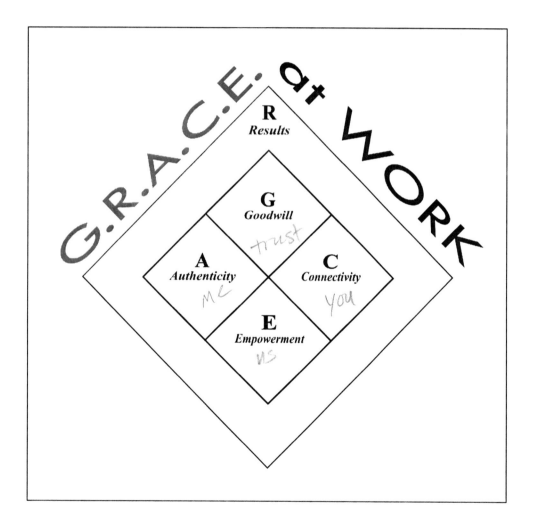

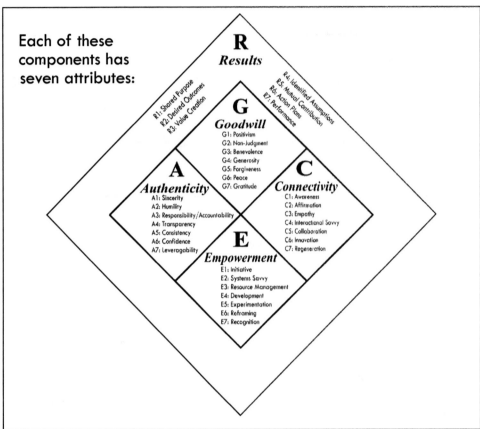

Each of these components has seven attributes:

R — Results
R1: Shared Purpose
R2: Desired Outcomes
R3: Value Creation
R4: Identified Assumptions
R5: Mutual Contribution
R6: Action Plans
R7: Performance

G — Goodwill
G1: Positivism
G2: Non-Judgment
G3: Benevolence
G4: Generosity
G5: Forgiveness
G6: Peace
G7: Gratitude

A — Authenticity
A1: Sincerity
A2: Humility
A3: Responsibility/Accountability
A4: Transparency
A5: Consistency
A6: Confidence
A7: Leveragability

C — Connectivity
C1: Awareness
C2: Affirmation
C3: Empathy
C4: Interactional Savvy
C5: Collaboration
C6: Innovation
C7: Regeneration

E — Empowerment
E1: Initiative
E2: Systems Savvy
E3: Resource Management
E4: Development
E5: Experimentation
E6: Reframing
E7: Recognition

GOODWILL	RESULTS	AUTHENTICITY	CONNECTIVITY	EMPOWERMENT
Positivism	Shared Purpose	Sincerity	Awareness	Initiative
Non-Judgment	Desired Outcomes	Humility	Affirmation	Systems Savvy
Benevolence	Value Creation	Responsibility/ Accountability	Empathy	Resource Management
Generosity	Identified Assumptions	Transparency	Interactional Savvy	Development
Forgiveness	Mutual Contribution	Consistency	Collaboration	Experimentation
Peace	Action Plans	Confidence	Innovation	Reframing
Gratitude	Performance	Leveragability	Regeneration	Recognition

Within each component are also certain dynamics necessary for the component to function properly within the system.

At the core of the **GOODWILL** component is the need to make certain choices. *Will I exercise goodwill in this relationship? To what extent or measure am I willing to do so?* The answers to these questions must be reached before attempting to employ the seven attributes associated with the Goodwill component.

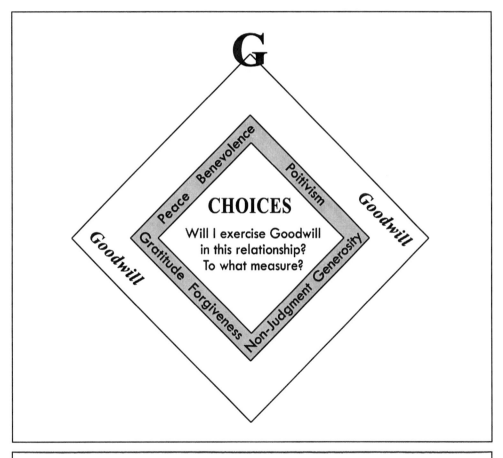

GOODWILL

In addition to the seven attributes that compose the **RESULTS** component, the understanding that all the other components reside within this "outer diamond" is critical. This knowledge allows us to comprehend that the measure and extent of how all the other components are practiced will very directly affect the realization of the desired outcomes, or Results. All the components are related to one another such that when more *Goodwill, Authenticity, Connectivity* and *Empowerment* are displayed in a relationship, the *Results* are larger. Conversely, the less the four inner diamonds are evident in relationship, the smaller the results.

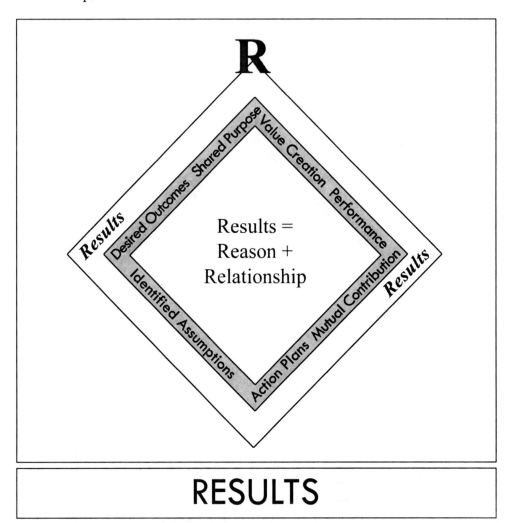

RESULTS

The **AUTHENTICITY** component may be the most complex. Not only does it consist of seven critical attributes, but its very existence (the ability to *be* authentic) relies upon what we have termed *Self Knowledge*. Self Knowledge is the thorough understanding of self, which is composed of Heart, Mind, Soul and Body. These four elements of self are manifested in physical ways and viewed by others in what can be called Leadership Presence. Leadership presence is simply what is seen and felt by others in relationship. Like those nesting dolls we referenced earlier, the core of the individual (heart, mind, soul and body) is inside leadership presence, and self knowledge dictates authenticity.

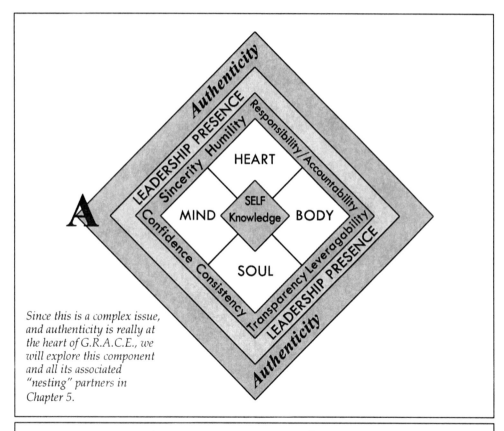

Since this is a complex issue, and authenticity is really at the heart of G.R.A.C.E., we will explore this component and all its associated "nesting" partners in Chapter 5.

AUTHENTICITY

CONNECTIVITY can be can be seen as the link between Authenticity and Empowerment. We can have Self Knowledge, but unless we have knowledge of others, we will not be able to empower them to action and to desired outcomes. Connectivity relies on this Other Knowledge linking up with Self Knowledge to create powerful connections that enable empowerment.

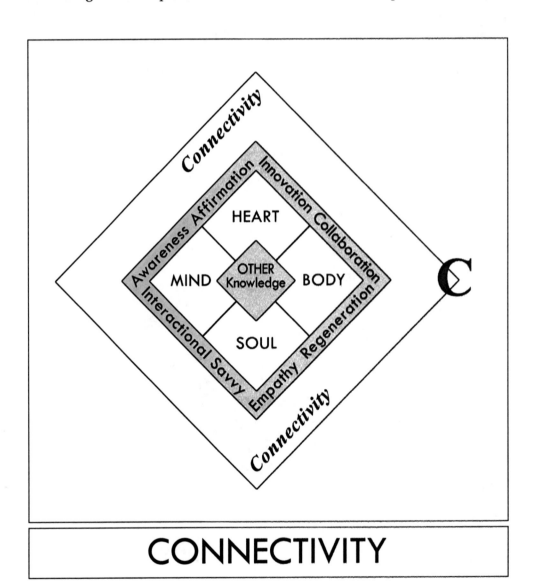

CONNECTIVITY

The final piece to the *G.R.A.C.E. at Work* model is the **EMPOWERMENT** component. The core of this last element is the combination of both the heart of Authenticity (Self Knowledge), and the center of Connectivity (Others Knowledge), yielding Shared Knowledge ("Us" Knowledge). This is the real power source of powerful relationships. We know ourselves well, then we know others well, then we explore and know who we are together, and what helps us work to our ultimate ability and potential.

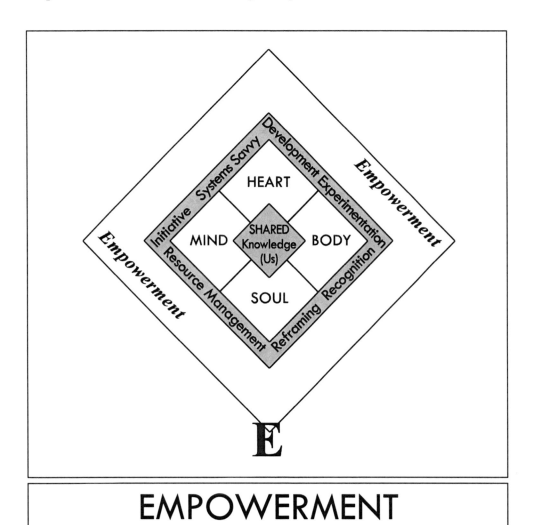

EMPOWERMENT

GRACE-full leadership occurs when all five G.R.A.C.E. components work together to create that purposeful, powerful and productive relationship, reflect a capacity to create value and recover quickly from mistakes.

If any one of these components is missing (even a few attributes) or exists in insufficient quantity, there is no G.R.A.C.E.

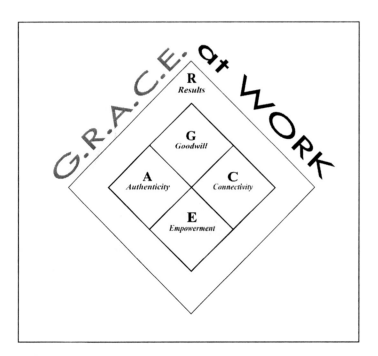

Let's put the model back together now *(next page)* and take another look, this time at the *master* model, which contains all of these components and their attributes. The diamond in the center is the "Bull's Eye" or "Sweet Spot" where all the components come together in equal balance, all in action. The circular arrow indicates they are all in motion, and there is interaction between all the components.

BALANCE

Strategy vs. Relationships

The Complete G.R.A.C.E. at Work Model

It's Not About Me

AFTER learning about the *G.R.A.C.E. at Work* model, you have probably determined that there is a foundational realization that undergirds the entire model. This model is not about you, or me, it is about all of us. This is not a popular sentiment among many people today, but it is essential for the GRACE-full leader. Team or organizational success sometimes demands individual sacrifice. And that requires doing what's best for the team, as opposed to pushing toward individual opportunity or pursuing individual honor and recognition. In the game of baseball, a sacrifice fly or bunt may result in a player sacrificing his personal performance statistics to advance the team. Similarly, a sacrifice in a powerful relationship may mean that a person gives up his or her agenda, his or her need to be "right," or the need to be first. This is the pure meaning of goodwill, and evidence of the capacity to lead with G.R.A.C.E. It is also a characteristic that, when successfully modeled, can be learned by others.

G.R.A.C.E.-Full Change

THOSE who work within the model of G.R.A.C.E. are also more apt to recognize when the opportunity to create mutual value no longer exists and it is time to move on. Organizational decisions involving downsizing, outsourcing or reorganizing will not come as a surprise or be perceived with a sense of betrayal when G.R.A.C.E. is at work. Employees and leaders realize that these actions represent the right business decision for the organization, and for the individual. If G.R.A.C.E. has been operational in the workplace, employees are better prepared for new challenges and opportunities. It is vital to remember that G.R.A.C.E. operates on the win-win assumption. Even if an employee moves on, it is a win for him or her, having been given every opportunity to thrive and prepare in a safe place of grace.

The concepts behind the word "grace" lend themselves to this model well.

Leading with G.R.A.C.E.

POWERFUL relationships can form the basis for achieving breakthrough performance and building the capacity for future growth. Whether you are an executive, manager, coach, or colleague, *G.R.A.C.E. at Work* can provide greater opportunities to build relationships and facilitate performance. Employees and leaders are authentic, achieve a special kind of chemistry for growth, empower each other and extend good will. It is the creation of a safe place for people to perform – within stated boundaries – without fear of failure.

The concepts behind the word "grace" lend themselves to this model well. Grace generally brings to mind two ideas. One, simply put, is unmerited favor. In other words, we are treated much better than we deserve. The other is a certain poise or elegance in movement. Both of these ideas contribute to leading with grace. G.R.A.C.E. leadership assumes goodwill, which will many times translate into unmerited favor. In the previously mentioned study involving Jim and Karl, Jim had grounds to fire Karl. Karl's poor performance was reason enough. But, instead, Jim extended unmerited favor, and with leadership elegance, created an environment in which Karl could, and did, flourish. In a leadership state of G.R.A.C.E., energy is abundant and performance effortless. Obstacles are anticipated, but with the expectation that they will be overcome. Failure is seen as an opportunity to learn. This does not imply that this kind of relationship is pain free or even easy. It requires effort, commitment and yes, grace. But the anticipation and realization of success supersedes pain and difficulty.

Leading with G.R.A.C.E. encourages people to learn new things and express themselves authentically in a safe environment. G.R.A.C.E. encourages commitment, not compliance, because G.R.A.C.E. assumes that development and high performance occur most effectively in the context of a purposeful relationship. This relationship is based on goodwill and a mutual commitment to a shared purpose that provides affirmation, inspiration and personal transformation. Without G.R.A.C.E., what remains is a series of transactional interactions that neither satisfy nor inspire.

Chapter 4

STRATEGY + RELATIONSHIPS = SUCCESS

The Case for G.R.A.C.E. at Work

"Courage and grace are a formidable mixture.
The only place to see it is in the bullring."
— *Marlene Dietrich*

*(While mostly true, I disagree with this quote.
You will also see it here in these award winning companies.)*

The Case for G.R.A.C.E.

G.R.A.C.E. AT WORK is about creating the context for people to rise up and do more than what they would normally do on their own. This model provides a framework and structure to help people determine their behavior and interaction attitudes with those around them, to gain the greatest results.

At the beginning of this book the Baldrige Criteria for Performance Excellence was introduced. This system is useful to explore the common components of organizational leadership, a standard guideline for excellence in these areas. To demonstrate how the *G.R.A.C.E. at Work* relationship model is balanced with a strategic model, the tables on the next pages list the seven major components of the Baldrige Criteria, and the five elements of the *G.R.A.C.E. at Work* model at work together. Here again are the seven areas of the Baldrige Criteria, and what they are intended to measure:

CATEGORY 1: Leadership
The personal actions of an organization's senior leaders, and how they guide and sustain the organization.

CATEGORY 2: Strategic Planning
Strategic objective and action plans, how they are deployed, changed and measured.

CATEGORY 3: Customer and Market Focus
Customer engagement for long-term marketplace success. Building customer-focused culture, listening to voice of customers, innovation.

CATEGORY 4: Measurement, Analysis and Knowledge Management
Selecting, gathering, analyzing managing and improving data, information and knowledge assets, including information technology. Use of performance reviews.

CATEGORY 5: Human Resource Focus
Engaging, managing, developing high performance workforce to achieve full potential, alignment with organizational mission.

CATEGORY 6: Process Management
Designing, managing, improving and sustaining work systems for customer value and organizational success.

CATEGORY 7: Business Results
Organizational performance, improvement, customer outcomes, financial and market outcomes.

These 7 areas of the Baldrige Criteria are intended to represent all processes within an organization.

The charts showing the G.R.A.C.E. at Work component relationships to these areas are found on the next pages.

BALDRIGE CRITERIA FOR PERFORMANCE EXCELLENCE	G.R.A.C.E. AT WORK COMPONENTS				
	GOODWILL	**RESULTS**	**AUTHENTICITY**	**CONNECTIVITY**	**EMPOWERMENT**
CATEGORY 1: LEADERSHIP	All leadership, especially senior, approaches leading first with goodwill to all parties, not personal gain, seeks place for growth, and assumes positive intent toward customers and all employees. Governance through goodwill and benevolence.	Leadership clearly understands reasons for organizational being, employee and/or customer relationships, and expected results, which drive all operations, and imparts sense of shared purpose, mutual value, and desired outcomes.	Leadership desires to be authentic (real, with integrity) in all relationships, and in tactical operations, openly and honestly communicates reality. Sincere, humble approach, transparent and consistent. Governance responsible and accountable.	Leadership has genuine desire to connect with employees, customers, stakeholders, etc., and finds ways to identify with and affirm others. Seeks collaboration and innovation, empathy. Has interactional savvy.	Leadership establishes a safe environment, resources, catalysts for organizational success with employee commitment and continued motivation. Takes the initiative, manages resources, experiments.
CATEGORY 2: STRATEGIC PLANNING	Strategic Planning is designed to achieve results, but with honest good intention for all parties involved, no personal gain or promotion. Planning also seeks to be generous to both employees and customers.	Strategies to achieve results are tactically sound, but are driven by understanding that relationships, and reason for being together, are what ultimately yield those results. Based on mutual contribution, shared purpose.	Strategic planning is completely aware of reality, does not contain hidden agendas or unrealistic goals, openly communicates and consciously designs strategy to maximize authentic relationships that yield results	Strategies include active development of connections that serve the processes to yield results. Plans encourage interaction, collaboration and innovation. Communication and complete awareness of strategies within organization.	Strategic planning always addresses and includes practical ways to empower employees to perform at optimum, with motivation to achieve results — but with goodwill toward them, not intent to enslave or drain dry.
CATEGORY 3: CUSTOMER AND MARKET FOCUS	Organization adopts and acts with attitude of goodwill toward customer to provide best product or service within means, protecting customers from harm with good intent. Marketing also assumes this intent and engages in truthful and ethical practices.	Understanding that customers drive results. Customer needs fully integrated into results oriented planning. Customer requirements, focus and priority are known and reinforced throughout organization. Customer satisfaction drives planning.	Customer communication encouraged, and is open, honest and collaborative. Customer is always right, company is humble. Marketing is honest, providing authentic information, no attempt to deceive or oversell. Marketing efforts are truthful, transparent.	Company aware of customer needs and wants, finds empathy with customer, knows how to interact. Market focus is innovative, knows how to connect with customers. Able to repair any disconnects in customer communication, or market servicing.	Organization seeks ways to empower the customer, through experimentation, reframing, recognition of customer needs. Takes initiative to meet needs. Marketing focuses on empowering the customer.

BALDRIGE CRITERIA FOR PERFORMANCE EXCELLENCE	G.R.A.C.E. AT WORK COMPONENTS				
	GOODWILL	**RESULTS**	**AUTHENTICITY**	**CONNECTIVITY**	**EMPOWERMENT**
CATEGORY 4: MEASUREMENT, ANALYSIS AND KNOWLEDGE MANAGEMENT	Information, data and knowledge are obtained and managed with an attitude of good will and positive intent — always! Knowledge management is positive, non-judgmental.	Knowledge management understands shared purpose and desired outcomes, based on value creation, mutual contribution. Used to improve performance, support action plans, etc.	Measurement and management of knowledge is honest and sincere, transparent and consistent. Information provides confidence, leveragability.	Information systems affirm connections and collaboration, invite innovation, help in regeneration and keep organization fully aware. Not hidden, but open to encourage and support connection in all areas.	Knowledge management used for resource management, development reframing and recognition. Always used for positive, helpful for taking initiative. Empowering, not limiting.
CATEGORY 5: HUMAN RESOURCE FOCUS	Human Resources focus is always positive, non-judgmental, and benevolent. People processes are generous, grateful and extending forgiveness as appropriate.	HR understands that results are achieved through people who have shared purpose. Strives for value creation, encourages mutual contribution and excellent performance. Uses action plans to achieve results, by balancing people needs.	Human Resources interactions are always sincere and honest, open and transparent, consistent. Department is confident in employee dealings, using and encouraging leveragability, responsibility and accountability.	HR is aware of how to make appropriate employee connections, has empathy and interactional savvy, encourages collaboration and innovation, affirms everyone equally, and knows how to regenerate broken connections.	HR major focus is to empower employees through resource management, development, experimentation, reframing and appropriate recognition. Understand systems well, takes initiative and encourages employees to empower others.
CATEGORY 6: PROCESS MANAGEMENT	Design, manage and improve work systems for positive benefit to employees and customers, undergirded with goodwill, generosity, benevolence.	All processes managed to achieve desired outcomes and shared purpose of all employees. Processes also create value and promote performance based on action plans and mutual contribution.	Systems and processes designed and maintained to be honest, transparent, consistent, and instill confidence in all stakeholders. Systems encourage leveragability, and promote responsibility and accountability.	Systems promote ready connections, reveal interactional savvy, encourage collaboration and innovation, and allow for regeneration of broken connections. Process management affirms, empathizes with people.	Systems encourage initiative, resource management, employee development and experimentation. All systems and processes designed to empower all stakeholders, allow for reframing, recognition.
CATEGORY 7: BUSINESS RESULTS	Desired outcomes become realized outcomes based on goodwill for all stakeholders. Results non-judgmental, forgiveness and gratitude given, attitude of benevolence seen in realized results.	Results focus on shared value, value creation, performance and mutual contribution. Evaluation of results identifies assumptions, customer value, efficacy of action plans	Results achieved through consistent, authentic relationships, sincere and humble attitudes. Responsibility and accountability are apparent, results transparent and leveragable.	Results enhanced through stakeholder affirmation, empathy, interactional savvy. Interactions and processes results-driven, but also collaborative, innovative connectivity-based.	Results directly affect all stakeholders, and empower all employees. Results improved through reframing, experimentation. Appropriate recognition and reward.

In every one of the seven areas of business focus that stand as the criteria for the yearly Baldrige Awards, the balance between strategies and relationships is always the deciding factor. Total revenue and bottom line results may be the ultimate goal for any organization or business, but it is a fact that the only way to actually reach these successes is through the careful building and maintaining of relationships with the people responsible for pursuing and achieving those desired outcomes. Whether those relationships exist among the workforce (including every level of leadership and "followership"), the customers, or other stakeholders, business victories and successes will be sadly elusive without overall well-being among the individuals who are the minds, hearts, legs, feet and hands of the organization. A business or organization is so much more than the brand, holdings or product. Without the people, those things are empty and hollow. This is not just a nice sounding business "tactic" or some sort of magical formula for success. It is a fact. Organizations thrive on the people, and die without them. If those people feel respected, honored and valued, the output increases. This view is supported by research, conducted by the Center for Creative Leadership.

Every year the Malcolm Baldrige National Quality Award is announced for outstanding businesses and organizations. Details of the winning entries are made public so others can see just exactly why these organizations were recognized. Year after year, without fail, you can expect to find that consistent relationship building is one of the major factors in these award decisions. Companies that place a focus on the people (employees, customers, other stakeholders) are the companies that succeed. And, again year after year, you will find evidence of *G.R.A.C.E. at Work* in the committee reviews of these award-winning organizations. Want to surpass your organizational goals? Want to be recognized as an award-winning company? Want to be the envy of leadership teams everywhere? Well, to use a popular colloquialism today — *"it's about the people, stupid!"*

It's always about the people. People do the work of the company, and happy people do better work than unhappy people. It is really very simple. Making the people happy is all about goodwill, keeping an eye on results, being authentic, connecting with others, and empowering everyone to do their best. It's all about the smart strategy of relationships.

If you researched the reports written about the Baldrige award winners, you would read the following sampling of actual comments about these exceptional organizations *(these were randomly selected and paraphrased from some of the winners in the last three years)*:

- "No blame" approach to leadership

- Empowerment and innovation ingrained in the culture

- Focus on developing lasting relationships with clients

- Treat each client as a guest in our own home

- Focus on prevention and process improvement rather than personal blame

- Open door policy...frank two-way communication with all organization's stakeholders

- Such policies as "It's OK to report errors or mistakes in my department..."

- Daily interactions with workforce, partners, suppliers, customers, and collaborators

- Reinforcing relationships through simple actions such as publicly praising staff members

- Senior leaders devote significant time and resources to communicating with and engaging the workforce

- CEO: *"It is my job to make this the best place you have ever worked. If I'm not doing my job, tell me."*

- Engage the workforce through informal settings... luncheons, celebrations and social events

- Established and maintained a culture of celebration

- Numerous reward and recognition opportunities

- Focus on people

- Turtle Award celebrates an employee's "sticking neck out" at some risk to pursue a desired outcome, regardless of ultimate success

> The foundational aspects of G.R.A.C.E. at Work are behind workforce and customer satisfaction.

- Employee incentive compensation programs
- Recognition of employee accomplishments
- Opportunities for work/life balance
- Enhanced employee development and increased visibility
- Numerous cross-functional teams
- Opportunities to manage home life situations, seek advanced education, etc.

> ...relationship building is one of the major factors in these award decisions...

And the list could go on and on and on. These are all actual comments about Baldrige Award winning organizations. They were important enough to mention as part of the deciding factors for their recognition. All of them indicate that *G.R.A.C.E. at Work* is present and practiced in these award-winning businesses. The foundational aspects of *G.R.A.C.E. at Work* are behind workforce and customer satisfaction. Take a look now at the 2009 Baldrige award winners, and some of the highlights of these organizational findings.

Honeywell Federal Manufacturing & Technologies, LLC

(management/operating contractor at National Nuclear Security Administration's Kansas City Plant contract; multi-discipline engineering/manufacturing specializing in electrical, mechanical, and engineered material components)

Highlights

- Overall customer satisfaction at or above 95% past four years

- Combined quality/reliability performance level at 99.9% for customers past three years

- Workforce satisfaction scores of 72% for "workforce feels appreciated" (compared to commercial best in class manufacturers of 67%), a score of 81% for "management listens to ideas" (compared to 76%), a score of 72% for "positive environment" (compared to 58%)

MidwayUSA
(family-owned, catalog/Internet-based retail merchant)

Highlights

- Overall customer satisfaction rating 93%
- Overall customer retention is 98%
- Overall customer loyalty, measured as "likelihood to shop again," is 94%
- Annual employee survey score improved from 60% favorable in 2002 to 82% in 2008

AtlantiCare
(non-profit health system in southeastern New Jersey, delivers acute and chronic care, preventive and at-risk services, and health information)

Highlights

- Customer satisfaction above that expected for these services
- Employee loyalty index score equals that of health care leader
- Workforce engagement survey are equal to or approaching 90th percentile national performance levels
- Nurse turnover rate declined from 7.75% in 2006 to 6.02% in 2008 (New Jersey Hospital Association average is 12.43%

Heartland Health
(integrated, not-for-profit, community-based health care delivery system, serves 22-county market, portions of Missouri, Kansas, Nebraska, and Iowa. Physician and hospital care services, Health and wellness programs)

Highlights

- Overall outpatient satisfaction 90%
- Employees' Individual Education Plans
- Workers' Total Rewards Program

Department of Veterans Affairs
Cooperative Studies Program Clinical Research Pharmacy Coordinating Center
(federal government organization supporting clinical trials targeting current veteran health issues)

Highlights

- "Overall Satisfaction" from 83% "good-excellent" (2003) to 100% "good-excellent" (2009)

- 75% of customer relationships exceed 10 years

- Majority of extramural funding from repeat business

- "Workforce Satisfaction" results exceeded Gallup's 75th percentile rating four consecutive years (2005-2008).

- Low turnover, supportive learning environment

- Federal Executive Board Employer of Choice for 2008 and 2009

- Top 10 ranking on the "New Mexico Best Place to Work for 2009" list

IT is also obvious these organizations have a good grasp on the fundamentals of good leadership and strategic planning and execution. However, the glue that holds all of these competencies together is the people. Take a look again at the exceptionally high percentages of both customer and workforce satisfaction. There is only one way to achieve these numbers. Those companies that make sure they build relationships on a platform of goodwill, and practice the components, elements and attributes of *G.R.A.C.E. at Work*, will rise to the top of both the award lists and the goal achievement lists. These are organizations that achieve results, and organizations that last.

...the glue that holds all these competencies together is the people.

Chapter 5

AUTHENTICITY

The Heart of G.R.A.C.E. at Work

"The authentic self is the soul made visible."
— *Sarah Ban Breathnach*

GETTING REAL:

Finding and Living Your Authentic Self

AUTHENTICITY has been defined here as the essential reality of a person. It is "knowing and showing" the real you. As a component of the *G.R.A.C.E. at Work* model, it is the central core that gives life to all the others. If we are not ourselves, then all our efforts of G.R.A.C.E. will not be real, and certainly not successful. G.R.A.C.E. can't be faked. It relies upon our ability to be authentic, and act authentically. The attributes (sincerity, humility, responsibility/ accountability, transparency, consistency, confidence and leveragability) of Authenticity were discussed in Chapter 2, and are characteristics visible to others that indicate either the presence, or the lack of, authenticity. In essence, authenticity is the real you, and that real you is observable by others.

The attributes of authenticity blend together into one entity that speaks to the world about who we are. We sometimes call this entity "presence." The typical definition of this word means the state of "being present." But exactly what or who is present? An empty shell, a phony, a persona "constructed" for public consumption, or the authentic person? Our authenticity is observed by others as our presence in the world. It is how we show up in the world. For leaders, we tack on the word "leadership." But if you believe as I do that we are all leaders of sorts, then all of us (whether in positions of leadership or not) will exhibit a "leadership presence."

> In essence, authenticity is the real you, and that real you is observable by others.

Our ability to be authentic is necessary for our health and well-being in every area of life. Many people live as if they were someone else. But the dark side of our inability to be authentic is that the very thing we don't want to do or be becomes the predominant expression of our presence. This is true whether seen in the business world, at home, or anywhere we have a presence. When we continue in personal and professional deception, being someone we are not (*in other*

> Leadership Presence manifests itself in the visible and observable attributes of the Authenticity component.

words, inauthentic), we are caught in the clutches of the very thing we vowed we didn't want to become or do. And in the moment of our deepest struggle, we lack the will and ability to make the transformation that would free us from self criticism, self loathing, and despair. Our overall health and welfare is in great danger at this point.

In the *G.R.A.C.E. at Work* graphic depiction of the model, the Authenticity component is illustrated with a number of "nested" elements. The outer diamond represents the entire Authenticity component. Moving from the outside of the diamond inward, Authenticity is seen through our "presence," and in the business case, our leadership presence. Leadership Presence manifests itself in the visible and observable attributes of the Authenticity component: Sincerity, Humility, Responsibility and Accountability, Confidence, Consistency, Transparency and Leveragability. These attributes have already been discussed in the previous chapter. A leader is only able to display these attributes in an authentic way when he or she has integrated all of his or her personal core components, the vital parts of heart, mind, body and soul. These components make up what we can call "SELF knowledge."

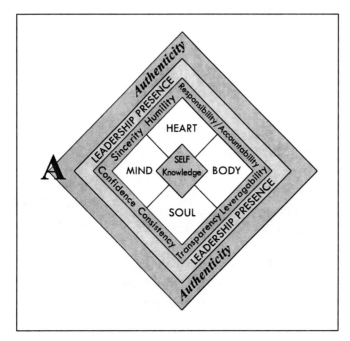

In its essence, Authenticity begins with self knowledge, and the inner commitment to be, as Shakespeare said, true to self. A lack of commitment to do this will cause breakdowns in our ability to be authentic, from the inside out. Looking at the Authenticity diamond again, this time moving from the inside core outward, we could place the big question of "am I true to self?" at the center of the SELF Knowledge core diamond. If the answer is "yes," you will be able to successfully integrate your heart, mind, soul and body, which will then allow you to be sincere, humble, responsible, accountable, confident, consistent, transparent and able to leverage strengths and weaknesses. In other words, you will be able to be authentic. This *authentic you* translates into powerful leadership presence, which is the outer core of real Authenticity in the *G.R.A.C.E. at Work* model. Conversely, if the commitment to be true to self is missing, a person will never integrate those vital core parts (heart, mind, soul, body), will most likely have great difficulty practicing or exhibiting the seven attributes of the Authenticity component, and will have pretty much zero or even negative leadership presence.

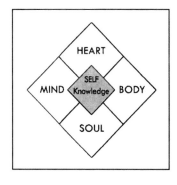

And it all begins with Self Knowledge. Trying to integrate your four self core components, absolutely necessary for Authenticity, without really knowing yourself, knowing what your passions and purpose are, what your physical skills and capabilities are, what you are really thinking, or what triggers your emotional responses, would be as fruitless as trying to get butter from butterflies. The purpose of this book is not to show you how to know yourself. There are many, many tomes written for this pursuit. The point here is to make sure you know that you must know yourself before anything else falls into place, and before you can ever hope to practice Authenticity with effective leadership presence. Let's take a look at these various "nested" components of Authenticity a little more closely.

Leadership Presence

LEADERSHIP Presence is a term that many people define in many different ways. If we break down these two words in their simplest forms, we can get a pretty good idea of what is intended here. We all know or can provide a definition of what *leadership* means. I will let you do that on your own. The word "presence," as defined by Wiktionary *(a wiki-based Open Content, free online dictionary)* can include the following:

- *The fact or condition of being present, or of being within sight or call, or at hand*

- *A quality of poise and effectiveness that enables a performer to achieve a close relationship with his audience*

- *The state of being closely focused on the here and now, not distracted by irrelevant thoughts*

◇
___

Presence is...
inescapable.

When presence is yoked with leadership, the idea emerges of a leader being able to focus on the here and now, *achieve a close relationship* with his or her "audience," and be truly present in any given moment without distraction. That is the essence of *Leadership Presence.*

1 Leadership Presence,
Bella Linda Halpern and
Kathy Lubar
Gotham
(October 14, 2004)
ISBN 978-1592400867

In their book by the same name *("Leadership Presence"*[1]*)* authors Halpern and Lubar define it this way: *"Leadership presence...the ability to connect authentically with the thoughts and feelings of others, in order to motivate and inspire them toward a desired outcome."*

Dr. James Bugental takes it a bit further: *"Presence calls our attention to how genuinely and completely a person is in a situation rather than standing apart from it as an observer, commentator, critic or judge...Presence is a name for the quality of being in a situation or relationship in which one intends at a deep level to participate as fully as she is able. Presence is expressed through mobilization of one's sensitivity – both inner and outer – and through bringing into action one's capacity for response."*[2]

2 <u>The Art of the Psychotherapist: How to develop the skills that take psychotherapy beyond science</u> James F. T. Bugental W.W. Norton & Co. (September 17, 1992) ISBN 978-0393309119

I'd like to offer a simpler and more practical definition, one that can inspire us to improve our presence in any situation:

> **Presence is the manifestation of the way in which we choose to give life to our heart, mind, body, and soul.**

Presence creates a "space" for us as individuals and for others as community. Presence can be understood as what other people see as a result of our personal alignment of heart, mind, body and soul. The more we are able to integrate and align our values and beliefs with our actions and behaviors the more powerful our presence. Alignment not only enables effectiveness, it also affords us efficiency by eliminating tolerations that distract us from being authentic.

Presence is not only important, it is inescapable. If we plan to be in relationship with others, in any way, in any place, we will literally "present a presence." That presence is a reflection of our authenticity. If we are not perceived as real and authentic, or if our presence does not powerfully connect and impress others, we will not achieve the results we desire. Halpern and Lubar state: *"Leadership is about results and outcomes, and so leaders want the hearts and minds of others directed toward some purpose, some result desirable for the group or organization. Presence is the fundamental way a leader can engage the full energies and dedication of others to a common end."*

> Our Leadership Presence is essentially the extent to which we can align and leverage our heart, mind, body and soul in the pursuit of excellence and the influence of others.

Many people relate presence to the outward and visible ability to speak well, look good, have appealing body language and high energy levels. While these are important, none of them will, in themselves, create a powerful presence. That kind of presence comes only from that *careful alignment of heart, mind, body and soul.* Our presence is a declaration of:

- Who we are
- What we stand for
- Where we are going
- What actions we are committed to taking in support of declaration

Our Leadership Presence is essentially the extent to which we can align and leverage our heart, mind, body, and soul in the pursuit of excellence and the influence of others. This presence manifests itself in the *ability to cause impact on someone else's heart, mind, body and soul.* This is the first attribute of leadership presence. The second, perhaps more visible, feature is the connection we are able to make with others to create something bigger than ourselves.

> In many ways we can say that what we do with our leadership presence is actually a moral act....

On August 28, 1963, Martin Luther King, Jr. spoke from the steps of the Lincoln Memorial to a crowd so large it spilled out onto the National Mall and around the large reflecting pool. His "I have a dream" speech electrified the crowd and ignited and advanced the cause of civil rights more than anything else in America's history. Dr. King had the ability to verbalize and demonstrate something much bigger than any one person, and through this allowed people to connect with this bigger dream, and therefore connect with one another. But it wasn't just King's speech—it was his life. He had an essence, what we can call "leadership presence," that came as a result of his personal journey and integration of the grand purpose and values of his soul, which when leveraged with the emotional responses of his heart, the sharp intellect of his mind, and his physical actions combined to yield a force that moved people. They were attracted to him, and to his message. And his presence rubbed off on others, who took that message to the ends of this nation, and across the globe. Dr. King was one of the best examples of what it means to have leadership presence, but there are many others out there who may not have had the same recognition, but just as surely have and will influence us and even change our lives.

Moral Responsibility

In many ways we can say that what we do with our leadership presence is actually a moral act, since a leader can use this presence for good or evil. In this regard, we must remember that leadership presence, and leadership in general, carries a big responsibility. We all have a presence. We've seen how a person in a really good mood can brighten up a room and affect the moods of others. Conversely, we have all experienced what happens when a person walks into a room with rain clouds hanging over his or her head. This is a simple way to illustrate this important concept. When we consider that the utility of presence can cause good or evil, we are reminded that leaders have to be thoughtful and mindful of their intentions. Great leaders realize there will be consequence, intended and unintended, resulting from their actions. This is one reason why being in relationship is so important, and also why Goodwill is critical. It is important to talk to people about what has transpired in this relationship, to clarify what is in mind and align it with what has actually happened. If people don't feel the leader is having an impact, or the impact doesn't match intentions, there will be a disconnect and dissatisfaction.

Intentionality

Presence is intentional. It is increased or enhanced through intention. If we are purposeful about what it is we want to do, we can become more effective and efficient with our decisions, our actions, and our impact

There are consequences, intended or unintended, that will result from every word, every action. This underscores the criticality of Goodwill starting and ending every action. This model is about enabling transformational relationships for all parties. These may even be strangers. There are new insights, new wisdom obtained when Goodwill is present in all words and deeds. The message received is that someone took the time to care, to listen, to explore with Goodwill. Sometimes this is all it takes to open the floodgates of opportunity.

on others. People have opportunity to see how well leaders are aligned with what they say they will do and what they actually do. If impact and intention are in sync, there is a greater chance that people will recognize and appreciate that presence, and that they will be "on board" with the leader.

Transparency

The concept of transparency is critical to leadership presence. People are looking for others they can affiliate with or relate to, and they resonate with positive attributes of leadership presence. If a leader has a way of creating transparency so that people know exactly what they are getting into (or not) this creates a basis for greater trust, allows synergy to build, and paves the way for collaboration. Transparency also assumes an element of education and training. When a leader is transparent, people understand his or her mind-set, paradigms, and passions. Part of the ability to create leadership presence is to train others to know those things, and to know what this leader stands for and is trying to accomplish.

Spontaneity

Intention and transparency are strengthened by spontaneity, which demonstrates a genuine expression of whatever is on a person's heart. It is through spontaneity that we can know a person's true values and substantive base. Spontaneity by nature is something not planned, so it is more difficult to "hide" the real person, thus revealing the authentic presence of any leader. Goodwill, which undergirds the entire *G.R.A.C.E. at Work* model, must also be spontaneous and natural. Planned goodwill works only when it reflects the leader's true self and presence.

> ...motivation must align with *doing* in order to preserve our authenticity....

Presence is the ability to use our authenticity to make connection with others. Presence only comes from that integration of heart, mind, body and soul, and *then being comfortable with who we are*. This integrated presence helps us understand what we stand for, and why we do what we do. Our own presence becomes the culture in which all other things reside, and the basis from which we are able to practice a relationship model like *G.R.A.C.E. at Work*.

Leaders with presence know their boundaries, parameters, strengths and limitations. They know what resonates with themselves, and with others. These leaders can engage people in conversation, relationship and ongoing collaboration for something aligned with their purpose and passion. They know they cannot be everywhere, nor do everything, at once, or by themselves. In order to serve the vision, the thing the leader stands for and has clearly aligned with, they must enlist the help and commitment of others. This requires leadership presence, which then takes on a life of its own at times, making a small thing a big thing, and accomplishing not just one thing, but many things. This is successful leadership, accomplished in large part by leadership presence.

Some leaders may have a "natural" presence. They just seem to connect well with people. Chances are, however, that this did not come until these people integrated heart, mind, body and soul. All leaders can enhance their presence by personally aligning these four components. And that is accomplished through some serious "soul searching" and finding the answers, and then the solutions, to these questions:

1. How well have I integrated all four components (or domains) of my life? *(heart, mind, body and soul)*

2. How comfortable am I in realizing the power I exert in the world through my heart, mind, body, and soul?

3. What is my declaration about myself in the world and how do my heart, mind, body, and soul support or undermine that declaration?

4. Do I exude a positive and inviting presence with others or am I conveying a negative presence with others?

Leadership presence is what drives your leadership, and your relationships. At its core is your heart, mind, soul and body profile, what can also be called your *personal presence*.

We need to comprehend what we are honoring with our very *being*. We must understand our motivation and that motivation must align with our doing in order to preserve our authenticity. This is about the time worn saying

Authenticity = full integration of heart mind, body and soul, + comfortable with who you are

of "walking the talk." It is wise also to be sure that our talk matches the heart and passions that drive who we really are. Are we really credible representations of who we are, or do we merely speak the "company line" or some other talk that we think others want to hear? If the walk does not match the talk, then the problem is either that the heart is not engaged, or the talk is not genuine. All of these things affect who and what we look like to others.

As leaders, if we expect others to follow and to engage in our agenda, we need to insure that others will believe us. What do we get excited about? What frustrates us? What are our emotional "buttons?" How strongly do we come across regarding our passions? Do we take up space in the room, do we demonstrate skills and competencies, and do we have and show passion for what we are doing?

Presence, and Playing in a Bigger Space

Leadership presence is a critical part of "playing in a bigger space" *(a subject to be covered more extensively in the next chapter).* You, the leader, see something others haven't seen. You are inside the box, and you see something you want. You must expand the boundaries of this box, pushing out the walls to achieve your desired results. To do this, especially in business, you have to recruit people, influence others, build champions for your cause or desired outcome, and personally appeal to them regarding their benefits. You must have a credible plan, and measurable data to support your hypothesis. You are putting yourself on the line here, which is necessary when pushing out boundaries and recruiting the assistance of others. You are remodeling your space, a job best done as teamwork of complementing skills and competencies. In order for these people to work in an orchestrated movement, all devoted to one shared outcome, you must have personal presence to take a stand and put your stake in the ground.

Leadership presence involves knowing what triggers your emotions, and how to leverage those to push out the current space into that bigger space you've envisioned. When things don't go well, you can demonstrate appropriate responses rooted in goodwill, and designed to bring things back on the track you have set. Understanding your own presence and authenticity allows you to point things out so others can connect the dots. Some people tend to operate only from the emotional point of view. This emotional response must be tempered with skills and competencies and an understanding of human dynamics. People will be look at you to see if you have what it takes to move forward. *Are you able to engage people, and get them to trust you?* Your leadership presence will demonstrate that you have a purpose and passion about something, that you've done your homework, that you appear to be physically capable to do whatever it is you've engaged others to do with you, and that you have the right "fire in your belly" to make this happen.

Consider a leader, *any* leader. How do you judge this person, and their leadership capabilities? On what basis do you say he or she has succeeded as a leader? Most likely your answers will come back to the fact that this person has achieved integration with heart, mind, body and soul. He or she is able to connect with others on these levels as well. These leaders have well defined and secure purpose and passions, and know how to make them visible and observable to others.

Think of someone you know who shows powerful leadership presence. Not just any presence, but a presence that is strong, inviting, and able to engage others. This is not just about appearance, although that is an element, but about a difficult-to-define "something" that just "is" in this person. The following list contains some of the most common elements of leadership presence. How many have your observed in others, or in your own presence?

- A seamless congruence of language, body and emotion
- Pleasant, neat appearance
- Genuineness
- Available and receptive
- Alert and aware of surroundings
- Present in the moment, not distracted
- Connected, part of his or her surroundings
- Flexible and open (can even be seen in appearance, facial expressions, etc.)
- Compassionate, yet firm
- Embodies and engenders trust
- Body relaxed, not tense
- Even pitch and voice volume
- Appropriate gestures while speaking
- Even mood and temperament
- Overall energy
- Appropriate emotional responses
- Generally inviting demeanor

What does
Leadership
Presence
look like?

CHAPTER 5: *AUTHENTICITY—The Heart of G.R.A.C.E. at Work*

Our Integrated Parts

Heart, Mind, Body and Soul

WE think of ourselves as a single entity, often ignoring that we are in fact composite creatures. Each of us is composed of heart, mind, body and soul, all of which contribute to authentic wholeness. Ignoring or discounting one or several of these components will result in a presence that is incomplete, dishonest, non-transparent and not authentic. This "partial presence" will result in harm, in some way every time, either to ourselves, others, or both. Our hearts are the *feeling* parts of us, our minds the *thinking* parts (the processing center), our bodies the *doing* parts, and our souls the *spiritual* parts, the essential being, or our purpose. Genuine authenticity depends on integration of *all* these parts. This integration is the very core of authenticity, which is the heart of the *G.R.A.C.E. at Work* model. Leadership Presence is the extent to which you can align and leverage your heart, mind, body and soul in the pursuit of excellence and the influence of others.

The Heart

The heart represents the emotional side of who we are. The heart tells us how we feel about the world, and about life in general. It reflects our mood and our emotions. Many people attempt to quash or hide their emotions, but life without emotions will generate the feeling of merely going through the motions of life. Life is much easier when we understand our emotions and how they provide a deeper richness in life. They reflect our assessments and expectations about what's going on around us and what we feel about the events and people we are experiencing at the moment. Emotions can be anchored in the past, present, and future and reveal the soul's condition in relationship to how we feel about ourselves and others important to us.

Emotions are triggered by the "stories" we maintain about ourselves and the world. They are responses to expectations we have. Learning to identify what triggers our emotions and how to manage them are critical to effective leadership, and satisfying relationships. Goodwill for ourselves and for others is critical to manage the inevitable risk and disappointment that we will all

feel *(not to mention the more common emotional responses like hurt, anger, and countless others)* when conflict or some "failed" action occurs in a relationship.

Being aware of our own hearts and emotions is only part of authenticity, and only part of practicing *G.R.A.C.E. at Work.* We must also be mindful of the emotions and hearts of others, and what we do to trigger certain emotions in others. Whether leaders in a corporate sense or leaders at home or anywhere in life, we need to create a safe place that provides freedom for emotional expression in an appropriate context. Leaders must also learn to help themselves and others articulate what kind of emotional state they are in and help identify the root causes. Identifying these causes allows us to begin addressing them. A safe place (the Place of G.R.A.C.E.) is required to do this, or we are just chasing rabbits. This safe place begins with a willingness to really hear others, connect with them, and help them connect with their emotional states, with their hearts that drive these emotions. This is one of the standout traits of any great leader.

It is incumbent on leaders, coaches, or anyone in relationship *(that's all of us!)* to create the environment so that all emotions can be "out there," bounded by appropriate expression. It needs to be okay for people to explore and express their feelings in appropriate ways in that environment. Having already been in tune with our own hearts, knowing what causes our personal emotional responses enables us to extend the gift of non-judgment to others. Being offended is a choice we make. The ultimate strength and endurance of the relationship depends on this.

The Mind

The mind is that vast receptacle of all the facts and data we have consciously or unconsciously acquired or been exposed to. It is the place where we sort through these bits and pieces of information, interpret them, shape them into perceptions and ideas, and attempt to organize them. The mind enables intellectual discernment by which we identify data points, information and high order thinking like analysis and synthesis to create some meaning. In other words, our minds are like vast super computers, processing information at hyper speeds, though at times it may certainly not seem that way. Each person has developed a unique manner and method of data collection, fact analysis, hypothesis testing and general navel-gazing. And for every individual, that process will be different. Essentially, our minds create a certain sense of what is real (or authentic) for us through the processes of analysis and discernment.

The mind reflects what we pay attention to and what we think the consequences are to our thinking. The mind reveals how we think about the world, or life, and will often drive our relationships. The mind represents the intellectual side of who we are. Our thinking can create or close down options or possibilities for us simply by the way in which we've structured our thinking and language. For example, if I need to lose weight, but I declare that I will never be able to drop those pounds, I may as well forget about the diet and have another chocolate, frappuccino, or whatever I desire. My mind has just shut down the possibility that I can take any action that will result in weight loss. Sometimes we make decisions based on incomplete or inaccurate data, thereby hurting our chances of creating a strong argument or case for a certain action.

The mind is where we determine our world view, how we end up believing or doing certain things. We formulate certain logic, data sets, tools of inference to shape our thoughts. We must realize that what people are in today, they won't be in tomorrow. And that includes ourselves. Because change is the nature of life, we need constant refreshing of our minds, mental models, certain disciplines, hypotheses, research, what we are willing to accept as true and false (something that is ultimately anchored in our purpose, our soul's work) and the rigor in which we pursue things. Many people fall short in this area, and don't keep up with changes in their fields, technology changes, and soon their jobs disappear and they wonder what happened. Change is a fact of life, and technology and tools in the workplace, or life in general, need to be fresh. We need to consider things like continuing education, training, and other ways to stay abreast of the changes in both work and life. The mind is where we do all this, and the mind is where we make this first step.

In this harried and hurried world today, sometimes *"mind time"* is at a premium. Keeping the mind fresh may mean creating opportunities for focused thinking, reflection, and reframing. Outside distractions keep us from truly visiting the mind's inner sanctum, and from developing the ability to visit other disciplines, other stories, and concepts beyond what we typically think about. Analytical thinking can be practiced and honed. And don't neglect the creative thinking, the dreaming that we never seem to have time to do. The mind is an amazing place of invention, discovery and breakthrough — if we give it enough room.

The mind is where we determine our world view.

A cautionary word is needed here. Today's technology and lack of social interaction (through the advent of e-mail, the internet, cell phones, etc.) can make our minds very sterile and uncolorful. (It is ironic that in this age of exploding technology people are still looking for deeper relationships.) We must be careful not to exalt the mind (or simple knowledge) too highly, or give it too much "face time" at the expense of the heart and the soul. Remember, just like the G.R.A.C.E. model itself, authenticity and presence are optimized through balance of all components.

The Body

The body represents the physical side of who we are. It reflects how we behave in life, and our capacity to take action. Besides the basics of maintaining our bodies in great shape through diet, exercise and sleep, the opportunity for us to impact and influence our world is directly tied to our capacity to take actions through skills and competencies, or by our ability to connect with others. The body (heart and mind included) is an expression of the soul's ultimate desires and passions.

Quite often the wellness of the body is not balanced, or given the same weight with the other components. People tend to overwork, not keep fit, not keep a proper diet, and hence don't sleep right. In essence, they are not physically well, but will continue to neglect the body's need for these things. The entire model of *G.R.A.C.E. at Work* is based on proper balance. The body is often the first to become out of alignment. Dealing with unheeded physical needs is much like trying to control a car with unbalanced tires on the freeway at 60 miles per hour. The vibration can shake your teeth loose and require every ounce of energy you have. The body will eventually get our attention, however, either by building stress indicators, sapping our zest and energy, or ultimately slamming us down with illness and disease. Along the way to this place, those indicators and messages may be read by everyone around us, even if we continue to ignore them. The well-being of the body will also be seen in the other components of mind, heart and soul. Ignore one, and all the others will scream for attention as well.

> The body is often the first to become out of alignment.

The Soul

The soul represents our faith declaration or commitment and is how we declare to ourselves what is most important to us in life. The body, mind and heart are receptors and transmitters of the soul. Quite simply, the soul acts as the "gatekeeper" for that which is taken in by us, and that which is transmitted to others from us, expressed emotionally, intellectually and physically. The soul fuels the heart, the mind and the body. The different attributes of who we are allow us to interact with or give and receive in different ways. They are different manifestations of the soul's identity. The soul represents the spiritual side of us, that is, our life's purpose and passion. From the moment we are born until the day we die, we are in pursuit of relationship and meaning to satisfy the soul. Each of us will determine our life passion, and the place where we are called to live, work, and serve others. For each of us it is something different. Until we seek and recognize our unique purpose and passion, we will be spinning our wheels, making our hearts, minds and bodies quite unhappy, and perhaps those around us as well.

We make a decision about how we show up in the world. Everyone makes a choice in what they ground their identity. Purpose and passion will dictate what you pay attention to, and the things and people you make investment in. Some people do this through a spiritual walk, and some through merely a material purpose. Without first identifying this passion, however, all of actions and our visible presence is ungrounded, and essentially ineffective.

Through the soul, we commit to relationships with someone or something that will ignite and feed our life's purpose and passion. Through the heart, mind, and body the soul manifests its values, beliefs, desires, and commitments. The soul's commitments will shape and determine what the heart, mind and body pay attention to, what they react to, and what they will present or manifest to the world. Fundamentally, the soul represents the "purpose" declaration while the heart, mind, and body represent the "works."

Self diagnosis for a healthy soul will include regular checks and management of the differences between our stated values and the values that we reflect in our actions and behaviors. Priorities that align our daily activities with our deepest passions result in soul-building and healthy expression of the soul through heart, mind and body. Being part of a community of like-minded people who share our passions is also a healthy way to feed the soul and mind with new ways of thinking and being.

Peace, contentment and satisfaction come only through the soul. The heart, mind, and body serve at the soul's bidding and desire. When we have breakdowns in life it is because the heart, mind, and body has hijacked the soul's role in determining and preserving who I am and what's most important in life.

Integration

These four components combine to present our whole selves. If these are fully integrated and combined to function smoothly together as a whole (one part not allowed to hijack the others), we are living authentically. The goal of focusing the heart, mind, body and soul is to create the greatest connectivity and personal authenticity. The soul is what fuels our presence, the heart, mind, and body are what connect us with the world.

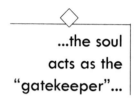

...the soul acts as the "gatekeeper"...

COMPONENT				OUR AUTHENTICITY
Heart	Mind	Body	Soul	**What Others See**
Absent	x	x	x	Merely going through the motions, no emotional evidence
x	Absent	x	x	Spontaneous, not rational
x	x	Absent	x	Not walking the talk (being and doing don't align), mixed messages
x	x	x	Absent	Material life only, no passion or purpose
x	**x**	**x**	**x**	**The ultimate Presence, fully integrated**

So how can we arrive at a fully integrated self, where heart, mind, body and soul are present and accounted for? It begins with the inner core, self knowledge, and radiates outward as we grasp the truth of who we are, and who we want to be. Not only is soul searching in order, but so is heart, mind and body searching.

A good place to begin is to take a look at the questions on the next page, and determine if you already know the answers, or need to do some work to discover them honestly.

COMPONENT and (Domain)	Helps me Know and Understand:	Internal Questions for Personal and Professional Authenticity
HEART (Emotions)	How I **FEEL** about life (or *specific issues, people, etc.*)	• How well do I understand my emotions and how well do I make them work for me? • How well am I able to identify what emotions I am feeling? • How well am I able to appropriately express my emotions? • What do I know about what triggers my emotions? • How well am I able to resolve my emotions for myself? • What do I notice about how my emotions impact others around me? • How well do I recover when I get knocked off balance? • What recharges my emotions after I've been knocked off balance?
MIND (Intellect)	How I **THINK** about life (or *specific issues, people, etc.*)	• What data and information do I pay attention to and what are the consequences of my thinking? • What do I notice about my language i.e., am I using encouraging language that creates possibilities or am I using language that is self-defeating? • How am I keeping myself current with data and information in the field I am working/world that I am living in? • How well can I present a logical and convincing argument for what I want to accomplish? • What do I notice about my ability to take multiple perspectives in any given situations?
BODY (Physical)	How I **ACT** (or behave) in life (or *in specific circumstance, with specific people, etc.*)	• How effectively does my body allow me to impact and influence the world? • What kind of presence am I creating in the places where I work or live? • How comfortable am in the presence of others? • What new skills and competencies would give me greater confidence and influence in the world? • How well am I taking care of nutritional requirements? • How well am I taking care of my sleep requirements? • How well am I doing with a physical fitness regimen? • What do I notice about the stress in my body?
SOUL (Spiritual)	How I define life, what is of value and importance to me	• Who do I declare myself to be? • What is most important in my life? • What is my purpose/passion in life? • What are the principles/values that guide my life? • How do I resolve competing claims to my principles and values? • What do I believe about transformation in life? i.e. what brings about growth and change in my life and the lives of others? • What am I tolerating and for the sake of what?

The way you show up as a person is the way in which you have integrated all of these pieces into one entity. If we have all four cylinders of our leadership vehicle engaged, balanced and operating at full power, life carries more excitement, enthusiasm and natural attraction. Our leadership is more attractive, more resonant with people, because we are authentic and real. We are also better able to offer forgiveness, and extend compassion and grace. When we have fully integrated our hearts, minds, bodies and souls, we operate from a position of strength, and others recognize those strengths. Because we are living in a state of strength, we can afford to be more G.R.A.C.E.-full.

> It's not enough to just *walk the talk*.... we must also *talk the walk*....

And it's not enough to just walk the talk, so to speak. We must also *talk the walk*, if we want others to know our motivation and understand why we do the things we do. In relationship, others must understand our message behind the "sale" of the package, not just the package. Our ability to create a presence around that one thing we are serving is solely dependent on our ability to prioritize what is important and unite that with our singular purpose. We must identify the appropriate tasks and the people we connect with in order to accomplish them.

Authenticity and Connectivity
Inseparable

AUTHENTICITY and Presence are by nature completely useless and of no purpose unless the element of Connectivity is also present. We can obviously be "authentic islands" but without others, our presence is of no consequence, and our fully integrated selves will have no means of accomplishing purpose. Our presence is how we show up in the world, and the world is composed of other people. Hence, by the very nature of presence, connectivity is required. Knowing and showing ourselves authentically is only one part of the path to accomplishing passion and purpose. The other part is knowing (and many times showing) others as well. The *G.R.A.C.E. at Work* component of Connectivity was detailed in the previous chapter, and this concept of

Authenticity paired with Connectivity will be the focus of several other concepts regarding this model. However, in regard to our authenticity, and our presence, how we show up in the world is inherently connected to other people, and that requires connecting with other people.

The *G.R.A.C.E. at Work* model shows that at the heart of Authenticity is self knowledge, and the heart of Connectivity is Other Knowledge. Both knowledge sets are required to practice any relationship model, or have any

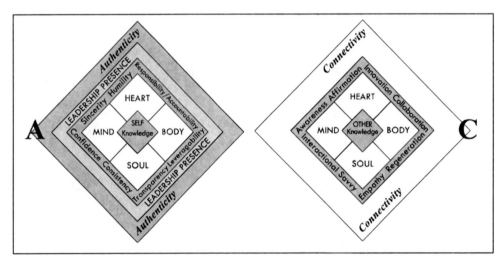

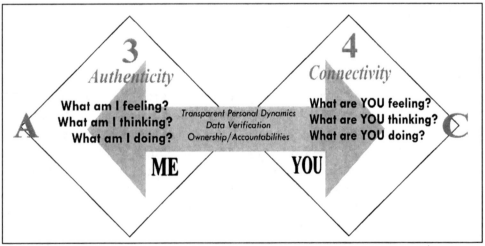

relationship for that matter. There is a line (in the case of this graphic, an arrow) that runs between the Authenticity and the Connectivity components. This line is called trust.

Authenticity requires knowing what I am feeling, thinking and doing. Connectivity requires that I also know what the other person is feeling, thinking and doing. There is much more about this exchange of knowledge in chapter 6 on G.R.A.C.E. in Conversation. This mention of Authenticity dynamically linked with Connectivity is presented here to remind us that presence is not a one way, dead-end street.

Decision-Making
Authentic Being and Doing

THROUGHOUT the course of any single day, each of us will make literally thousands of conscious and unconscious decisions. These decisions are based on who we are, knowing who we are, and what is right for us. The process we use to arrive at these decisions is critical to making choices that are sound and right for us and those around us. Some people make those decisions based only on the emotional component. Others make them solely on the hard data available. Some ignore the body and physical element, not entirely aware of the ramifications of certain decisions. People who work 100 hours a week have come to believe that is what their life is all about. They have decided money is the focus, so attention to physical needs slips off the radar — until a devastating health crisis develops.

Some people take action because they *can* take the action, and do it *only* because they can. Most of us, most of the time, do not consider the effects of certain decisions on the other components of who we are. If we are composed of the four distinctly different yet integrated components of heart, mind, body and soul, all of these elements should be considered for the best and healthiest decisions, with the fewest negative repercussions down the road. A large part of being, living and doing life authentically (both personally and professionally), is making decisions using a sound process that arrives at choices in alignment with our total authentic selves.

Decisions reflect opportunities to advance, maintain, or reshape our identities, responsibilities, or relationships. It opens and closes possibilities, and allows us to make a declaration or statement about our identity and commitments. Decision-making helps us identify with others, or with a purpose greater than ourselves. Through decision-making we prioritize what is important in our lives. It preserves, or destroys, our integrity or commitments. It has consequences and implications. Powerful, effective decision making rests on our ability to incorporate every aspect of our identity: our hearts (emotions), our minds (intellect), our bodies (the physical), and our souls (our essence, purpose, or being).

If I am perfectly aligned with my heart, my mind, my body and my soul I am more likely to make a decision that fully reflects my identity and my ability to withstand the consequences and possible unintended repercussions of my decisions. The problem with decision making is that sometimes one aspect of my being hijacks my identity.

For example, I live in Richmond, Virginia. My favorite pizza place in the whole world *(and I've visited many across the globe)* is Donato's Pizza out of Columbus, Ohio. It's not just the taste that makes this pizza and the outfit so great, it is the memories my family created when I was much younger. We would celebrate achievements, holidays, birthdays and life in general with Donato's pizza. The folks who own this enterprise are "great people" who give back to the community. I identify with their mission in life and in their work. Unfortunately, there are no Donato's in Virginia, where I live. Consequently, when my family and I make the eight-hour journey to Columbus, you can bet the house that I will visit Donato's at least once during our trip. My body's cravings for the best pizza in the whole wide world and my emotional memories completely hijack my intellectual recognition that just a little bit of that pizza is all I really need. The reality of the situation is that before I know it I've consumed far too many calories in much too short a time. *(I must also add that the reality of the situation is that I really don't care that I eat way too much while I'm there...but it still makes a great example!)*

So if we break this example down, from an intellectual perspective, I can tell you that I only need about 650 calories to satisfy my real nutritional requirements. I know that pizza contains about a *bazillion* calories. Intellectually it probably makes sense not to starve myself all day thinking that I'll make it up when I get to Donato's. By the way, you can smell the pizza two miles away before the restaurant comes into view. The aroma is taken in by my body, which helps fuel the emotional aspects of my desire. This "pizza perfume" on the air instantly triggers the *"feed me now"* response in my body. The mind now responds by reminding me yet again that Donato's pizza is the best pizza in the whole wide world. At this point my emotions are stimulated to ask *"did someone say Donato's?"* It brings back a flood of memories from the past, and the desire to create more for today. My soul, the guardian of my purpose and passion, recalls its mission to keep me balanced in my heart, mind, body and soul, but now declares a hiatus from its commitment to preserving my body through a state of self-control and joins in the potential feeding frenzy. The result? Total bliss, accompanied by that pleasantly stuffed sensation, accentuated by guilt. Oh well, I'm not back in Columbus for another six months.

For positive, powerful decision making, all four essence components must contribute equally to the process. This is illustrated by the figure here. The decision to be made is the diamond in the center, composed of two pieces, representing contrasting decisions.

Now let's see if we can picture what is happening here in our pizza mini-drama. In the diagram the decision to be made is represented in the center, with two parts. One part is a decision in one direction *(represented by the #1, or "no" but can be any other type of response, as indicated by the *)* and its opposing decision *(represented by the #2, or "yes")*. In my example of the pizza hijacking, it was not as simple as a yes or no decision. The decision would *always be yes*, in the case of Donato's

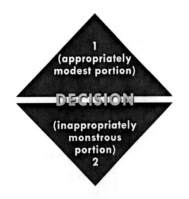

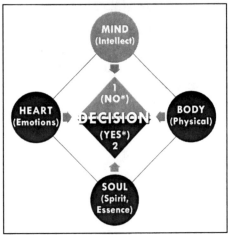

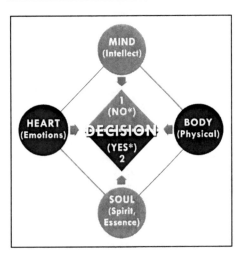

pizza. It was a matter of *how much* yes. The body's desire for pizza shuts out the mind's more intellectual contribution to this decision, effectively diminishing my capacity to make authentic decisions that are best for me. Now, with the mind or intellect shut out of the process, the best I can hope to do is a 50% effort on the authentic decision making scale.

Because my emotions (about family memories) have also formed an alliance with the body, the desire to consume without restraint is a force to be reckoned with. Now, my ability to make a 100% integrated or effective decision has just been reduced by half. Consequently my soul makes a valiant attempt to try to remind me of my desire to be a "lean, mean fightin' machine," but in the end loses out to the ever-strengthening emotional appeal of *"well, you are only here two to three times a year, so shut up and enjoy your pizza."* With the soul effectively shut down also, we are down to just a two-component argument, with no real counterbalance to offset the desire to indulge. All that's left to do now is to consume as much Donato's pizza as my stomach will allow.

And later I will have to deal with the mind and the spirit that inevitably say *"I told you so, but you wouldn't listen!"*

In many ways, until we learn how to manage this process, decision-making can resemble four opponents coming from every corner of the ring to battle each other and win the decision.

Not all of our decisions will be of the pizza-indulging variety. Some will be quite serious, others without major consequence. If we don't learn how to properly integrate all of four components into one being with an automatic decision-making process, or if we allow one or more components to hijack the others, we will not make solid and sound decisions. Once again, we are back to the concept of balance. Powerful and positive decision making rests on the balanced input and feedback from heart, mind, body and soul.

The Decision Diamond
A VISUAL DECISION-MAKING TOOL

Successful decision-making is not just the simple matter of consulting the mind, or the heart, or the body, or the soul. Every part of us must be integrated to provide feedback in order to arrive at right and positive decisions for us. It is often difficult to do this without the assistance of visual helps. For that reason, the Decision Diamond was developed to enable individuals to utilize a visual process so that all factors involving any decision can be viewed. Some decisions lend themselves to careful and critical thinking through the process. Others, however, require either immediate or very quick responses which do not allow this critical thinking time frame. In these cases, enough practice with this decision making Decision Diamond™ model will allow you to automatically consult all parts of you in a quick but authentic manner, even a matter of seconds, to make sound, decisive and rapid decisions. With enough experience and practice, this model will become your "default" system process for decision making, and one which will enable you to make decisions that have the greatest positive impact and the least negative consequences for all parts of you, and others.

This process begins by understanding that you will be utilizing information and feedback from all four essence components of your authentic self.

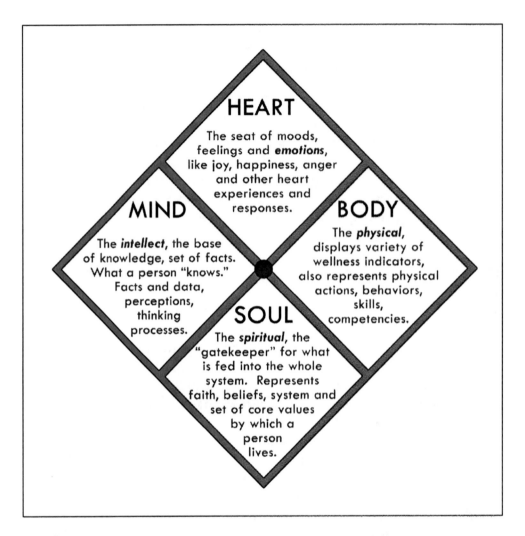

This is a simple process, but powerful. Start by considering all the decision criteria, determining what you know and feel about them, and assigning them positive or negative values. You will be plotting your responses to these simple questions on a diamond worksheet similar to the one on the next page. You can use this sheet, make copies, or draw your own. Start by writing out the decision you want to make at the top of the sheet.

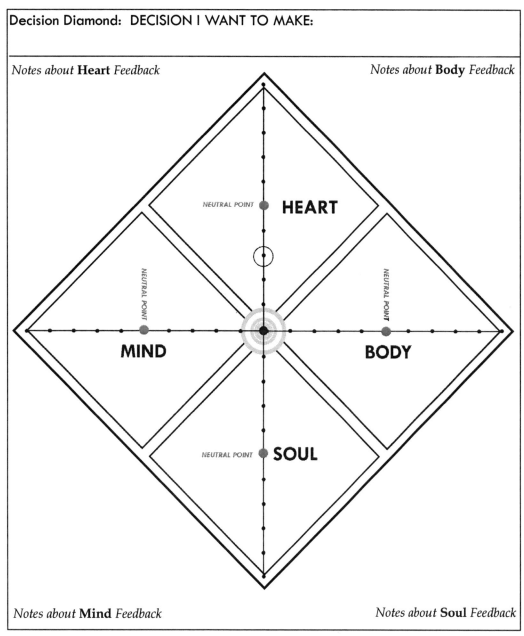

Next, carefully consider the following questions, using the rating system shown on the next page and plot your responses on this diagram.

Use this rating scale:

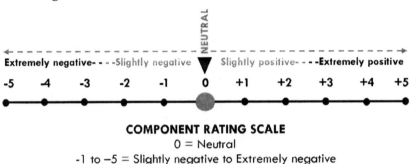

COMPONENT RATING SCALE
0 = Neutral
-1 to −5 = Slightly negative to Extremely negative
+1 to +5 = Slightly positive to Extremely positive

Decision Feedback from THE MIND

What do you KNOW about this decision? Write simple descriptions of this knowledge in the box labeled "MIND." (These will be called "criteria") Assign a value to each criteria reflecting its impact, on the scale of –1 to –5 being slightly to extremely negative, +1 to +5 being slightly to extremely positive, or neutral. If you like, you can write the criteria on the scale value that applies to each *(see example),* or write them on another sheet of paper and assign value points on the scale. Average these values for **ONE** "Mind" position on the scale and circle that position.

Decision Feedback from THE HEART

What emotional responses do you have to this decision? What are your "gut" feelings? How do you feel whenever you think of this decision, or attempt to process it? Write and plot the criteria as above. Determine ONE average position based on all your responses, and circle your position. *(Note: for each of the four essence diamonds, you should end up with only ONE average point, the one you circle.)*

Decision Feedback from THE BODY

What is your body saying to you about this decision? (stress, not sleeping, worry, anxious, etc.) Distinguish between stress (negative) and excitement (positive). Write and plot the criteria in this box the same as for the previous box. Circle your average as before.

Decision Feedback from THE SOUL

How does this decision impact your values, beliefs, and core ideas? Do you feel any guidance or leading for this decision? Write and plot the criteria same as the others. *(See the sample on the next page.)*

READING THE DIAMOND

Connect your circled "average dots" to show a diamond (of sorts) inside the larger structured diamond. Chances are your inner diamond will be somewhat "misshapen" and probably not a true diamond. The resulting shape of your plotted feedback will reveal where you have the largest gaps, the least confidence about this choice or decision. Perfect "+5's" in all feedback responses will obviously "hit the bull's eye" yielding a positive and confident decision, but the chances of this happening are very rare. In the meantime, the resulting diagram can give you more visual feedback for further consideration. Look for the areas where the shape you have drawn extends more toward the outer edges of the larger diamond. This indicates your feedback may be somewhat negative in any or several of the essence diamonds, requiring you to perhaps take a better and deeper look before making the final decision.

Why is my diamond misshapen?

Your feedback in each of your essences components may look something like the diagram on the next page, but most likely you will have many more data points. Notice that the responses for the body and the soul are farther out toward the larger diamond, indicating that these two areas are struggling somewhat with this decision. Since the body is often a component that will provide "honest" feedback, at least if we allow it to and observe it honestly, and the soul is that "gatekeeper"

SAMPLE DECISION DIAMOND

Decision Diamond: DECISION I WANT TO MAKE HERE: *"I have been offered a better position in the company, but it requires a major move for the family. Should I take it?"*

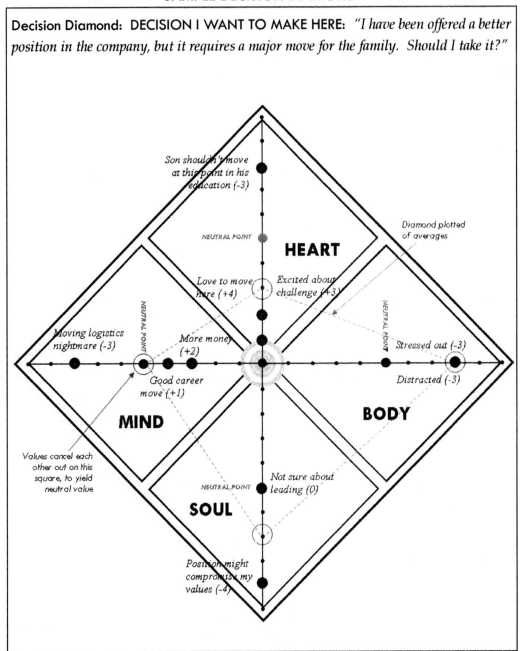

of our core being, the somewhat negative responses here should be seriously evaluated. The heart and the mind tend to want this, but why? Are the reasons enough to outweigh the concerns seen in the body and the soul diamonds? In a situation like this, consider asking the following kinds of questions:

- What is my body trying to tell me?
- Is the stress I feel merely from the decision making process, or does it relate to consequences of this decision?
- Why are my soul responses so low?
- Of what importance, relatively speaking, are all the criteria on this diamond? *(On this set of responses, for example, the decision to move his or her son at this point in his education may weigh more heavily than the prospect of more money, etc.)*
- Does this decision compromise my values?
- Am I willing to make such a compromise under any circumstances? *These* circumstances?
- Have I weighted all criteria appropriately in relation to the others?

If, after all criteria and potential gaps are considered, and the resultant average diamond is still misshapen or very large (indicating more negative responses), then the decision may be "no" to this particular choice at this time. If the diamond becomes more regular shaped, and smaller, approaching the center bulls eye, then the choice may be "yes." Keep working the diamond until your responses are completely set, and you have explored all consequences of the decision and weighted them appropriately. By the time you have done all this, your decision will most likely make itself.

THE 4 PARTS OF YOU
For Balanced Decision Making

HEART
The emotional "you." This is the seat of your moods, feelings and emotions like joy, happiness, anger and other heart experiences and responses.

MIND
The intellectual "you." The mind and intellect, the base of knowledge, or set of facts. This is what you "know." Includes facts and data, perceptions, and thinking processes.

BODY
The physical "you," which displays a variety of wellness indicators, and also represents your physical actions, behaviors, skills and competencies.

SOUL
The spiritual "you." Your "gatekeeper" for what is fed into your whole system. The soul represents faith, beliefs, system and core values by which you live.

Perhaps considering more possibilities and data points might help nail down this decision. Or perhaps it is a matter of simply deciding to honor the soul's feedback over all the others. These are choices only you can make. It is likely, however, that after you complete this kind of exercise, you have "consulted" each of the four components of your authentic self, and will have given them voice in your ultimate decision-making process, thus making it a more balanced and well-thought out choice. This exercise can often reveal indicators that were not previously recognized or even considered. You are more likely to make a solid and balanced decision based on who you really are, rather than immediate or hasty emotional or intellectual responses. For many people decision making is agonizing. Hopefully this simple tool will enable you to develop your own methodology that becomes reflexive *(automatic, the default mode)* and reflective of your authentic self.

Authenticity and Values

WE all have a set of values and beliefs that we use as a foundation for our identities. These values help us make decisions and shape our passion and purpose, which resides in the soul and drives the heart, mind and body into action. Whether we are aware of it or not, we generally act in ways that are basically consistent with our values and beliefs. Authenticity requires that we each know ourselves, so it follows that we also know our values. Yet, when asked, many people have a difficult time identifying those values. Values come in all shapes, sizes, and labels. Can you readily identify yours? Do you know *why* you make certain decisions, or what values drive your behavior? It is always helpful to take a few moments to do some "values clarification." The following pages contain some worksheets that will help you quickly identify what is important to you, what makes you authentic, and what fuels your passion and purpose. Knowing our values can be the beginning of self knowledge.

This exercise may seem rather rudimentary, especially for those who are certain of their values. However, values can and do change. If it's been awhile since you seriously evaluated your core value system, you will benefit by this quick journey into what is really important to you. Knowing our values (*the first step of knowing ourselves*) helps integrate the heart, mind, body and soul of who we are.

#		Value	#		Value	#	
1		Accomplishment	51		Honor	101	
2		Accountability	42		Independence	102	
3		Accuracy	43		Individuality	103	
4		Acknowledgement/Reward	54		Inner Calm, Peace	104	
5		Authenticity	55		Innovation	105	
6		Balanced life	56		Intelligence	106	
7		Best Performance	57		Integrity	107	
8		Challenge	58		Justice	108	
9		Change	59		Knowledge	109	
10		Collaboration (Teamwork)	60		Leadership	110	
11		Commitment	61		Learning		
12		Communication	62		Loyalty		
13		Community	63		Lifestyle		
14		Compassion	64		Meaning		
15		Competence	65		Openness		
16		Competition	66		Orderliness		
17		Concern for Others	67		Organization		
18		Consensus	68		Perfection		
19		Continuous Improvement	69		Perseverance		
20		Control	70		Personal Growth		
21		Cooperation	71		Pleasure		
22		Courage	72		Positive Attitude		
23		Courtesy	73		Power		
24		Creativity	74		Practicality		
25		Decisiveness	75		Privacy		
26		Developing Others	76		Progress, Improvement		
27		Direction, Purposefulness	77		Prosperity		
28		Discipline	78		Quality (of work, etc.)		
29		Diversity	79		Resourcefulness		
30		Efficiency	80		Respect for Others		
31		Empowerment of others	81		Responsibility		
32		Environment, Concern for	82		Results-oriented		
33		Equality	83		Safety		
34		Ethics	84		Security		
35		Excellence	85		Service (to others)		
36		Fairness	86		Simplicity		
37		Faith	87		Sincerity		
38		Family	88		Skill		
39		Flair	89		Solitude		
40		Flexibility	90		Speed		
41		Freedom	91		Stability		
42		Friendliness	92		Status		
43		Fun	93		Strength		
44		Generosity	94		Success, Achievement		
45		Goodwill	95		Timeliness		
46		Happiness	96		Tolerance		
47		Hard Work	97		Trust		
48		Harmony	98		Values		
49		Health and Well-Being	99		Variety		
50		Honesty, Truthfulness	100		Wisdom		

1. Look over the list of 100 values on this page. Consider each one, and place a check mark in the boxes that reflect your values and beliefs. There is space to add up to 10 more that are not included on this list.

2. Look at the values you checked, then narrow them down to your Top 25 values. Write them in the table on the next page.

3. From your list of top 25 values, further narrow them down to your absolute Top 10, write them in the table space provided.

TOP 25 VALUES	
1	well-being
2	authenticity
3	service
4	trust
5	courage
6	independence
7	collaboration
8	change
9	inner calm - peace
10	direction, purposefulness
11	creativity
12	integrity
13	ethics
14	learning
15	leadership
16	meaning
17	openness
18	perseverance
19	success, achievement
20	intelligence
21	wisdom
22	accomplishment
23	flexibility
24	progress
25	variety

TOP 10 VALUES	
1	courage
2	trust
3	calm / peace
4	authenticity
5	service
6	creativity
7	learning
8	change
9	leadership
10	achievement
11	purpose

Did anything surprise you here? Have your values changed at all since the last time you mentally reviewed them? What difference will this make in your authentic self? In your Leadership Presence?

Chapter 6

The SPACE of G.R.A.C.E.

Playing in a Bigger Space

"The sign on the door of opportunity reads PUSH."

--Unknown

WHEN I WAS A KID, *the neighborhood gang used to play our own rendition of baseball, usually with old discarded bats or a well-selected stick, chewed up balls, and hand-me-down gloves. When gloves weren't available, an old garden or work glove stuffed with sponges worked well. These games were usually played in someone's back yard, but were limited by fences, clothes lines and other yard impediments. We always had the bases marked with some sort of imaginary plate, sometimes an old cushion or even a ragged piece of cardboard. But the outfield was a problem. No space. When we moved our games to a bigger space, usually to a front yard, our new boundaries collapsed with the shattering of the neighbor's living room window. We were relegated to the backyard, with a severe reduction in our team rosters, and a painful reduction in allowance committed to repairing windows. We weren't close enough to vacant lots, parks or schools where our games could expand to playing in a bigger space with virtually unlimited participants. We could not advance past the cramped back yard. We often imagined our own "Field of Dreams" where everyone could play and the game could be expanded.*

Life and business often seem like that cramped baseball game. Our limited boundaries don't grow, and our achievements do not yield what we'd like to see. The players don't increase, and the results don't improve. We only *dream* of "playing" in a bigger space. Life and business results have a common denominator, the need for human dynamics. Results depend on relationships. Expanded results depend on expanded relationships.

We've already discussed the fact that *G.R.A.C.E. at Work* is a relationship model designed to improve and expand relationships of all kinds, business, personal, and organizational. The goal of expanded relationships is expanded results, of whatever nature desired. It is a simple model, yet profound in its ability to produce results, on any level, with any one. It is successful quite simply because it is based on the principles of human relationship. When we humans imagine or dream of something we'd like to achieve, that achievement will often depend on our proper use of the five components of *G.R.A.C.E. at Work*. We do not achieve anything in a vacuum. Our results, whether in business or on a personal level, are dependent upon relationships with others. And playing in a bigger space, or achieving expanded results, depends on building and expanding powerful relationships.

Playing in a bigger space, or achieving expanded results, depends on building and expanding powerful relationships.

Powerful relationships are based on goodwill and a mutual commitment to shared purpose that provides affirmation, inspiration and personal transformation. These relationships emerge only through the presence and practice of the five key components of the *G.R.A.C.E. at Work* model. Let's picture our baseball diamond to illustrate this model in a little different way. It starts at the pitcher's mound, with Goodwill, and a first pitch toward the results preferred–a run scored. Goodwill is the "safe space" where all successful relationships begin. This is where the game focuses, no matter what team is up to bat. The action starts here. Goodwill sets the tone that enables all the other actions and reactions, the game dynamics. The same is true with relationships, whether professional or personal.

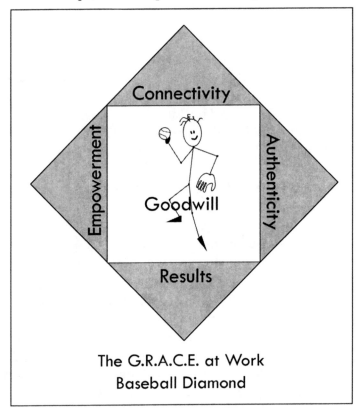

The G.R.A.C.E. at Work
Baseball Diamond

The other components make up the bases, eventually coming back to home plate, the results we desire. In order to score, all the bases must be tagged. We can't skip any of them. GRACE-full leadership occurs only when all five G.R.A.C.E. components work together to create purposeful, powerful and productive relationships to produce greater and greater results. If any one of these components is missing or exists in insufficient quantity, there is no G.R.A.C.E., and generally no increased results.

Playing in a Bigger Space

If you have a desire for greater results, you need to play in a bigger space. The first step toward building this space is to take a look at what you have now, comparing it to what you would like to achieve. The *G.R.A.C.E. at Work* model allows you to perform diagnostics and build plans for growing and expanding results. Here's a simple way to begin this expansion on a practical level. Take a look at these questions and give serious consideration to the answers.

1. How would you describe the space you are currently playing in?

2. What would it mean to you to be playing in a bigger space?

3. Who are you connecting with to achieve your desired results, and for the sake of what?

4. Who else would you like to connect with, and why?

5. What results are you currently capable of delivering?

6. What results would you like to be able to deliver?

7. Where do you believe you have opportunities to expand your results, or play in a bigger space?

Now take a closer look at the relationships within your current "playing field." Evaluate what exists now, based on and related to the five components of the *G.R.A.C.E. at Work* model. Remember, building and growing results will depend in large part on building and growing relationships.

Try sketching out a quick worksheet showing a diamond shape *(see figure next page)*, with the G.R.A.C.E. components listed *(move results to the center, and put goodwill at home plate)*. Jot down your current results in the center box, then write bullet points to indicate expanded results in the bigger diamond. This is a valuable exercise and works for any relationship, so you may wish to make copies of the next page to keep and use as convenient worksheets.

How can you achieve this bigger space, these expanded results, through the application of each of the five G.R.A.C.E. components? For example, try asking yourself the following questions:

1. To whom can you show greater goodwill to further your results?

2. Who do you need to connect with on a better, or more authentic level?

3. How can you empower others to help achieve these greater results? *(For each of these questions, it is helpful to try focusing on a particular person, or individuals on a team, with whom you are currently in relationship for these results.)*

4. How would you rate yourself on each of the five attributes of G.R.A.C.E.? How can you grow each of these attributes *(how are you displaying them to others)*?

5. Where do you possibly sense stress, frustration or unrealized potential?

6. Why can't you achieve desired results in your current space? *(i.e., what is missing, or what is getting in the way?)*

7. How can you further leverage your purpose and passion with others to achieve greater results?

8. What attributes of G.R.A.C.E. do you think are currently missing or unrealized?

Playing in a Bigger Space

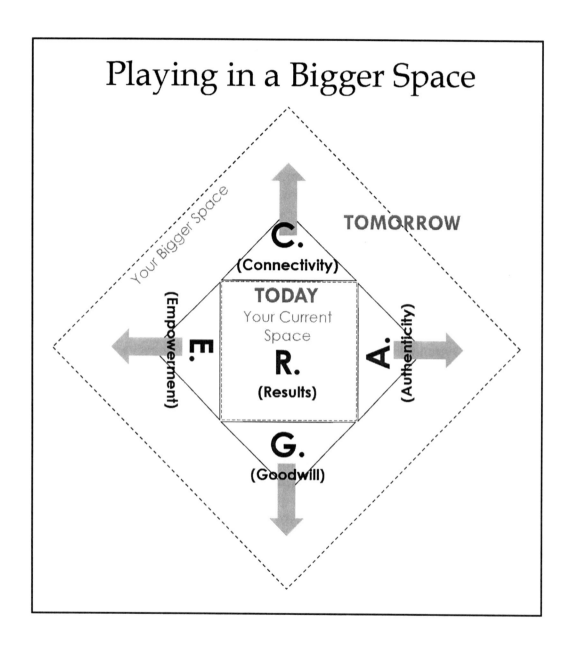

Growing Your Playing Space for Growing Results
Worksheet

Now what can you do to practically build these relationships to achieve great results? Take your worksheets and your notes to develop a purposeful and powerful plan for growth. This is similar to a development plan, but the development project is a bigger playing space which will yield larger results.

It is both eye-opening and very constructive to try this exercise with others in this relationship. Ask them to do the same thing you have done with the worksheet and the questions. Often individuals have differing perspectives about these areas, and subsequent discussion about those viewpoints can facilitate impressive breakthroughs and altered behaviors that lead to greatly expanding playing fields.

Knowing Self and Sharing Self

Sometimes playing in a bigger space is all about knowing yourself well, and how you interact with others. This aligns with the previous chapter on AUTHENTICITY: The Heart of *G.R.A.C.E. at Work*, but these exercises are placed here in order to help you know how to expand your relationships in order to expand your results.

Life Story Exercise

This first "workout" is one that may seem unnecessary initially, but life experiences shape who we are and how we react in relationship. Take a few minutes to consider, and possibly journal your answers to, the following questions. Sometimes a written record of our own authentic profile is revealing and helpful for relationship-building.

Life experiences shape who we are and how we react in relationship.

Who are you today, and how did you get here? Think about what *experiences and backgrounds* (and people) in your life have significantly shaped who you are, *at various times* in your life. If you are journaling, write those things down. If not, just make a bullet list in the blank sidebars on these pages, using headings such as **CHILDHOOD, SCHOOL AGE, HIGH SCHOOL, COLLEGE, WORK/CAREER, GENERAL RELATIONSHIPS, OTHER.** Consider your personality, likes, dislikes, prejudices, strengths, weaknesses, competencies, attitudes, behaviors, highlights, lowlights etc. What made you this way? Caution, you might need more room for this! *Ignore the urge to forget or abort this exercise.* It is always amazing what such a simple effort can produce, a revealing picture of self in relationship with others that may need some adjustments. And with just a few "tweaks" you can enlarge your playing space dramatically.

> **The Great Motivator:** How can doing these things help you play in a bigger space, and realize greater results?

When you have finished, re-read what you just wrote about yourself. What themes do you see emerging? Can you see places in your relationships (work or other) when your life experiences and backgrounds have influenced what you say, how you react to others? What are positive influencers? What are the negative influencers? What can you do (a plan) to mitigate/temper the negative influencers? How do you maintain your authenticity? What do you need to do to insure a greater probability of successs for future opportunities? How can doing these things help you play in a bigger space and realize greater results? The answer to this last question is the real motivator for willingness to change and extend beyond our comfort zones.

Reality Check Exercise

Knowing yourself is only part of the equation in relationships. The other part is SHARING yourself, and knowing others. The *G.R.A.C.E. at Work* model relies on authenticity and connection with others to achieve results. If you want to grow your playing field and realize greater outcomes, but you don't seem to be having any success doing the same old things, you might want to reflect on the following questions and statements. *(You may wish to journal here and use another sheet of paper for your answers).* Sometimes all it takes is thinking through the answers to find the missing ingredients, unresolved issues that might be keeping you from the results you want.

1. Can you "be yourself" in your relationships at work? If so, how? If not, why not, and what can you do about it?

2. Are you free to express yourself openly in your working relationships? Why or why not?

3. Do you know the values and beliefs of others you work with? If not, how can you do this?

4. Do you give others the "safe space" in which to be open with you, and share their values, concerns, opinions, emotions, etc.?

5. Do you respect the values and beliefs of others in working relationships? How, or why not?

6. Do others around you know your values and beliefs? *(What might be getting in the way of others understanding your values and beliefs?)*

7. Do you know your strengths, AND your weaknesses? What are they?

8. How do you leverage your strengths and manage your weaknesses?

9. Do you know the strengths and weaknesses of others? How do you deal with those?

10. How are you really authentic? How do your actions match your values (not just lip service!)? How transparent are you to others? *(Give this some serious and honest thought.)*

It becomes a helpful and eye-opening exercise to go back and answer these questions from an individual *(what can be called "targeted")* point of view. For example, think of *one* person you work with, then put his or her name in the blanks above (in relationship with you, substitute for "others"). Are your answers still the same? Why or why not? How can the mismatches be resolved?

Whether your playing space is a giant international entity, or a few individuals, its *growth depends upon relationships*, and making the most of human connections.

Partners Worldwide is a faith-based international partnership of business and professional people who work at eliminating poverty and transforming lives. Their approach is to grow businesses and create jobs in areas of need, by developing business partnerships, offering business mentoring and training, increasing access to capital and advocating on behalf of the poor. They are active in 21 countries across the globe. Doug Seebeck, the Executive Director of Partners Worldwide, sums up the *attitude* of service through *G.R.A.C.E. at Work*:

> *"The poor are more talented than I am, and if I was in their shoes I would be worse off than they are. The biggest thing they need is capital, opportunity, relationships and encouragement. If we actually listened and served them, we'd have a world transformed. We need to treat them as equals and customers and stop trying to serve our own egos and ideas about service. There has to be a relationship to have a partnership..."*

Mr. Seebeck obviously understands expanded results through relationships based on goodwill, results, authenticity, connectivity and empowerment. So can you. Playing in a bigger space is all about partnership, and partnerships require relationships. If you are looking to expand your results, to play ball in a much bigger space, keep the *G.R.A.C.E. at Work* model in front of you. Draw bigger and bigger diamonds. Consistently grow your relationships by growing the five components of G.R.A.C.E and playing in ever enlarging spaces to yield ever growing results.

> **Playing in a bigger space is all about partnership, and partnerships require relationships.**

Refer to Chapter 9: "Relationship Architecture" which expands on the concept of playing in a bigger space and provides some practical and deeper methodology to do this.

Chapter 7

The Dynamic Tensions

Creating and Maintaining Optimal Balance

"Wisdom is your perspective on life,
your sense of balance, your understanding of how the
various parts and principles apply and relate to each
other. It embraces judgment, discernment, comprehension.
It is a gestalt or oneness, and integrated wholeness."
— *Steven R. Covey*

DYNAMIC TENSIONS:

The Pursuit of Balance

DYNAMIC TENSION is a "coined term" that describes just about everything in the natural world, and should describe everything in the business world and even our personal worlds as well. The concept of balance was introduced in Chapter 1, as the argument for balancing strategy with relationships was presented. The universe, all inclusive, is on a perpetual quest for this balance. Without it, catastrophe occurs. These disasters may take the form of natural storms, business hurricanes, or personal tornados. Dynamic tension can be used to describe this constant conflict of forces to yield balance. The word "dynamic" relates to

energy and objects in motion. Very little in our world, or universe for that matter, is static or unmoving. Everything is in a state of flux, of constant movement and change. Tension describes the balanced relationship between opposing elements, or the interaction of those elements with one another. A Dynamic Tension, then, is the constantly balancing relationship between two elements, always implying movement and correction between the opposing ends over the fulcrum point of balance.

Just as the case was made for balancing strategy with relationships, the whole point of *G.R.A.C.E. at Work*, it is also important to note that everything else also requires balance. In the quest for organizational, professional or personal results, all things must be in balance. This applies to the model itself first. The *G.R.A.C.E. at Work* model consists of the five elements of Goodwill, Results, Authenticity, Connectivity and Empowerment. As mentioned earlier, each of these elements is, in a sense, seeking a balanced relationship with each other in order to allow the model to work successfully. The right and equal amounts of each component is necessary to yield productive relationships. Without this balance, the model can be "flat," not producing the desired results. Flats can cause the vehicle to be out of alignment, they impede forward motion, and eventually require fixing or replacement. If

Results-Stopping
"FLATS"

The current
value and
potential
future of any
relationship
are linked to
the dynamic
tension, the
balance, of
Goodwill and
Empowerment.

one component is short or lacking, the *G.R.A.C.E. at Work* wheels on the relationship vehicle go flat, and the forward momentum halts.

Goodwill and Empowerment

Perhaps the most critical of all the dynamic tensions for the *G.R.A.C.E. at Work* components is between Goodwill and Empowerment. This is the theme that runs throughout the model, and throughout this book. It is critical to create a balance between these two components, which will enable all the other components to also maintain balance. Assuming the positive, Goodwill in its essence is at the core of all successful relationships. If we take the "G" (Goodwill) out of the *G.R.A.C.E. at Work* model, we are left with RACE. This, then, removes the relationship aspect for the most part, and returns the relationship to one of transaction, not transformation. The partnership or relationship simply becomes a race for results, and only results. Most people, whether in business or professional liaisons, are looking for transformational relationships, with all partners contributing to something larger than self. Yet none of us is perfect, and sooner or later conflict will arise. We must have the ability to give self permission to try something new, something bigger. Goodwill goes beyond support, and is the "something bigger" effort. We support each other with process, resources, policy, procedures, tools and equipment, but we must also support with encouragement and genuine concern. These don't always imply relational components, but these are indeed empowerment attributes. Goodwill and Empowerment are inextricably linked to one another. If I have given someone tools and responsibility and resources to go and get things done, but I have not really understood their fears and concerns, goals and aspirations from a Goodwill perspective, all the empowerment in the world won't matter much. There must be a blend, an integration of these two for the relationship to take root and go somewhere. The current value and potential future of any relationship are linked to the dynamic tension, the balance, of Goodwill and Empowerment.

Static or Dynamic?

As indicated, the word *dynamic* implies energy, or growth. Something is in movement, as opposed to something not moving, or static. It is important to pause for a moment here to discuss the vital realization that in relationships, and in the tension between task and relationship, there is always potential for something to grow, to get bigger and better, but we don't always capitalize on that potential. To fully understand Dynamic Tensions, and the entire *G.R.A.C.E. at Work* model, we must first understand that all relationships are either growing or dying. If it is growing, it must be continually fed and nourished. Without this care and feeding, the relationship is dying. This is an intentional choice. If we are not intentionally growing the relationship, then we are allowing it to die off. And if we are intentionally maintaining a healthy dynamic tension between components, growth requires an increase in the opposing elements. For example, in the Goodwill and Empowerment balance, an extension of Goodwill will most likely enable, and require, an extension in Empowerment. The relationship grows through the management of the balances between the components.

This concept is important because we will have

> The relationship grows through the management of the balances between the components.

to make choices along the way since humans don't have unlimited energy and time to invest in every person that comes our way. We have circles of family, friends and professional alliances and connections and each one will require our own balancing act. This does not mean that we can't treat people well, and with goodwill at all times, but it does mean that our own energy is limited and will require us to make decisions about which relationships we will invest in for long term results. And if we want long term successful results, it will require growing the relationship and extending the amounts and balances of the dynamic tension components. Each of us must decide which relationships we will grow and which we allow to die out. That term may seem harsh, but it is an accepted fact of life that people come and go within our circles of relationships whether in personal or professional settings.

> The transformational relationship will last much longer than the transactional ones, and those are the relationships that require long term investment to ensure growth.

We don't always know in the moment which of these relationships will be short or long term. We don't always know the current or potential value of any particular relationship. We do know, however, that the transformational relationship will last much longer than the transactional ones, and those are the relationships that require long term investment to ensure growth. And that growth depends also on maintaining the tension, a growing balance, between the components.

All the dynamic tensions are tied back to the concept of balance, not just for static stability, but for growth. This may mean pushing the envelope, and adopting the philosophy that it is not *either or*, but *and*. How do I make sure that I am taking care of the results for the day, but also developing the capacity for the potential of tomorrow? This notion of growth has to be for both current and future potential and in sync with what I think to be the space I'm supposed to be playing in.

Goodwill and Empowerment are also balanced in today and tomorrow. From a business perspective, I make sure I have my things to do, doing my normal work, but I am also seeing and preparing for the possibility of the future by making and growing relationships, to grow the space and grow the results. It is not necessarily about trying to secure my own future on my own merit. Much like a farmer there is always another harvest to plan for, to plant, water, and weed. It is a continuing process in which the planning for the future begins with the plans that you have for today. Whatever it is that we have in mind for the future, the actual work begins now. Advance planning for relationships is not just about physical stuff. Part of it is conversation in which you talk about what's important to you, what's emerging, and what is critically important for both parties. It is a way of expressing your own desires and goals, while also learning about what each other person is feeling and thinking. This is authenticity and connectivity working together in dynamic balance.

Conversation is also critical to potential and growth of any relationship. Look at your conversations. In any particular relationship, the current state of your conversation is the state of your relationship and the state of your future relationship. Conversations are a major diagnostic for the welfare of any relationship. Do your conversations double back on themselves, yielding only an endless circle of questions with no answers, or do they allow for the deliberate growth of such components as goodwill and empowerment? This is one of the ways you can see at a glance where a relationship may be headed.

Growing a relationship requires us to be thoughtful and intentional. Relationships don't just happen or evolve on their own. Like any other dynamic life form, a relationship requires constant feeding for growth, or it will languish, eventually go static, and die. Hence, a dynamic tension is one that implies continual balancing and feeding to maintain proper conditions for growing results.

Authenticity and Connectivity

Authenticity and Connectivity are both more fully understood in the context of Goodwill and Empowerment. In its basic format we have two people in the equation, me and someone else. Authenticity, is fundamentally about both parties being real, open and interested. Connectivity is seeking ways in which these relationship partners can connect on emotional and productive levels, in authentic ways. Growing a relationship means growing Authenticity, then balancing that with growing Connectivity. These two components are the inner dynamic mechanisms of the Goodwill and Empowerment dynamic. It all begins with Goodwill, but Empowerment depends on Authenticity and Connectivity, all of which are in tension and in balance in order to achieve results. The results are the evidence, the manifestation of the commitments of each person in the relationship. The five components are interwoven and must be balanced with each other. One is not more important than the other.

Balance between all other aspects of working or personal relationships are also subject to countless Dynamic Tensions. Just one element out of balance can

throw the entire system into dysfunction, causing chaos to reign and storms to rage, whether we are speaking of business or our personal lives. Just as every vehicle, at least the ones we expect to move, require frequent and regular checks and balances. Are the tires inflated correctly? Are the fluid levels adequate? Is the engine tuned for optimal performance? The same checks, and balances, must be present for organizational, professional and personal performance. The G.R.A.C.E. practitioner will sometimes need to perform diagnostics in order to determine the working order of the relationship, or even the entire organization. Fine tuning of these tensions can also result in growing a bigger space, a larger playing field to yield larger results. There are an unlimited number of Dynamic Tensions that exist within organisms and organizations. When it comes to leadership, however, there are some we would always expect, and some we will most likely encounter at some time or other.

The Big Three

Later in this chapter we will present some common Dynamic Tensions found in most organizations. The list is really endless, as each organization is unique, creating and maintaining its own set of tensions. However, leaders of anyone in anyplace will always encounter these three tensions that consist of six dynamic elements that are generally in opposition to one another to create the right balances to achieve results:

- Challenge and Support
- Inquiry and Advocacy
- Task and Relationship

As we talk about relationships we have to remember that we are talking about joint ventures. You have your goals and your agenda, others also have theirs. Now while much of what can be described in the relationship will be dictated by organizational design, job descriptions, processes and the like, these are the inanimate structural components that simply do not engage the heart and soul of the people you are working with. The people working in those structural components must accept the boundaries and parameters of the position, but you are also looking to tap into the passion they may have for the organizational vision and for the purpose that drives their energy. If you don't create a shared sense of purpose all you will end up with is compliance, not commitment. This shared sense of purpose is critical to understanding the dynamic tensions. Just remember that balance requires at least two forces, two tensions, pulling in opposite directions – your direction and my direction. Our shared purpose is the fulcrum, the place where both of our needs are met.

> If you don't create a shared sense of purpose all you will end up with is compliance, not commitment.

Challenge and Support

One of the keys to successful learning and leadership, and productive relationships, is learning how to create the right kind of balance between challenge and support. There are inherent dangers to the viability of the relationship with an absence or abundance of either challenge or support. Too much challenge and you invite fear into the relationship. People, by nature, will either resist or reject outright your requests. If there is too much support, people will feel stifled or bored, and withdraw. The key is determining the right balance. The only way to do this is to have productive conversations about all

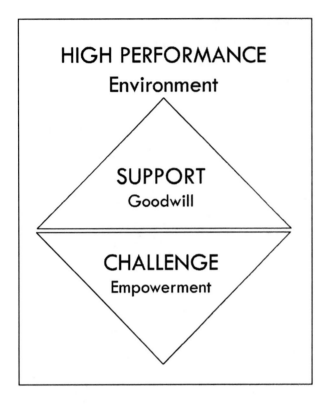

the perceptions and needs that are present in the task at hand. Candid conversation about assessments and aspirations are critical before you can discuss terms for autonomy.

Challenge and support is a dynamic tension that is about creating the space, balancing the tension, and providing sufficient safety (yet sufficient challenge). This balance can be achieved by engaging others in the conversation in a way that enables them to feel free enough to reveal their challenges. It is the balance of Goodwill and Empowerment as discussed earlier. The leader still has deliverables, but he or she also wants to create opportunity for others to learn, perform and recover if they don't meet expectations the first time around. A challenge is not a command, and a command is not a challenge. The leader facilitates meeting challenges with appropriate support—advancing goodwill and empowering for results. This balance creates a high performance environment.

Advocacy and Inquiry

This dynamic tension is between Authenticity and Connectivity. The Authenticity component represents what is important to me, my agenda, my view of the world, assumptions and expectations. On the other side is Connectivity, putting self in the other person's shoes, understanding what is important to them, demonstrating my concern and understanding for their concerns. This requires creating a blended agenda and conversation. There are now two or more people playing in the diamond space. This is blending my agenda with your agenda, and having "our" agenda conversations. Advocacy implies support, for a particular position and for the other person, while inquiry is about gaining information. These two ideas are balanced along the axis between Authenticity and Connectivity by seeking to know others, advocating for them, and inquiring about them and their work. It is making strong connections through authentic interaction. Inquiry without advocacy is often seen as a

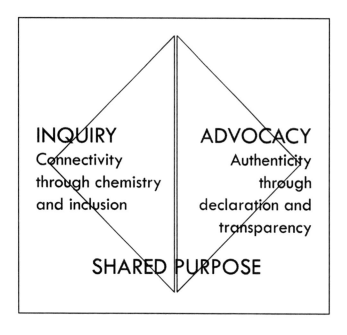

threat or intrusion. If the other person knows you are an advocate, he or she does not mind providing the information you need. Inquiring involves seeking answers to questions that are in the best interest of all parties. This balance cannot be maintained without the use of "chemistry" and full inclusion. Advocacy is enabled through authentic declaration and transparency by all parties in the relationship, and all of this rests on the fact that we have a shared sense of purpose in what we are doing, and why we are together in the first place.

Task and Relationship

Balancing task and relationship is similar to the overall concept of balancing strategy and relationships. The work we do with others is not just about the task, and it is not just about the relationship. There must be sufficient integration of these two components that builds a unified whole that is much bigger than either one separately. Contract workers and consultants have been typically conceived as all about the task, but employees must be about both. If it is just about the relationship, then there is no production, no money,

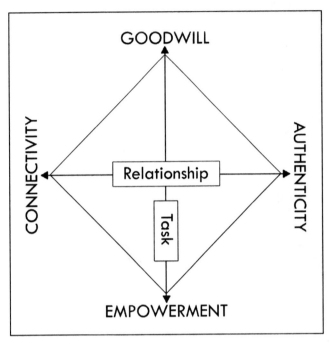

and no worth. Tasks alone may be able to drive some relationships, but they will not enable them to thrive. Tasks can be completed without relationships, but the results will most often be less than what would be achieved if these same tasks were balanced with relationships where people played in safe spaces, knowing they can recover from failures, and will be rewarded for successes. In the term of any working relationship, one of these components, task or relationship, may take precedent over the other at times, but for the long haul must have good balance.

The task portion of this dynamic balance is managed along the Goodwill-Empowerment axis, the same one that facilitates Challenge and Support. This "north and south" line is *task oriented*. The Authenticity - Connectivity axis, related to Inquiry and Advocacy, is *relationship* oriented. To balance any relationship, then, both axes, and all the components of *G.R.A.C.E. at Work* must be balanced. A healthy tension between all components along both axes will yield results well beyond what could be achieved only through a task orientation.

These "Big Three" dynamic tensions are further summarized in the following tables which indicate how these are balanced (what it looks like) and what happens when they are out of balance. You will find these three dynamic tensions required in every aspect of every leadership role.

DYNAMIC TENSION: High Performance
The balance and tension between Challenge and Support

DYNAMIC TENSION	CHALLENGE	SUPPORT
IN BALANCE	• Motivational • Inspire interdependencies for team work, appropriate connections • Create context for innovation • Allow for complete engagement • Fully utilize abilities • Clearly stated, desired results known • Match employee skills, passions, development path	• Appropriate encouragement given • Appropriate, consistent communication • Resources available to do the work • Allows people to be able to leverage their competencies while creating the capacity for growth • Genuine desire on leadership part for person(s) to succeed
OUT OF BALANCE	Goals, expectations are: • Overwhelming, or not clearly stated • Not challenging, motivational (underwhelming!) • Do not utilize individual skill sets, passions • Inappropriate for person/team	• No encouragement • Communication sporadic, missing, or inconsistent • Resources not available to do the job • "Cold," impersonal leadership attitude • Inauthentic
LEADERSHIP IMPLICATIONS	• Know employees, skills, abilities, motivators, strengths and weaknesses • Have people in the right positions • Facilitate conversations so can share strengths and weaknesses openly • Establish a learning environment where successes are celebrated, mistakes honestly evaluated and reviewed • Identify performance gaps, and discuss possible action steps to mitigate potential problems • Communicate pro-actively • Identify and understand difference between novice and expert, establish development plan • Create learning opportunities to develop targeted skill sets • Be available, in touch, open, operating from goodwill	
CONSEQUENCES OF BEING OUT OF BALANCE	• Boredom • Resentment • Frustration • "At risk" feeling • People not effectively or efficiently engaged • People guarded, not open • Less synergy, team work • Employee and production value compromised • No growth, in individuals or in bottom line	

DYNAMIC TENSION: Conversational Synergy

The balance and tension between Advocacy and Inquiry

DYNAMIC TENSION	ADVOCACY	INQUIRY
IN BALANCE	• Allows you some measure of self-determination • Allows you to build confidence in what you want • Provides others with an opportunity to understand where you are coming from • Creates possibility of taking a leadership stance	• Learn what the other person wants • Demonstrates a desire to lead collaboratively • Can determine what a win-win situation might look like • Creates some avenue for relationship building
OUT OF BALANCE	• Leadership style can be viewed as authoritarian • You limit the potential contribution of others • You miss opportunities to see things from a different perspective	• Can cause suspicion about the quantity of questions • Can lead to paralysis by analysis • Can provide interesting conversation but may not lead to any consensus action • Can mask intent of the person asking question
LEADERSHIP IMPLICATIONS	• Powerful conversation is balanced conversation • Powerful relationships require a balanced approach that demonstrates a desire to take a stand and to engage the other person • Asking open ended questions creates an open approach to inquiry • The power of the balance is in creating an opportunity for mutual collaboration in generating value • Learning how to frame assessments, requests, declaration, and offers create the foundation for balancing advocacy and inquiry	
CONSEQUENCES OF BEING OUT OF BALANCE	• An over emphasis on either attribute limits the potential of the resources and perspectives that people bring to the relationship • You limit the opportunities to create the win-win • The opportunity for people to be "heard" or "listened to" is limited with an overemphasis on advocacy. • You may never establish mutual respect for people in the relationship because other issues prevent people from establishing a deeper level of trust and transparency in the relationship.	

DYNAMIC TENSION: Results Integration

The balance and tension between Task and Relationship

DYNAMIC TENSION	TASK	RELATIONSHIP
IN BALANCE	• Consideration of business and people implications • Execution of excellence with integrity and goodwill • Graceful execution/actions • "Organic" interactions not simply compliance	• Ability to defer to a better solution • Ability to "see" that the task is a manifestation of the relationship • Trust that the other person can deliver
OUT OF BALANCE	• Everything else becomes subservient to the task • May not act in ethical ways • May view people as expendable	• May not address conflict or have the difficult conversation • May not act in ways that serve the greater good
LEADERSHIP IMPLICATIONS	• Need to have clear vision about the end state • Need to understand the needs and motivation of the people they lead • Give people the chance to learn and grow • Lead with a give and take mentality • Ability to play with tension between task and relationship that delivers with quality and allows freedom of expression • Create a synergy by looking for ways to leverage and optimize the transformation of one with the other	
CONSEQUENCES OF BEING OUT OF BALANCE	• Too much emphasis on the task and those involved may feel used to achieve your ends • Too much emphasis on the relationship and the long term sustainability of the business is jeopardized (you'll go out of business) • Without relationship, task performance can lead to individualized approaches or very transactional based interaction	

As in all life, balance is required in all relationships, including business, in order to achieve desired outcomes. This need for balance will be observed in many different areas, and necessary in all kinds of situations, general or specific. When intended and anticipated results are not being realized, one of the best evaluation tools is to check the balance in a number of common areas that can easily reveal dynamic tensions that pull too heavily to one side or the other. In addition to the "Big Three" mentioned earlier, there are several tensions that can be assessed and can serve as indicators of a need to re-establish proper balance. Some of these are included in the table on the next page. Following this table, a handful of these dynamic tensions are highlighted again *(random samples)* in tabular form *(like those presented for the "Big Three")* in order to more fully explore their dynamics. Neither this list, nor the tables, are exhaustive. In any given organization, or any particular relationship, there are an unlimited number of tensions that must be balanced for optimal outcomes. Following these next tables, you will be given an opportunity to discover and investigate your own dynamic tensions, perhaps some that do not appear here.

EVERYTHING
must be in
balance.

Again, life is all about balance. *Everything* must be in balance. Like a car traveling at high speed with out-of-balance tires, your leadership vehicle will shake, rattle and be difficult to control without these critical tensions in sound balance. Use these tables to evaluate your alignment and balance.

BUSINESS AREA OR ISSUE		DYNAMICALLY BALANCE TWO TENSIONS	
1	ORGANIZATIONAL IDENTITY	Preserving the Core	Stimulate Progress
2	RELATIONAL ALIGNMENT	Intentions	Impact
3	PERFORMANCE FOCUS	Results	Process
4	VISION	Strategic	Tactical
5	BOUNDARY MANAGEMENT	Empowerment (Commitment)	Control (Compliance)
6	LEADERSHIP FORMATION	Action	Reflection
7	RISK MANAGEMENT	Certainty	Ambiguity
8	WORK CONTEXT	Structured	Open
9	RELATIONAL DYNAMIC	Extroverted	Introverted
10	ENERGY	Calm, Controlled	High energy, Enthusiastic
11	COMMUNICATION	Clarity	Quantity
12	INFLUENCE	Initiating	Cooperation
13	LEADERSHIP STYLE	Formal	Informal
14	LEADERSHIP AGILITY	Letting Go	Holding Firm
15	LEADERSHIP PERSPECTIVE	Pessimism	Optimism
16	MANAGEMENT APPROACH	Compliance	Laissez-faire
17	CONVERSATIONS	Direct	Indirect
18	EXPERTISE	Generalist	Specialist
19	POWER	Formal	Informal
20	PROCESS DISCIPLINE	Control	Flexibility
21	STANDARDS	Precise	Relaxed
22	TRUST	Earned	Assumed
23	CAPACITY FOCUS	Today's Results	Tomorrow's Capacity
24	INTENTIONALITY	Spontaneous	Methodical
25	EVALUATION ATTITUDE	Quick Judgment	Positive Intent
26	PERFORMANCE FOCUS	Process	Results
27	INTERNAL FOCUS	Self	Others
28	NAVIGATIONAL FOCUS	Details	Big Picture
29	SELF-CONFIDENCE	Pride	Humility
30	ENGAGEMENT INTERACTION	Independent	Dependent

DYNAMIC TENSION: Leadership Perspective

The balance and tension between two leadership perspectives:

Optimism and Pessimism

DYNAMIC TENSION	PESSIMISM	OPTIMISM
IN BALANCE	• Maintains realistic assessment of threats or downsides • Identifies/Checks assumptions • Provides safeguard against blind optimism • Identifies boundaries of comfort zone	• Generates enthusiasm for the task • Creates a positive can-do attitude for the group • Supports a culture of innovation or continuous improvement • Reinforces goodwill and gratitude
OUT OF BALANCE	• Creates a spirit of negativity • Promotes inertia • Stifles recognition • Encourages a victim mentality	• Ignores real threats • Minimizes concerns • Glosses over pain • Contributes to a false sense of invincibility
LEADERSHIP IMPLICATIONS	• Secure real trustworthy data to make assessments • Intentionally assign competing resources to solve problems • Communicate widely assumptions and expectations regarding desired actions and goals • Assign people to play devil's advocate roles • Celebrate innovation, continuous improvement, and other actions that overcome obstacles or inertia • Recognize efforts that highlight and overcome real threats/dangers	
CONSEQUENCES OF BEING OUT OF BALANCE	• Can create a culture that stifles and ridicules action or risk taking • Can create a culture that ignores real threats and commits to irrational or misguided actions • People don't feel like their needs or concerns are being addressed appropriately • Decision making becomes inefficient as people either have to overcome inertia or unexpected obstacles	

DYNAMIC TENSION: Organizational Identity
Balancing the Core of the Present and the Emerging Promise of Tomorrow

DYNAMIC TENSION	CORE	EMERGING
IN BALANCE	• Keeps focus on the central identity of the organization • Provides stability in challenging times • Leverage efficiencies for maximum results	• Capitalizes on latent capabilities • Keeps people motivated • Offers renewed energy to move forward • Creates opportunities for others to join and contribute • Invites people to a part of the creative/generative process
OUT OF BALANCE	• Doesn't allow for growth • Organizational purpose can be rendered obsolete • Stifles creativity	• Attempt to be something the organization isn't • Need to manage a steep learning curve • Can potentially break the trust of customers and employees
LEADERSHIP IMPLICATIONS	• Leverage the organization brand by preserving the core while stimulating progress • Know what's happening with the market and customer demands • Know what's happening with employee engagement and commitment • Identify pressure points and appropriate change management issues and opportunities • Identify implications for employee development • Be mindful of how to balance organizational vision, mission, values, and goals when addressing future opportunities and threats • Manage the organizational "story" • Reward behaviors and results that demonstrate a successful combination of leadership for honoring the core and nurturing the emerging future	
CONSEQUENCES OF BEING OUT OF BALANCE	• Organizational purpose and mission can become confusing • Company may not be able to present compelling vision/product for future • Shareholders won't desire to invest in a company without a strong value proposition or identity in the marketplace • Organization will lose ability to be competitive • Employee value proposition diminished, leading to retention issues for high potentials	

DYNAMIC TENSION: Engagement Interaction

The balance and tension between two engagement interactions/attitudes:
Independent and Dependent

DYNAMIC TENSION	INDEPENDENT	DEPENDENT
IN BALANCE	• Keeps groupthink in check • Leverages your strengths • Provides fresh perspective • Offer a perspective that honors your unique abilities	• Able to rely on each others' commitments or goodwill • Demonstrates mutual commitment to the end goal • Leverages each other's strengths
OUT OF BALANCE	• Tend to function in isolation • Isn't conducive to creating synergy in using resources • Limits connectivity • Limits toleration for dissent • Limits accountability • Reinforces need to be "right"	• Creates undue burden in a relationship by having to "carry others" • Threatens personal space • Limits effective use of challenge and support • Limits initiative taking • Relies on others for self-worth
LEADERSHIP IMPLICATIONS	• Manage the expectations and balance between individuality and team work • Must create proper incentives for individuality and team work • Create development opportunities that fosters both individual and team development • Facilitate employees' ability to hold each accountable for actions • Equip employees with the ability to hold both powerful and difficult conversations	
CONSEQUENCES OF BEING OUT OF BALANCE	• Can create an environment that creates inertia through group think • Can create an environment that supports mavericks and doesn't leverage each other's gifts and talents • Can create unhealthy dependency and co-dependency issues • Limited leadership effectiveness without true followership	

DYNAMIC TENSION: Self-Confidence
Balancing Pride and Humility to Yield Authenticity

DYNAMIC TENSION	PRIDE	HUMILITY
IN BALANCE	• Provides feeling of accomplishment • Encourages accountability • Conducive to generating quality • Creates boundaries • Communicates/demonstrates values and commitments • Provides motivation	• Helps us keep perspective • Helps us identify our strengths and weaknesses • Demonstrates our need for others • Demonstrates our gratitude to others • Encourages us to own our mistakes
OUT OF BALANCE	• Overestimate our abilities or contributions • Keep us from asking for help • Isolate us from others • May avoid certain tasks that we deem are "beneath us" • May try to achieve too much in order to prove our "worthiness"	• May discount our own abilities • May create dependencies on others for self-esteem or confidence • Keep us from standing up for our needs or agenda • Keep us from trying new things for fear of failure
LEADERSHIP IMPLICATIONS	• Create a culture of direct, open, and honest feedback • Implement measurement systems that provides people with accurate assessments of their behaviors/contributions • Ensure that all parties contributing to an accomplishment are recognized/rewarded commensurately • Facilitate After Action Reviews that focus on process and accountability issues • Provide training or structures that facilitate conversations for engagement, conflict resolution, and managing our internal dialogue	
CONSEQUENCES OF BEING OUT OF BALANCE	• Run people over with your own agenda • Being run over with other people's agenda • Increases the possibility of hidden agendas • Aggressive behavior • Can create passive-aggressive behavior • Can create culture where people don't assume ownership/ accountability for actions • Can create atmosphere of victimization	

DYNAMIC TENSION: Leadership Agility
Balancing the need to Let Go with Holding Firm

DYNAMIC TENSION	LETTING GO	HOLDING FIRM
IN BALANCE	• Allows flexibility in thinking and behavior • Invites new possibilities • Allows others to participate in a more meaningful way • Can relieve the pressure/strain of the leader to do everything themselves	• Demonstrates resolve or a constancy of purpose • Demonstrates to others what's important or less important • Provides basis for leadership authenticity
OUT OF BALANCE	• Doesn't provide sufficient structure or direction to get things done • Abdicates responsibility or accountability for action • Failure to make connections for people • Limit ability to leverage synergies	• Stifles creativity/innovation • May limit the strength of response • Actions puts some people/ideas on the outside
LEADERSHIP IMPLICATIONS	• Know your core values and how they play into your decision making • Know what you consider negotiable vs. non-negotiable • Look for trends in the industry and global market place • Reflect on your own growth and development and the changes this may imply on your identity • Realize that your decision to hold firm or let go is a choice – how is it serving you to do either one?	
CONSEQUENCES OF BEING OUT OF BALANCE	• People will resent not having the opportunity to pursue what they feel they have the capacity to do for themselves • Ambivalence in making decisions regarding empowerment is counter productive and drives mistrust • Your own ability to make a difference will be limited and will contribute to inertia • You can lose your ability to create a distinctive leadership approach or philosophy	

DYNAMIC TENSION: Standards

The balance and tension between Precise and Relaxed standards

DYNAMIC TENSION	PRECISE	RELAXED
IN BALANCE	• Increased confidence in meeting exact specifications • Clarity on performance expectations • Creates parameters for process controls • Highlights cost benefit ratio of different levels of performance	• May demonstrate high levels of process performance standards • Can allow people to learn or perform without undue fear • Allows for exploration of innovative opportunities • Allows people to focus on multiple issues
OUT OF BALANCE	• Standards could be used as a hammer • Cost of excellence could exceed what the customer is willing to pay • Lose sight of the relationship opportunities • Could get too caught up in the details	• Disregard for standards could diminish the value of the product or service for the customer • Lack of operational or financial controls could drive up costs • Relaxed approach could cloud goal and role expectations
LEADERSHIP IMPLICATIONS	• Identify the right balance between task and relationship • Identify the cost/benefit ratio for quality standards • Improve the capability of your processes to deliver quality product or services at the least cost to the performers • Create appropriate rewards for exacting performance • Identify and communicate your understanding of the sacrifices employees make to deliver quality products or services	
CONSEQUENCES OF BEING OUT OF BALANCE	• Could alienate/frustrate employees with the work standards • Could adversely impact the brand of the product or service • Could lose profitability with too stringent or too relaxed standards	

What about *your* organization, your team, your relationships? Where are your most critical dynamic tensions? Even if they are the same as those appearing in the tables previously, you will benefit from this exercise.

Give your Dynamic Tension a name. Identify the two opposing elements that must be balanced. Write in the blanks on the table. Complete the table on the next page by filling in the appropriate boxes:

1. Write the opposing elements into the blank top boxes.

2. Identify at least 3 things that show what each element in balance looks like.

3. Identify at least 3 things that reveal when each element is out of balance.

4. List at least 3 things that show the leadership implications for this Dynamic Tension

5. Provide at least 3 consequences for being out of balance on this Dynamic Tension. *(Obviously, for any of these areas, you can provide more than 3 responses.)*

Make copies of this worksheet to outline and debrief all the Dynamic Tensions in your organization and your professional or personal life that you suspect may need some fine tuning and balancing.

DYNAMIC TENSION: _____

The balance and tension between (1)_____ and (2)_____

DYNAMIC TENSION	(1)	(2)
What this Dynamic Tension looks like **IN BALANCE**		
What this Dynamic Tension looks like **OUT OF BALANCE**		
LEADERSHIP IMPLICATIONS		
CONSEQUENCES OF BEING OUT OF BALANCE		
OTHER COMMENTS		

Chapter 8

G.R.A.C.E. in Conversation

Powerful, Difficult and Internal Conversations

"The true spirit of conversation consists in building on another man's observation, not overturning it."

– *Edward G. Bulwer-Lytton*

CONVERSATIONS:

Fueling Results

CONVERSATIONS are the connecting tissue of relationships. They hold everything together, whether the relationship is based on professional associations or personal connections. Conversations not only make relationships interesting, but it is through the use of conversation that we make things happen. Often the conversation *is* the relationship. It is the medium for getting work done in organizations and other networks.

> Conversations are the connecting tissue of relationships.

Every relationship requires powerful and productive conversation to thrive, but we all know only too well that this may not always be the case. There are essentially three basic types of conversation: Powerful, Difficult and Internal. The Powerful Conversation is one that results in advancing the relationship, or the desired results of this relationship. The people in this conversation have moved forward toward expected outcomes. The Difficult Conversation may or may not always be powerful, but can be, if it is based on some simple guidelines. These are the conversations we usually dread, generally dealing with things we would rather avoid and shove under a convenient rug somewhere. But with the right attitude and approach these can be some of the most productive conversations, turning difficulty into powerful solutions. The Internal Conversation is one we all know about. It is that constant dialogue we have with ourselves, parrying and jousting often with our internal critic and our internal champion. The *G.R.A.C.E. at Work* model can provide helpful templates to turn all conversations into productive and powerful tools. Powerful conversations fuel powerful results. Results are a function of the conversation and the relationship.

Before we present these conversation models, it is helpful to have some simple tools in our conversation toolkits. Let's take a look at some of the most basic, yet most often abused, concepts about conversation in general.

Facts and Opinions

In conversation we often confuse facts with opinions and personal perception. It is important to understand that when we speak what we consider to be fact, it should be verifiable and true, not based on our own perceptions. Perceptions are really opinions, and they are *not* verifiable. Our opinions may or may not be shared with others in the conversation, and cannot be assumed as fact. Facts are not subjective. They do not belong to observers, but to objects, via an objective measuring tool. Facts are assumed to be true, until proven otherwise. Opinions are either grounded or ungrounded. It is very important to understand the difference between these two types of information. Unless we are specifically asked for our perceptions and opinions, it is almost always safer to "stick to the facts, Ma'am."

> Results are a function of the conversation and the relationship.

One person in conversation may make the statement "It's hot in here." This is an opinion and may not be shared by someone with a fever who has the chills. Another person may be standing next to the thermostat and state "It's 72 degrees in here." One is an opinion, the other a fact. Some conversations are casual enough that these differences may not be as critical as at other times, but there are times that it is essential to know and maintain the difference. If we approach all conversation with this foundational guideline, of distinguishing in our speech and assumptions the differences between fact and opinion our conversations will not be easily derailed, misconceived or ill-received.

Requests and Agreements

Many conversations occur as the result of one or more persons needing to make a request, asking for something. That seems pretty straightforward, but so often confusion, misconceptions and even total communication breakdowns happen because we don't follow a few simple guidelines. To get desired and effective results from making a request, we must employ effective requests.

EFFECTIVE REQUESTS MUST:

- **State specifically what you want.**
- **State specifically who you want it from.**

- **State what will create satisfaction (time frames, outcomes, etc.)**
- **Establish common understanding (same terminology, restatement of request by the party requested, etc.)**
- **Arrive at common agreement regarding the request**

Clear agreements that everyone understands and commits to are based on established specifics regarding the elements of the request. If this isn't possible, then the request needs to be renegotiated, either with a new request, or reformulated expectations. All parties need to have clarity (check this!) about what the expectations and agreements are.

This might sound like a lot of work or unnecessary steps to take in a normal conversation, but it really becomes easy with a little practice, and the results are pleasantly surprising. We all make assumptions about what another person might hear, or might agree to, but without verifying these, we are disappointed by the results. For example, when mom asks her teenage son to mow the lawn, he might mumble something and slink off to his room. Mom assumes the lawn will be mowed before her party on Saturday night. But without further clarification, and stated expectations, that grass may not get cut until a hay truck is necessary to cart away the bales. Mom is now not only disappointed in the results, she is angry with her son. The outcome of their conversation is lose-lose, a bad situation for them both, and certainly does not advance this relationship anywhere but backwards. Next time mom might want to stop her son, look him in the eye, state her expectations (including when this is to be done), get his agreement to the terms, and his commitment to fulfilling them. It's not that hard to do.

We also sometimes make requests that aren't really requests at all. Which of the these are effective requests?

- *"Will you please mow the lawn?"*
- *"Can you help with this project?"*
- *"Will you fax this mileage report to our branch office by 3:00 pm today?"*
- *"The last three meetings you led ran over their scheduled time."*
- *"This conference room is a mess. We have a meeting here in one hour!"*

The first "request" on this list results in knee-high grass. There are no specifics, no expectations, no commitments, no agreements. The second is the same. It can be answered with a simple yes or no, which hopefully is followed by more specific details of this request. The last two statements are just that—statements. They are not requests, but hidden agenda comments with unstated expectations. People should not have to read our minds, and we should not attempt to "shame" them into what we really should have asked them outright. If we give a little thought to making requests and pursuing agreement, we will all find life and work goes much smoother, conversations are more productive and the desired results are pleasing, and not surprisingly disappointing.

> **People should not have to read our minds.**

G.R.A.C.E.-Full Conversations

BUILDING on these basic tools of conversation regarding facts, opinions, requests and agreements, there is a way to dramatically increase the odds of making any conversation productive and powerful.

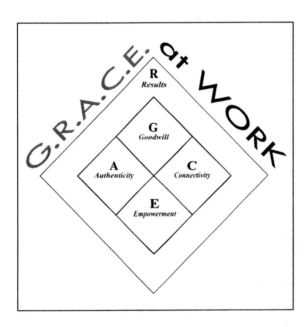

By now you are familiar with the classic diamond that represents the *G.R.A.C.E. at Work* model. We have discussed the five components of Goodwill, Results, Authenticity, Connectivity and Empowerment. When these are employed in conversation, the results are often startlingly powerful, especially when previous conversations have not yielded desired outcomes. Try it again, using this model, and we can pretty much guarantee much different, more acceptable results.

The Powerful Conversation Model presented on the next page can be considered the treasure map to conversation gold. The guidelines, boundaries, questions and processes it provides will keep conversations headed for the best outcomes.

Keep in mind that "conversations" are what meetings are made of. This chapter is not just about those casual personal or workplace conversations "around the water cooler." These conversations, the ones discussed here, are those intended to yield tangible results. Meetings are nothing more than conversation between two or more people intended to produce some desired outcome, some shared purpose. All of the elements of a "Powerful Conversation" are the same elements of any powerful meeting.

> The Powerful
> Conversation
> Model can be
> considered the
> treasure map to
> conversation gold.

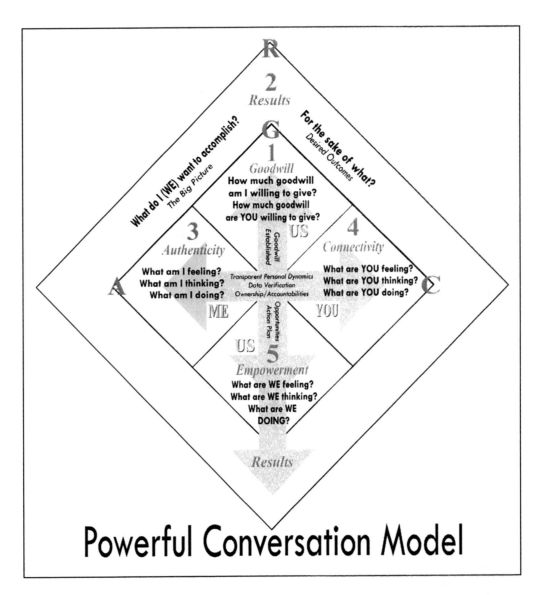

Powerful Conversation Model

Powerful Conversation is facilitated by answering a series of questions for each of the five components of G.R.A.C.E. These questions may be openly stated and placed squarely on the table for discussion, or they may be internally processed through guided conversation designed to yield the answers to these questions. Each of these questions is important, and has the ability to either facilitate further conversation, or terminate meaningful dialogue. There is also a process and order through which these questions are answered. The questions are designed to elicit answers that enable the following process:

1. Establish mutual **goodwill**, and goodwill boundaries

2. Determine the intended **results**, desired outcomes of the conversation

3. Practice mutual **authenticity**

4. Make **connections** through transparent personal dynamics

5. **Empower** one another to achieve the desired outcomes through available opportunities and action plans

The groundwork for successful and powerful conversations is laid at the very beginning of any dialogue. As with anything else that employs the *G.R.A.C.E. at Work* model, it begins with the first component of Goodwill. Goodwill is the medium in which grows the culture of dynamic, powerful conversation and relationships.

GOODWILL in Conversation

Without the presence of goodwill, every conversation is doomed to failure. Goodwill comes even before the reasons for the dialogue. It is the platform on which every other element of the conversation is built. The questions that must be asked and answered before anything else are:

1. How much goodwill AM I willing to give?
2. How much goodwill ARE YOU willing to give?
3. What does goodwill mean to YOU, ME, to US?

While Goodwill may begin with one party in conversation, it must extend to both. No matter how hard the one expressing goodwill tries, if the other parties in conversation have not chosen to also extend goodwill, the conversation is over before it begins. In most typical conversation, goodwill is often assumed and there is no question or discussion about its presence for all contributors. However, there are also times when parties will come together in dialogue sporting boxing gloves, or at the least, a goalie's mask.

By openly addressing the element of goodwill to be present in the conversation, through the questions stated above, those gloves and masks can be laid aside. Defensive, or offensive and aggressive, conversation and attitudes end at the goodwill diamond on this model. Goodwill is about "US," two or more in shared conversation to achieve shared results through shared goodwill. It is not about YOU or ME, it is about US. Can WE agree to continue bringing the same level of goodwill to the conversation? Once all parties come to agreement on the level of goodwill to be practiced, *throughout* the conversation, Goodwill provides all the other components a safe basis of operation.

The presence of mutual Goodwill provides the "safe space"or trust for productive conversation.

G

1

Goodwill

How much goodwill am I willing to give? How much goodwill are YOU willing to give?

US

Authenticity

Connectivity

Goodwill Established

Empowerment

Results

Goodwill is the level ground of conversation, which enables ME−YOU Authenticity leading to Connection, which eventually Empowers to yield Results−desired outcomes and shared purpose for all parties. Without establishing Goodwill, the entire process will break down. The ensuing Results will be less than hoped, and often move a relationship back rather than forward.

RESULTS in Conversation

Since Results are generally the entire purpose (reason) for any conversation, especially those related to business results, it is essential that these are fully identified up-front. This seems logical, yet so many times we jump into conversations without determining, stating and agreeing upon, the desired outcomes. Not only is a great deal of time wasted when this critical step is skipped, but often the results of these conversations don't come anywhere near what was intended originally. Results determine the process, boundaries and flow of dialogue, moving conversation along toward realized outcomes. Have you ever had a conversation, then walked away and scratched your head wondering *"what was all that about?"* having no clarity around what you were supposed to do with this dialogue? We have all had those moments, and they are the end-product of undetermined, unagreed upon results, the very reason for the conversation.

Sometimes meetings and conversations are originated with previous stated goals and outcomes, where everyone in conversation is aware of, and has had time to process, these. At other times no advance notice of purpose or intended results is given for such conversation, and it is at these times that the actual dialogue must include a thorough discussion and opportu-

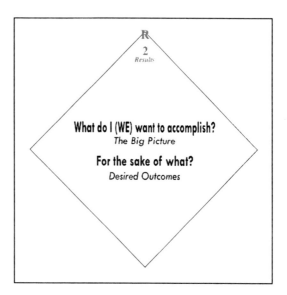

nity for agreement of the intended results. There are two foundational questions that must be asked and completely answered:

1. What do I (we) want to accomplish? *(the big picture overview of the intended conversation)*

2. For the sake of what? *(the specific desired outcomes)*

Most often conversations are originated from the desire or necessities arising for one party first. We'll call this person the conversation "originator." This originator spends time fully answering the questions above so that he or she will be able to guide the flow of the entire dialogue to achieve those results, and is ready to explain the intended results to others, making the "I" of the conversation a "WE." Unless all parties in conversation are informed of, and agree to, the intended results and reason for the conversation, those desired outcomes will not be achieved. Not only is information vital, *agreement is critical*. Agreement is the basis for accountability.

AUTHENTICITY and CONNECTIVITY
in Conversation
In order to yield productive results, any conversation must establish and maintain connections with all parties. In order to achieve these connections, all parties must be authentic. Hence, it is virtually impossible, and moot, to discuss one without the other. These two components of the *G.R.A.C.E. at Work* model are a matched set, inseparable. By its very nature, conversation implies more than one party *(unless it is an internal conversation which will be discussed a bit later)*. Authenticity and transparency on the part of only one person does not allow for essential connections. *Mutual* Authenticity enables Connectivity, and Connectivity facilitates the Empowerment to achieve desired outcomes. Again, there are a set of questions that will lay the foundation for these components to function together to yield productive results in conversation.

1. What am I feeling?
2. What am I thinking?
3. What am I doing?

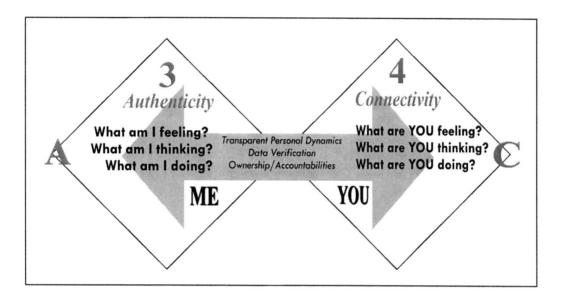

Honest answers to these questions facilitate transparent personal dynamics for all individuals in the conversation. Hidden agendas, unexpressed emotions and less than truthful answers will only serve as roadblocks on the path to powerful results. These questions begin on a personal level, with each individual. This is about first being authentic with yourself, then having a willingness to express the same authenticity in connection with others. Remember that Goodwill is the underlying platform on which these conversations are built. Self transparency and authenticity do not contribute much if there is no willingness to show goodwill and openly hear and accept the authenticity of others.

Connections are made once these questions are extended to include the public awareness of all parties to the answers to the questions above. Time to explore answers — honest answers — to the following is necessary to stay within that "safe place" where

> Not only is information vital, agreement is critical. Agreement is the basis for accountability.

conversation is not hindered by non-transparency, or less than authentic dialogue:

1. What are YOU feeling?
2. What are YOU thinking?
3. What are YOU doing?

After Authenticity has been openly established, the work of plugging in, connecting, begins. The facts, figures, perceptions, opinions, assertions and assessments of the conversation are then verified. Once connections are established, they are strengthened by this "data verification" stage, where the "nitty gritty" of the conversation makes the rounds of dialogue. Again, remember that Goodwill is to flow throughout the conversation, and Authenticity is a given requirement throughout. If either of these components is lacking or breaks down in any way, connectivity is broken. Since we don't always have perfect conversations, it may be necessary to re-visit these components and re-establish them in order to proceed to productivity.

Quite often the bulk of conversation happens in the back and forth interplay between Authenticity and Connectivity. This is the free-flow exchange of ideas and discussion that ranges from personal dynamics to verification of data. In this interchange a vital ingredient is ownership and accountability. These are explored, discussed, assigned, accepted and agreed upon, enhanced and strengthened again by Goodwill, Authenticity and commitment to shared purpose. As stated in the earlier discussion of the *G.R.A.C.E. at Work* model, all five components must work in unison to travel the road to results. With even just one component "flat," the entire vehicle comes to a halt.

EMPOWERMENT in Conversation

It is through the interchange of Authenticity and Connectivity that the ME and YOU become US again. There are no singular or unknown personal agendas. All the pieces have been contributed into one purpose. The data has been verified parties have come together in agreement and understanding.

The final component of this model is where the rubber hits the road. This is where opportunities are explored and strategies and actions plans are developed. Before any action can be taken to achieve intended results, the following questions are answered, now for the single unit (parties having become WE instead of ME or YOU):

1. What are WE feeling?
2. What are WE thinking?
3. What are WE doing?

Movement forward is now unified. There may be individual action plans, responsibilities and accountabilities, but the parties in conversation are now highly functioning as a whole—fully informed, fully committed, fully agreed, and fully accountable.

By exploring the answers first to personal emotions, thoughts and actions, (MINE and YOURS) a group dynamic can be achieved that identifies those of the unified parts into one forward moving entity. In many respects, a new "team" evolves as the result of powerful conversations. A team can be defined as a cooperative unit with shared purpose. It is only through the combined functions all five components of the *G.R.A.C.E. at Work* model in conversation that this unit is created for powerful results.

5 Steps to Powerful Conversations

1

GOODWILL

- It always begins, *and continues*, with goodwill.

- Resolve to work through all steps with this foundation.

- Return to, and remind of, commitment to work from goodwill for all parties.

- Discuss what attributes of goodwill you need for this interaction, this engagement.

2

RESULTS

- What is the "big picture" bringing these people together?

- What are the desired results, goals, or target outcomes?

- Describe all aspects fully.

- Obtain agreement.

3

AUTHENTICITY

- How does everyone "resonate" with this big picture?

- What does this big picture mean to each person?

- Is each person energized by the big picture?

- What are the moods, attitudes and feelings about the desired targeted outcomes for each person involved?

- Explore all personal dynamics, ensuring that they are fully transparent, and known to all involved (*and honored and respected*).

CONNECTIVITY

4

- What is known, and verified by hard data, about the current situation, and the desired target?

- Explore all data, information, commitments, conditions, resources, etc. relevant to the desired results.

- How are people (and things) connected in the big picture?

- What is known to hinder, deter, or limit, or what might be considered a challenge to reaching the desired target?

EMPOWERMENT

5

- What opportunities exist, or could exist to enable reaching the big picture?

- What steps need to be taken?

- What commitments need to be made?

- What resources are required?

- Explore all requirements for successful pursuit of the desired target.

- Develop an action plan that delineates all components of the strategy developed.

- Execute the plan with accountabilities.

It works.

Preparing for Powerful Conversations

Are you planning an important conversation or meeting? Do you want to be sure that you achieve your desired results? Taking a little time beforehand to map out the answers to all the questions presented here will give you a solid foundation that will have a much higher potential to reach those goals. You can develop your own personalized template for this conversation by utilizing the diamond model and the instructions on the worksheet that follows.

To provide a simple usable template, write your answers in the form of brief bullet points inside the diamond diagram. If you need more room, draw your own template on a larger sheet of paper. You may also find it useful to merely make lists and comments, as you work through these steps, then transfer them in bullet form to your template.

CONSTRUCTING A TEMPLATE
For Powerful Conversations
Go through the questions below and complete each diamond in the model.

Step 1: THE RESULTS DIAMOND
Describe the big picture of what you want to achieve *(your desired results, and for the sake of what)*. Describe all aspects and intended results *(goals, target outcomes)* completely. In essence, what is inspiring this conversation, and what do you hope to achieve by it?

Step 2: THE GOODWILL DIAMOND
Determine how much Goodwill you are willing to give and express in this conversation. What is your commitment to work from this base of goodwill? Will you extend this goodwill beyond this conversation and into action and behaviors to achieve the results? How will you hold yourself accountable, and remind yourself, to do these things? It is also helpful here to identify the parties in this conversation, and why they are included. You might even explore what you think their own answers to these questions might be. Remember, however, you are not in their heads. You may be able to theorize responses, but also allow for unexpected replies.

Powerful Conversation Template

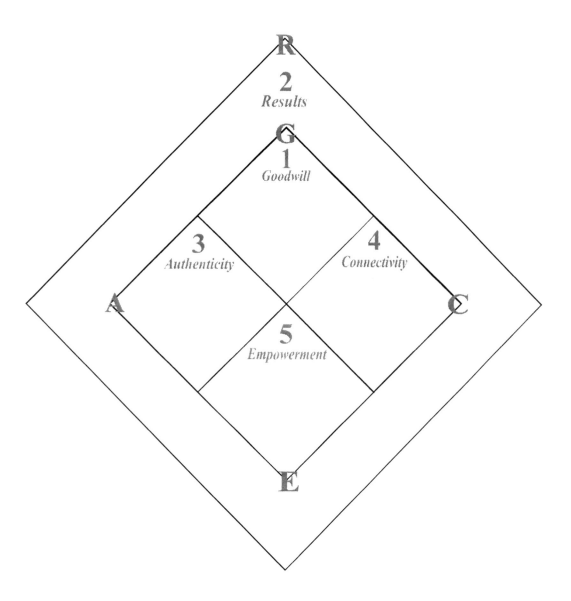

Step 3: THE AUTHENTICITY DIAMOND

This step is where transparent personal dynamics begin. Think about the words you will use to state how you resonate with the big picture, what it means to you, and how you are energized by it. How you will energize your partners in conversation to understand and commit to the big picture and specific details? When we have something in mind that resonates with us, there is a certain amount of energy involved. That energy has parts of its own, including the heart, mind, soul and body. The heart can be a critical part

◇
_____

How will you energize your partners in conversation to understand and commit to the big picture and specific details?

of this energy, expressing the emotional aspects. The mind creates intellectual understanding, and the soul will house the passion (if appropriate). The body cannot be neglected in this picture, which includes the physical elements of sleep, nutrition, stress, skills, etc. When preparing for an important conversation, don't sabotage your results by not paying attention to your physical needs. How will you share this with others? Mentally consider your answers ahead of time to the three questions: *What am I feeling? What am I thinking?* and *What am I doing?* as they relate to your big picture. Knowing your own answers first will facilitate your knowing those of others, in order to seek connectivity.

Step 4: THE CONNECTIVITY DIAMOND

Craft a plan that will easily allow you to help others to go through the process of personal authenticity, just like you did in the step above. Asking the right questions is a powerful tool in this endeavor. Allowing time for thoughtful responses, adequate sharing and discussion will keep your ultimate goals in sight and eliminate unexpected and unpleasant surprises. When connections occur, through transparent authenticity for all parties, the actual hard data (the meat) of your conversation is on the table. How will you present what is known about the current situation and the desired target? Be sure to include thinking about potential hurdles, limitations or other challenges to meeting your goals. Making a list of the information, conditions, commitments, resources and other relevant details can streamline discussion and further progress toward desired outcomes. If you have done your homework in this area *(in any of these areas)* your conversation is more likely to stay on track *(less likely to be derailed)* and more apt to produce immediate results, or concrete plans to achieve results. When thinking through this Connectivity component, however, remember that you are only thinking from one perspective—yours. Are you willing to receive other perspectives, other thinking, other ideas, even if they might seem to conflict with yours? How will you facilitate the "safe space" for this exchange? How will you move toward consensus and real connection? Commitment?

Step 5: THE EMPOWERMENT DIAMOND

Consider what opportunities exist, or could exist, to enable realizing your big picture results. What steps, commitments and resources would be needed? What constitutes a successful plan or strategy of pursuit for this big picture? Sketch out a brief action plan that delineates all the elements of your strategy, including responsibilities and accountabilities. In other words, what will get you from where you are now to where you want to be? How will you measure the progress? How will you make corrections? Obviously, this is again from only one perspective. As indicated above, how will you encourage discussion and agreement on one unified strategy?

Once you have completed this preparation for conversation, you might also want to consider actually bringing it to the conversation and working through it "diamond-by-diamond." By doing so, you are modeling for others how to have a productive and powerful conversation. You might want to even use the checklist *(based on the summary steps)* on the next page as a working process model. Copy this page and distribute it to every member in the conversation. Ask everyone to be responsible, and accountable, for seeing these steps completed fully. You can effectively turn your meeting or conversation into a powerful training session as well.

POWERFUL CONVERSATION TEMPLATE AND CHECKLIST	DONE? NOTES?
GOODWILL	
1 Explore and establish extent of Goodwill.	
2 Resolve to work through all steps with this foundation.	
3 Return to, and remind of, commitment to work from goodwill for all parties.	
RESULTS	
1 What is the "big picture" bringing us together?	
2 What are the desired results, goals, or target outcome?	
3 Describe all aspects fully.	
4 Obtain agreement.	
AUTHENTICITY	
1 How does everyone "resonate" with this big picture?	
2 What does this big picture mean to each person?	
3 How is each person energized by the big picture?	
4 What are the moods, attitudes and feelings about the desired targeted outcomes for each person involved?	
5 Explore all personal dynamics, ensuring that they are fully transparent, and known to all involved (and honored and respected).	
CONNECTIVITY	
1 What is known, and verified by hard data, about the current situation, and the desired target?	
2 Explore all data, information, commitments, conditions, resources, etc. relevant to the desired results.	
3 How are people (and things) connected in the big picture?	
4 What is known to hinder, deter, or limit, or what might be considered a challenge to reaching the desired target?	
EMPOWERMENT	
1 What opportunities exist, or could exist to enable reaching the big picture?	
2 What steps need to be taken?	
3 What commitments need to be made?	
4 What resources are required?	
5 Explore all requirements for successful pursuit of the desired target.	
6 Jointly develop an action plan that delineates all components of the strategy developed, including responsibilities and accountabilities.	
7 Execute the plan with accountabilities.	

G.R.A.C.E. for Difficult Conversations

JUST reading the words "Difficult Conversation" will most likely bring to everyone's mind a specific conversation experienced in the past. We have all had them, and we will all most likely have them again. We could spend a great deal of time analyzing why Difficult Conversations happen, or what constitutes a Difficult Conversation, but essentially conversations become difficult as a result of having to confront the fact that one person has made interpretations or assessments differing from another. Quite often there is a defining "event" which prompts these assessments and interpretations. All humans tend to have differing opinions and perceptions of what is observable in our world. It is always so noteworthy in the event of a "fender bender" on the highway that fifteen witnesses to the same event will have fifteen differing assessments and interpretations of what they witnessed. This has always baffled police investigators, but it is something they expect. We all see things differently, processing the hard facts through very subjective internal filters. Most often these differing views will culminate in some sort of rift or separation between the parties, requiring a Difficult Conversation in order to move forward. And often conversations can *become* difficult when we don't act from a basis of Goodwill. We consider these "difficult" conversations because we lack the confidence or the tools to express ourselves authentically and connect with the other person.

> We all see things differently, processing the hard facts through very subjective internal filters.

Difficult Conversations are usually full of competing claims to what is right and true, differing perceptions and opinions, what each person wants out of the relationship, and differing ways we express (or don't express) our personal authenticity. They reveal the story lines about our personal world view, and how we choose to live out that world view. And without some sort of guiding influence, these conversations may end in complete estrangement, failure to reconcile, and wounded egos and spirits. In extreme cases, failed Difficult Conversations will lead to violence, and sometimes even wars. The history of America is littered with the southern-style "feuds" of the 19th century, quite often started because of a failed Difficult Conversation. We still feud today, we just do it a little more civilly (*at least in most cases...*).

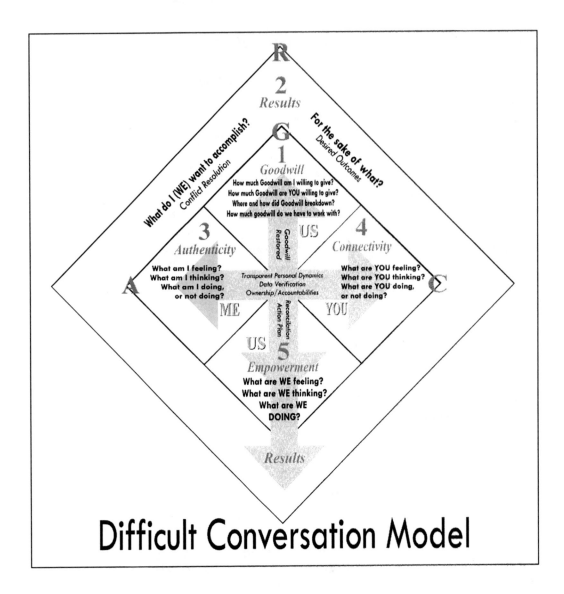

Difficult Conversation Model

The Coherency of G.R.A.C.E. and Broken Coherency

Coherency is a term used to describe the ability or state of certain things to "stick together" or remain connected and uninterrupted. It is the logical, orderly and consistent relationships of parts. When applied to the *G.R.A.C.E. at Work* model, it means that all the components or parts stick together, remain linked and function as a whole for powerful relationships. We can apply this also as the concept of "chemistry" in relationship, which describes how the people in the relationship converse in such a way where all the components of G.R.A.C.E. come together to create, enhance and maintain a powerful relationship.

On occasion this coherency is broken, generally through some "defining event." One or more of the G.R.A.C.E. components is either omitted, neglected, or not present in suitable strength. Any one of the components in this state will contribute to broken coherency. And broken coherency will always be found as the reason for the need for a Difficult conversation. If you are having difficulty determining "what happened" to cause this Difficult Conversation, all you have to do is trace back through the five components of G.R.A.C.E. until you discover which were not consistently practiced in full measure. Some of the signals that would indicate broken coherency of G.R.A.C.E. might include the inability to express yourself authentically, the inability to make connections with others in relationship, confusion regarding expected outcomes, reluctance to apply some measure of goodwill, and generally feeling un-empowered to make this a successful and productive relationship.

> ...the knowledge of how to have powerful conversations is critical to the creation of anything.

The Context of Coherency

In both action and words, we declare certain things to be true about ourselves and the world. Those truths manifest themselves in how we "show up" emotionally, intellectually, physically, and spiritually, especially as we relate with others. Successful interaction with others depends on our ability to communicate our truths, negotiate shared expectations and meaning for the future, and the extent to which we invest in the relationship. Conversations allow us to create possibilities for ourselves and for others. There is nothing in the world that has been created that didn't result from someone employing conversation, whether with someone else, or with ourselves (Internal Conversation). That is certainly a sobering thought. Therefore, the knowledge of how to have Powerful Conversations (difficult or otherwise), is critical to the creation of anything. The consistent employment of every one of the G.R.A.C.E. components provides coherency in relationship that enables powerful results. And G.R.A.C.E. begins and ends with Goodwill. Progress or development toward growth or resolution begins with a statement of intention (stated Goodwill) and is authenticated with evidence of fulfillment (actions to support Goodwill).

Individual Coherency

As individuals, our personal coherency also plays a large role in successful relationships, and is determined by the manner and measure we have integrated ourselves emotionally, intellectually, physically and spiritually. Our coherent "truth" is based upon our personal world views, which are the collective fundamental assumptions, values and beliefs about "who I am." Personal and cultural history and commitments to our internal Champion and Critic all contribute to our fundamental assumptions about the nature of the world. When we have integrated or aligned ourselves in all these areas, we will "show up" and be present as individuals who are confident and competent in our personal purpose and passion. The greater an individual's integration and commitment to Goodwill, Authenticity, Connectivity and Empowerment, the greater the possibility for establishing a powerful relationship to achieve powerful Results. When a relationship breaks down for any reason, requiring a Difficult Conversation, one of the first things to visit is individual personal coherency. When alignment on an individual, personal level is achieved, then exploration of the coherency of G.R.A.C.E. (and any brokenness there) can proceed.

The Challenges of Broken Coherency

This broken coherency will create multiple challenges, including becoming defensive and looking for ways to make ourselves "right," usually while discounting what the other person says or does. Broken coherency is typified by suspicion, isolation and disconnection, and may even include feelings of betrayal. The chart on the next page shows some of the many challenges present when the coherency of G.R.A.C.E. is broken.

CHALLENGES OF BROKEN COHERENCY	
Goodwill	• We allow our internal critic to punish ourselves mercilessly. • We find ways to justify ourselves. • We find ways to find fault with the other person. • We tend to allow the relationship to spiral into becoming transactional instead of transformational.
Results	• We lose track of shared purpose. • We question shared purpose. • We forget we are in relationship for mutually desired expectations. • We lose desire to achieve unclear or questioned results.
Authenticity	• We don't declare what we want or need. • We live in a state of resentment, anger, or disappointment with ourselves. • We waste time creating alternative options to "put up" with the situation. • We waste time in battling conflicting emotions and commitments. • We waste time creating an alternate reality full of "what if's" and needless worry, anticipation and drama.
Connectivity	• We lose interest in the wants and needs of the other person. • We tend to read into their situation more from our bias of what we think or want. • We don't make it a priority to make offers or give G.R.A.C.E.-fully. • We tend to minimize the concern of our impact on the other person. • We tend to lose interest in co-creating shared purpose or results.
Empowerment	• We don't create possibilities for breakthrough. • Instead of empowering, we actually tend to undermine the other person. • We question our commitments. • Responsibility and Accountability morph into personal justification. • We do not work the plan, so we become stuck in place.

The Consequences of Broken Coherency

Broken coherency of *G.R.A.C.E. at Work* components will create very definite and real consequences, and generally those consequences represent a decision point in the relationship. This decision involves one of two choices:

1) Decide to leverage Goodwill and work toward reconciliation for a powerful relationship and breakthrough results, or

2) Decide to journey toward the path of transactional interaction where there is either insufficient or no trust, and no hope of a powerful relationship capable of breakthrough results.

And, even worse, in some case, a third decision presents itself: **an end to the relationship altogether.**

The insidious reality of broken coherency is that in many instances, the decision to journey toward the second option, that of a transactional interaction, is often done in silence. Neither person shares this decision with the other, and the relationship slowly degenerates. Words that could create the context for reconciliation often become the fuel for Internal Conversations that feed the painful and destructive moods and attitudes of anger, resentment, cynicism, and pessimism. And, if the trust element is missing, often the third decision, to end the relationship seems the only recourse.

Decide to leverage Goodwill and work toward reconciliation for a powerful relationship and breakthrough results.

Re-Establishing Coherency of G.R.A.C.E.

Resolving Difficult Conversations means reestablishing the coherency of G.R.A.C.E. for all parties in the relationship. Restoring this coherency requires conversation that identifies and clarifies each person's assumptions and expectations, and serves to bridge the gaps between intentions and impacts to restore the mutual offering of Goodwill. This big point is, of course, just how do you do this? In very basic terms, you will be addressing each of the five components of G.R.A.C.E. thoroughly and separately, in an orderly and directed fashion whose aim is the re-assembling of the components into one coherently functioning whole. The "how" of all this can be simply stated in five steps:

1) **Integrate Goodwill** in every conversation. Describe what attributes of Goodwill are offered and needed (*review the model, if needed*)

2) **Identify the Conflict** and redefine and describe the desired outcome (both of the conflict, and of the relationship in general)

3) **Create mutual transparency and authenticity** in the relationship. Agree to open exchange.

4) **Sort out ownership and accountabilities** for the relationship (only after establishing mutual Goodwill!)

5) **Plan for reconciliation**, action and ultimate results.

Whatever the cause, Difficult Conversations can be managed to become *Powerful* Conversations with very acceptable, and often surprising, results. Successful outcomes to Difficult Conversations will most likely have several facets, and they can often lead to breakthroughs, reconciliation and stronger relationships. These Difficult Conversations can serve as a defining moment in manifesting your commitments, and demonstrating how you wish to define and present yourself to others.

Managing a Difficult Conversation

> The need for the restoration of Goodwill is the essential difference between a Difficult and a Powerful conversation.

A Difficult Conversation is the same as any other conversation, with the exception that it is most likely necessary due to a breakdown in Goodwill, and will only be resolved by a reconciliation via restoration of Goodwill. The model for this Difficult Conversation is essentially the same as that for a Powerful Conversation, but gives special attention to conflict resolution and reconciliation, through the restoration of Goodwill. The model acknowledges immediately that Goodwill has broken down and is the cause for this conversation. In addition to the two questions for conversation participants to answer for a Powerful Conversation, the Difficult Conversation also asks:

- When and how did Goodwill breakdown?
- How much Goodwill do we have to work with?

It is critical to talk through the breakdown in order to repair Goodwill, the most important factor to restore the connection and yield desired results.

A productive framework for managing a Difficult Conversation consists of:

1) Declaring and describing the breakdown in the relationship

2) Clarifying what is important to you

3) Determining what is important to the other person

4) Describing where the assumptions of positive intent broke down, and what the gap is between intentions and impact, and

5) Creating agreement about what both parties need to move forward.

The following table contains coaching pointers and questions for talking through the repair of Goodwill. This is the essential difference between a Difficult and a Powerful Conversation. Once Goodwill is restored, the conversation can then become a Powerful Conversation. Use this template to prepare for a Difficult Conversation.

DIFFICULT CONVERSATION TEMPLATE AND CHECKLIST (The Advance Work for a Powerful Conversation)		DONE? NOTES?
DECLARING AND DESCRIBING THE BREAKDOWN		
1	Establish mutual Goodwill, and agree to work from this premise.	
2	When and how did Goodwill breakdown? (describe the breakdown)	
CLARIFYING WHAT IS IMPORTANT TO YOU		
1	What exactly are you trying to accomplish?	
2	What didn't you make clear enough about what was/is important to you? (i.e., how are you feeling, thinking, doing?)	
3	Why is this important to you?	
4	Why and how do you think this creates a win-win situation?	
5	How do you feel about your interactions with the other person?	
DETERMINING WHAT IS IMPORTANT TO THE OTHER PERSON		
1	What do you think the other person is trying to accomplish?	
2	Why is that important to the other person?	
3	What do you believe might be frustrating the other person about your relationship?	
4	Is there an issue of broken trust for either party? If so, how can this be resolved enough to move forward?	
5	How might the other person be interested in securing a win-win situation for the relationship?	
DESCRIBING THE GAPS BETWEEN INTENTION AND IMPACT		
1	Where did the assumption of positive intent break down for you?	
2	How would you describe the gap between intentions and impact?	
3	What didn't you understand about what was important to the other person?	
4	What did you do to contribute to the breakdown?	
5	What do you believe the other person did to contribute to the breakdown?	
CREATING AGREEMENT TO MOVE FORWARD		
1	Reestablish and clarify shared purpose.	
2	Re-verify all the facts, data and assessments.	
3	Secure firm agreements for the next steps.	
4	Move to the template for Powerful Conversations and move through all the steps from the beginning, starting with re-establishing mutual Goodwill.	
5	After working through all the diamonds on the Powerful Conversation model, including your new action place...MOVE FORWARD.	

Declaring and Describing the Breakdown

Even before taking this first step of declaring and describing where Goodwill may have broken down, or has been missing, it is very important to establish up front what Goodwill exists now, and what can be made available for this conversation. In order for the Difficult Conversation to have a fighting chance, the parties involved must agree to approach even these beginning steps with a declaration of *mutual* Goodwill. Goodwill must be assumed, and must be the basis of all further dialogue. Without this foundation of positive intent on both parties, declaring and describing the breakdown would only lead to a shouting match or a quick and sudden death of all conversation beyond this point. The objective of this step is not to point fingers or assign blame. It is merely to explore the breakdown as objectively as possible, in order to discover the disconnects, the basic facts of when and how Goodwill was broken to the point that this Difficult Conversation became necessary. This is essentially where the premise for the conversation is stated *so that forward progress can begin.*

Clarifying What is Important to You

After the assertion that this conversation can be approached with a certain level of Goodwill, and the breakdown has been factually declared and described, the following questions will be helpful in helping you clarify your importance factors. These are questions directed at *you*, in order to help *you* state *your* truth during this exchange:

1) What exactly are you trying to accomplish?
2) What didn't you make clear enough about what was/is important to you? (*i.e., how are you feeling, thinking, doing?*)
3) Why is this important to you?
4) Why and how do you think this creates a win-win situation?
5) How do you feel about your interactions with the other person?

It is best to consider these questions *before* entering into a Difficult Conversation. Give each question some thought, and consider how you would frame your responses to the other person so he or she might best understand your position. Again, this is not about blame, shame or the pointing fingers

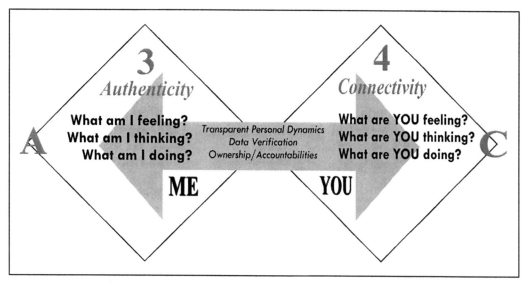

game. Do not frame your answers in a way that places blame. Make them as factual as possible, not just emotion-based. Create transparency and connectivity with how each party feels, thinks, and does. Make the conversation as complete as possible, *including* thoughts and feelings, but not based solely on one or the other.

Determining What is Important to the Other Person

Obviously this conversation will have a two-way exchange of personal feelings and information regarding the breakdown of Goodwill. The following questions are to enable you to hear and understand what the other person is sharing with you. They are the reverse of the questions stated above:

1) What do you think the other person is trying to accomplish?

2) Why is that important to the other person?

3) What do you believe might be frustrating the other person about your relationship?

4) Is there an issue of broken trust for either party? If so, how can this be resolved enough to move forward?

5) How might the other person be interested in securing a win-win situation for the relationship?

Describing the Gaps Between Intentions and Impact

In a situation that requires a Difficult Conversation, chances are that a breakdown of the assumptions of positive intent occurred, creating gaps between intent and impact. This means that what was understood as intended did not translate into actual impact. It can also mean that one person understood intent one way, and another a different way. In order to repair this disconnect, the intentions and the impacts must be explored, and existing gaps between them identified. These questions are helpful for all parties to consider and discuss openly:

1) Where did the assumption of positive intent break down for you?

2) How would you describe the gap between intentions and impact?

3) What didn't you understand about what was important to the other person?

4) What did you do to contribute to the breakdown?

5) What do you believe the other person did to contribute to the problem?

> **What was understood as intended did not translate into actual impact.**

It is important that both parties consider their own, as well as those of the other person, responses to these questions. Each person should express his or her understanding of the other person's perceptions of the breakdown.

Creating Agreement to Move Forward

Moving forward is undoubtedly the objective of any Difficult Conversation, but doing so is completely dependent upon moving progressively, objectively and hopefully peacefully through the previous four steps. Once all the needed information has been exchanged, it's time to figure out how to move past this place. Moving forward cannot proceed until Goodwill has been restored. At this point, the Difficult Conversation is really no longer a difficult conversation. The broken starting element of a Powerful Conversation is repaired, so now the conversation can proceed as any Powerful Conversation would, according to the model previously shown for these conversations.

All of the steps presented so far for the Difficult Conversation have been for the sole purpose of restoring the Goodwill diamond on the Powerful Conversation. Now it is time to move through the other diamonds: Results, Authenticity, Connectivity and Empowerment. Just as for a Powerful Conversation, the Results piece must be re-clarified with shared purpose and desired outcomes. It is quite possible that this clarification was inadequate in the first place, causing the need for a Difficult Conversation. The purpose of the relationship and its intended and desired results must be absolutely clear and understood by all parties before proceeding. Then it is time to work through the Authenticity and Connectivity diamonds, exchanging facts and data and all assessments. This is where data verification occurs, both parties engage with transparent personal dynamics, and the critical factor of ownership and accountabilities is thoroughly discussed, determined and detailed, with firm agreement on the next steps to be taken together. These processes are exactly the same as those for a Powerful Conversation.

At this point the Difficult Conversation is really no longer a *difficult* conversation.

This conversation is not complete until you have moved *through the last diamond*, Empowerment. This is where all the talk up to this point has prepared you to actually physically move forward. Without the Empowerment piece, it's just talk. As stated earlier, this is where opportunities are explored and strategies and actions plans are developed. Review the earlier process for Powerful Conversations *(pp 210-216)*.

A template for Powerful Conversations was provided in the earlier section. Such a template is also helpful for repairing Goodwill in Difficult Conversations. These would be *preliminary steps* that will transform the Difficult Conversation into *the beginning* of a Powerful Conversation.

Always remember,
POWERFUL RELATIONSHIPS:

- are never static.
- require a lot of work and energy.
- must be a priority to both parties.
- are all about momentum.
- will result when we increase the things that build momentum and address and decrease the things that hinder momentum.

G.R.A.C.E. for Internal Conversations

ONE of the most overlooked, yet most practiced, conversations is the one we have with ourselves, throughout the day, every day. These Internal Conversations may be supremely simple, with outcomes easily achieved to our satisfaction. Others, however, can be complex and stressful, requiring hours and days of internal struggle. These conversations can leave us drained, and uncertain, even after endless hours of internal turmoil. I have stated before that Goodwill is where everything begins in the *G.R.A.C.E. at Work* model, including all conversations. While it may be somewhat difficult at times to practice this Goodwill with others, it is seemingly even more difficult to extend it to ourselves. It is a similar concept as the ability to forgive others, while finding it hardest to forgive ourselves. Internal Conversations do not have to be Difficult Conversations, the kinds that cause our bodies to reap the unpleasant consequences of sleepless nights and twisted digestive tracts. The same model, with a few adjustments, that works for both the Productive and the Difficult Conversations, will also work for Internal Conversations. It is a simple matter of training and practice, until it becomes habit.

Coherent Self

In the last section I spoke of the concept of individual coherency, the manner and measure in which we have integrated ourselves emotionally, intellectually, physically and spiritually. If we are aligned in these areas, we can be present with others authentically. The same applies to be "present" with ourselves. The two internal "beings" of Champion and Critic, which reside in each of us, are usually the ones who will be engaged in most Internal Conversations. These two sometimes distinctly different entities must come to an agreement in these conversations. Sometimes, however, they are so polarized that meeting in the middle in order to make decisions, arrive at conclusions and move forward is difficult, even agonizing for some. Our internal "champion" is the self that feels good, the one at the top of our game, positive and confident. The champion encourages us, and sends positive messages. The internal critic, on the other hand, is that part of self (which we all have) that highlights our shortcomings and shows up to criticize our performance. The critic in us can tear down the good, and place the champion and the critic at odds with one another, creating a potentially painful Internal Conversation. Both the critic and the champion are part of our authentic selves. They both exist in us, and they both vie for position. Understanding, balancing and managing their union into one self, and how we present and show up, make decisions and have these Internal Conversations, requires us to promote self coherency – the integration of all parts of us into one articulate self.

> While it may be somewhat difficult at times to practice this Goodwill with others, it is seemingly even more difficult to extend it to ourselves.

Managing an Internal Conversation

Any Internal Conversation is generally the result of some need for a decision, or determining some course of action. Oftentimes it is about balancing competing claims of priorities or values. There is something that needs to be accomplished, the whole purpose and reason for the internal dialogue. This is the starting point in working the model to achieve satisfactory, and relatively easy, results – the end point of the conversation. And just like the Powerful and the Difficult Conversations, Goodwill is the key for the end point. This model works just like the others, only instead of conversing with others, we are conversing with self. Knowing your desired outcomes and extending yourself Goodwill, will enable you to work through the rest of the of the model conversation. The table on the following page is the same template and checklist that works for other conversations, with adjustments for this internal dialogue. Doing this prep work for your Internal Conversation will eliminate the former inner turmoil of arriving at satisfactory outcomes.

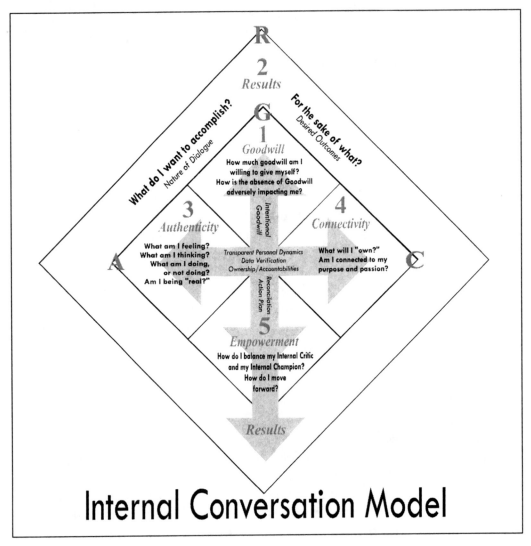

Internal Conversation Model

INTERNAL CONVERSATION TEMPLATE AND CHECKLIST (The Advance Work)	DONE? NOTES?
GOODWILL	
1 How much Goodwill am I willing to give myself?	
2 How is the absence of Goodwill adversely impacting me?	
3 How might I be able to extend myself more Goodwill?	
RESULTS	
1 What exactly am I trying to accomplish? (what is the nature of this dialogue?)	
2 What are my desired outcomes for this internal conversation?	
3 Why is this important to me?	
AUTHENTICITY	
1 What am I feeling?	
2 What am I thinking?	
3 What am I doing, or not doing?	
4 How am I being "real" about what is important?	
5 What are my honest appraisals of my skills, abilitites, past experiences, contributions, strengths and weaknesses?	
6 Have I fully investigated and corrected any potential misconceptions, hidden agendas and negative thought patterns?	
6 What are potential unintended consequences of my decisions and choices?	
CONNECTIVITY	
1 Am I connected to all parts of me, including my purpose and passion? How can I integrate my being better?	
2 Do I really know who I am, know my values and core beliefs?	
3 How can the core of who I am, including passion and purpose, help me in this conversation?	
4 What will I "own" in this conversation?	
5 Are there any ways others can help me in this internal conversation?	
EMPOWERMENT	
1 What is my internal Critic saying?	
2 What is my internal Champion saying?	
3 How can I manage the critic and champion to arrive at a working balance?	
4 Am I jumping to any conclusions, making guesses or surmising things (outcomes, etc.) with no real evidence?	
5 How can I empower myself to move forward from here?	

Sometimes we find ourselves in the middle of an intense internal conversation, and we don't even recall how we got here. We engage in these internal dialogues throughout our waking moments. Learning how to manage (reconcile) your internal critic and your internal champion for a healthy balance will remove the struggle aspect so you can arrive at faster and easier conclusions. Can you identify any "negative" thinking habits that you can replace with more balanced and productive habits? Can you detail a plan for keeping your internal dialogues balanced for positive results?

Reconciling your internal critic and your internal champion will remove the struggle...

To maximize your effectiveness in resolving internal conflict and conversations try developing a set of personal reminders to help keep these conversations in balance. This can even take the form of an action plan, something you determine you will follow in the future. Each time your critic and champion seem to be at odds, prolonging any given decision or internal argument, put this plan to work.

Internal Champion | Internal Critic

The battle between our two internal selves is the largest contributor to any personal struggle and difficulty in these internal conversations. It is helpful to review the information on the Internal Critic and the Internal Champion found in Chapter 3, under the Authenticity component.

HOW TO DEVELOP AN ACTION PLAN FOR INTERNAL CONVERSATIONS

1. Identify any negative thinking habits.

2. Determine how you can replace these with more balanced and productive habits.

3. Identify the authentic character of your internal champion. What does this part of you usually say during internal conversations? Is this real? Is it practical? Is it helpful?

4. Identify the authentic character of your internal critic. What does this part of you usually say during internal conversations? Is this true feedback, or is it based on assumptions and not evidence? What usually happens when your internal critic shows up? Does it outshout your champion?

5. Determine how you can reconcile these two parts of you. What will bring these into a healthy balance? How can you quickly achieve this balance within internal conversations?

6. Write down the steps of an action plan for your next internal conversation. What will you do, and in what order? Revisit your purpose and passion, internal values and core beliefs. Where do these fit in your plan?

7. Determine how you can quickly identify an internal conversation, and how to defuse the turmoil by using your action plan. What personal habits can you develop and use for this?

Asking Great Questions

THE best way to have great conversations is to ask *great questions*. Like everything else worth doing right, there is a skill, an expertise and an art, to constructing and asking great questions. Questions can be considered the currency of powerful conversations, reshaping transactions into transformations. These questions are investments in change, and the more you invest in the question, the more you get from the answer.

The Nature of Questions

Questions are designed to elicit conversation in order to provide critical information to advance the ultimate purpose of conversation. Questions are like synapses that allow movement across gaps, from one point to another, always progressing toward some specified goal. Asking great questions allows us to "connect the dots" and fill in the gaps. The essential character and impact of questions is in their ability to:

- **Uncover intent** (explore motivations, real meanings, purpose)
- **Integrate purpose** with assumptions (make sure intent and purpose are aligned with assumptions, integrate the physical (*Body*) with the emotional (*Heart*) in order to engage the passion (*Soul*), through conversation (the referee and filter of the *Mind*)
- **Initiate, maintain and close action** (introduce, determine, facilitate and complete desired actions)
- **Provide stability** (shore up areas that are unstable, provide reinforcement, remove obstacles, etc.)
- **Verify facts,** data, information
- **Engage the passion and the imagination** (give life, vitality and personal ownership to the conversation)

Great questions will do all this and more. They will focus on the *being* (who the people are) as opposed to mere *doing* (what they do). Great questions will open the door to future possibilities, delve deeper than the surface to the very core of anything (and anyone), and will create momentum and passion.

The Functions of Questions

There are four basic functions to questions. Questions should be pre-thought and crafted to meet at least one of the following criteria:

1. **FOCUS** on what is important to the other person.

2. **DISCOVER** the possibilities available to that person, and to others.

3. **MOTIVATE** by creating action to drive the desired results.

4. **CONFIRM** any requests, offers and promises

There is also a progression during the course of inquiry. Questioning can expand and build to eventually yield a plan of action. **Focusing, discovering, motivating and confirming**, *in that order*, will most often culminate in ACTING.

> Questions can be considered the currency of Powerful Conversations, reshaping transactions into transformations.

FOCUSING on what is important to people involves engaging their purpose and passion, identifying opportunities and gaps, exploring all assessments or perspectives, determining motives and intentions, clarifying capacity, seeking and labeling the impact of the past, present and future, and ascertaining commitments. Questions that create focus will include any that are framed to determine the items listed above. They can be basic, simple and straightforward, yielding simple answers, or they can be specific and targeted to yield very specific and detailed answers. Remember that the more thought and care given to questions, the better the answers.

DISCOVERING the possibilities available will mean leveraging the passion and imagination of people through questioning and dialogue exchange. It will seek to identify any limitations that may hinder reaching desired outcomes, as well as the possibilities and potentials that also exist. Through careful questioning, discovering possibilities really means generating options, finding ways, processes and paths that could not be previously detected. Part of this discovery questioning process will also need to clarify distinctions and definitions, so everyone is working on the same page, toward the same goals. Questions that serve to discover possibilities may begin with simple, seemingly "common" knowledge types of inquiries, progressing to the more involved and detailed questions designed to elicit the deeper meanings, the hidden possibilities, and the unforeseen hurdles.

MOTIVATING by creating action to drive the desired results will depend on gaining clarity on declarations, seeking solutions, setting goals, developing the metrics and measurement of the results intended, setting time frames, obtaining clarity on roles, and even specifying appropriate rewards and recognition. All of this is achieved through careful and artful questioning. All of the "loose threads" must be followed, by inquiry, to arrive at a strategic plan for action. But this plan does not merely focus on transaction, but on the transformation of all participants. Great questioning does not just seek to achieve a transactional result, but also seeks to transform those who both question and answer, to achieve something that could not be previously achieved.

> Great questions will open the door to future possiblities... and will create momentum and passion.

CONFIRMING the action plan, requests, offers and promises is a critical piece in masterful questioning. By inquiry, data and information are verified, assumptions and expectations are clarified and understood, resources are explored, boundaries and parameters are established, "walked around" and settled. All requests, offers, and promises are fully stated, questioned and understood.

G.R.A.C.E.-Full Questioning

There is a G.R.A.C.E.-full way to ask these transforming questions. *Without* G.R.A.C.E., or any element of G.R.A.C.E., questions can often seem to be:

1) **Judgmental,** stated or framed to pass judgment or criticism on the other person,

2) **Self-serving,** designed to influence an outcome favoring someone in particular,

3) **Disempowering,** to deny the other person even the possibility of change, or

4) **Meaningless,** not providing a clear "for the sake of what?" purpose, or merely a redundant statement made into an unanswerable question.

These G.R.A.C.E.-*less* questions at the least just fill up air time, and at the worst can turn a potentially powerful conversation into a difficult conversation, and without G.R.A.C.E. will become *no* conversation. On the other hand, practicing G.R.A.C.E.-*full* questioning creates that "safe space" which enables parties in conversation to identify, explore and express:

1) What **attributes of goodwill** they need or desire

2) What they **want to accomplish**

3) How they define and express their **authenticity** within a problem or opportunity;

4) What it is they are trying to connect with (*and how to make those connections*), and

5) What they need to feel **empowered**

A CONVERSATION can turn on a single question. That turn can either be toward more truly productive dialogue, or toward no dialogue at all. That makes questions critically important to any conversation, and the ability to craft great questions even more important—a leadership skill that cannot be left out of the leader's tool kit.

Chapter 9

Relationship Architecture

The 5 Building Blocks
for Bigger Spaces

"Design is a plan for arranging elements in such a way as best to accomplish a particular purpose."

– Charles Eames

DESIGNING BIGGER SPACES:

The 5-Block Foundation

ONE of the biggest reasons to practice *G.R.A.C.E. at Work,* and to adopt and apply any relationship model, is to grow the space in which you and your partners play. The object of this larger space is, of course, to realize greater results, regardless of current outcomes or stated expectations. This idea was first introduced in chapter 4 "The Space of G.R.A.C.E." In this chapter this concept will be further explored, but this time with very practical drills and methods useful to play in this bigger space.

The *G.R.A.C.E. at Work* model was designed to achieve transformational relationships. Every relationship will have a certain "space" to play in. Transforming relationships is about playing in a bigger space. Before we can do this, the space in which we are currently reside must be defined. If it is not serving us, we can create a bigger space. There are five basic conversations, requiring five different kinds of context, which need to take place before this transformation. These can be summarized through the 5 Building Blocks of Relationship Architecture.

1. Managing the Context
2. Point CounterPoint
3. Standing in the Issues
4. Looking for Possibilities
5. Catalyst for Change

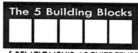

These steps have been termed The 5 Building Blocks of Relationship Architecture. Relationships should always seek to "grow the space" in which they exist and play and produce results, and these steps form a foundational platform on which to have conversation and interact in order to realize bigger spaces, and bigger results.

BLOCK 1: Managing the Context

This first block sets the context, identifies what we are talking about, and what we want to happen. This is illustrated with a dotted line diamond. The dotted line indicates there is some flexibility and fluidity about this context. In this step, we loosely hold the conversation in our minds, and set the boundaries and parameters around it.

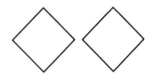

BLOCK 2: Point CounterPoint

The second step involves getting deeper into our unspoken assumptions about what is truth and what isn't. The "facts and data" of people's perspectives are often different, and this step is about discovering how each person understands those facts. It is about truth telling, seeing the world differently, and being open to new possibilities. The two solid diamonds illustrate the two different perspectives. This conversation may at first involve some ambiguities, some touchy subjects and declaring alternative perspectives. This is where we challenge what is possible and what is not, determine different ways to hold assumptions about where we are going, and reframe the past and future.

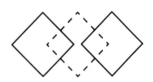

BLOCK 3: Standing in the Issues

Once the context is determined and managed, and all perspectives are identified, it is time to take a stand. We must understand what is at stake, and act authentically to take that stand. We may not always get what we want, but we need to declare what is important to us. The two diamonds must merge into one after the issues are declared and the context is fully defined in order to move forward. While taking individual stands, we realize competing claims and priorities, allegiances or other issues that need to be resolved, reaching some kind of agreement, becoming in sync rather than separate.

BLOCK 4: Looking for Possibilities

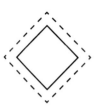

Once we have gotten through the first three conversations, it's time to go forward looking for possibilities. Options are identified, looking outside our own perspectives. There will be new stories to develop for new approaches and new futures. The diamonds are nested now, one inside the other. The larger dotted diamond represents what can be. The inside solid diamond is what is. How do you expand to next diamond? How do you play in this bigger space? Sometimes people have difficulty identifying with the future when today's goals still must be met, and this very real concern precipitates the discussion regarding needed change.

BLOCK 5: Catalyst for Change

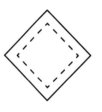

It's time to give up sacred cows and acknowledge there are often other ways of doing things, other ways of accomplishing higher goals. This is where personal and corporate change management occurs. This can be a difficult conversation as we may upset people's comfort zones, identities, and other established perspectives. Again we have two nested diamonds, but the outer diamond is now solid, representing the common goals and future of all parties. Clear communication and identification of what is important is critical. Processes are put in place, potential hurdles and resistance are identified and circumvented, and time is allowed for people to test and learn, bring closure to the old way of doing things and become truly engaged. Agreements are now in place to provide accountability. This step is what puts the R back in the Results component of the *G.R.A.C.E. at Work* model.

These 5 foundational blocks of Relationship Architecture are summarized in the following tables, and can serve as useful tools as you Know, Prepare, Do, and Review your conversations about growing the space of G.R.A.C.E..

BLOCK 1: MANAGING THE CONTEXT		CONSIDERATIONS
KNOW IT	1. Identifying and clarifying assumptions and expectations. 2. Identifying and clarifying values and beliefs. 3. Identifying and clarifying conditions of satisfaction. 4. Identifying and clarifying intentions and impact.	• Some people may not fully understand or appreciate the dynamics of a "systems" approach.
PREPARE IT	1. Know the benefit of understanding the other person's context and sharing your own. 2. Develop some questions you can ask that would help you better understand the other person's context. 3. Consider what challenges might arise in this process and how you will handle those challenges. 4. Know the G.R.A.C.E. model and how exercising intentional goodwill, being authentic, seeking genuine connection and enabling empowerment will help you and the other person better Manage the Context.	• Some people may not be aware of their patterns of thinking, feeling, or behaving. • Some people may be more comfortable with the situation they know, rather than the situation they don't know. • Think through potential challenges of Managing the Context, including the comments above, and how you will work through them.
DO IT	1. Describe a particular situation in which you feel a need to better understand the other person. 2. Ask questions to discern the attributes and components of the other person's context, i.e. "what do you believe to be true about this?" or "what do you want to have happen?" Seek clarity, and continue asking questions until both people know the parameters, components, attributes of the context. (Be sure both parties have shared their responses to the questions or items.) 3. Seek to understand the importance of those attributes and the implications for the person's identify, worth, etc. and at the same time voice your own. 4. Mutually confirm the context for the conversation.	• Use thoughtful questioning to determine understanding. • Craft questions that are empowering, not threatening. **1**
REVIEW IT	1. How well do you feel each party understands the context of the other now? 2. What gaps do you think might still exist in understanding, and what can you do about them? 3. Which questions were asked that allowed the best bridging of gaps in perception? 4. Was the G.R.A.C.E. model evident and in balance during this process?	

BLOCK 2: POINT COUNTERPOINT	CONSIDERATIONS
KNOW IT 1. Sharing your perspective as you see it. 2. Challenging unspoken assumptions. (i.e., reframing how you see things) 3. Challenging the basis for facts and opinions. 4. Providing accountability.	• Point CounterPoint may require courage to discuss the "undiscussables." • This process may require an individual to forego an identity that has served him or her well for a long time. • PCP may mean having to acknowledge failure.
PREPARE IT 1. Identify how this process can help both parties gain clarity on their stance or options. 2. Know where you are coming from. 3. Know ahead the kinds of situations where you can use PCP. 4. Consider what challenges might arise in this process and how you will handle those challenges.	• This process may require having to embrace ambiguity or uncertainty in order to move forward. • One of the goals of G.R.A.C.E. involves helping people see an alternative to their current thinking or stance. It also helps each party establish self-accountability for their declarations or commitments.
DO IT 1. Share your story and identify how the current story serves you (both parties). 2. Acknowledge the differences and similarities of each other's story. 3. Identify perspectives or assessments that the person has made that hinder his or her ability to create forward momentum. 4. Create a "third" story that honors intentions, acknowledges impacts and reflects a deeper shared understanding of what happened.	• Sometimes people don't fully appreciate the limitations they put on themselves or the consequences of their thinking or behaviors.
REVIEW IT 1. How well do you feel the other person understood your assessments? 2. What were the issues/challenges the other person had in responding to the Point CounterPoint? What was at stake for both parties? 3. What shift, if any, was the person able to make in his or her perspective, and what created the catalyst for the change? 4. Was the G.R.A.C.E. model evident and in balance during this process? How?	

BLOCK 3: STANDING IN THE ISSUES		CONSIDERATIONS
KNOW IT	1. Focusing on the real issue(s) or opportunity, and not just symptoms or sidebars. 2. Balancing advocacy and inquiry to discover what is really important. 3. Creating priorities and boundaries and preserving authenticity. 4. Helping yourself and others create breakthroughs.	• Standing in the Issues may require time and much reflection for a person to identify the real issues. • Questions must be tied to the person's purpose and/or passion.
PREPARE IT	1. Determine to be an advocate for the other person and their important issues. 2. Know how to ask the right questions and listen for the reality behind surface responses. Create a list of questions to help you "dig deeper." 3. Identify what you want the other person to know about what's important to you. 4. Understand how to balance advocacy and inquiry, and what that looks like in practical application.	• Try to determine the key question that needs to be resolved before success can be achieved. • Try to "think ahead" to potential challenges and how to overcome them. • Understanding the dynamic tension of advocacy and inquiry is critical to this process.
DO IT	1. Listen carefully and attempt to identify what aspect of the person's purpose or passion he or she wants to advance. Ask them to describe what new result they could achieve with a breakthrough. 2. Identify competing claims to the other person's priorities or issues. 3. Peel back the onion to get to the root issue. Focus on asking WHAT and HOW questions, and do not be tempted to accept the first answer. 4. Identify what may be hindering the person's ability to create forward momentum, and ask key questions about what needs to be resolved to advance.	• Look for ways to define the priorities and boundaries of the issues. • "Stand in" the issue, remain there, until fully resolved. **3**
REVIEW IT	1. How well do you feel the real and key issues were explored? Can both parties describe what matters most to the other person 2. What gaps do you think might still exist in this exploration, and what can you do about them? 3. What shifts or discoveries were made and what is, or will be, the catalyst for change? 4. Was the G.R.A.C.E. model evident and in balance during this process?	

BLOCK 4: LOOKING FOR POSSIBILITIES		CONSIDERATIONS
KNOW IT	1. Creating options for a new future, one you didn't have before. 2. Reframing or reinterpreting how you see things. 3. Getting clear on what's at stake. 4. Exploring possibilities that haven't yet been realized.	• Human beings, whether they realize it or not, act in an integrated manner. • Human behavior makes sense once you understand what the protected values are. • By helping people reframe their perspective, you help them create greater alignment emotionally, intellectually, physically, and spiritually. • Often reframing is helping people address competing claims to values or priorities. • Understanding the issue we're living in helps us to create priorities, boundaries, and plans, and preserves our authenticity.
PREPARE IT	1. Identify what breakthrough you'd like to accomplish for yourself and the other person. 2. Describe what you would now like to embrace and what you would like to "let go of." 3. Identify "outside the box" possibilities to look at for inspiration or alternative ways of doing things. 4. Identify what challenges each of you will have in creating a commitment to moving forward.	
DO IT	1. Ask both parties to describe "What is the bigger picture for each? For both parties?" Describe what's at stake in the absence of a new solution and what could benefit from a new approach. 2. Identify other people, processes, or industries that might provide insight for alternative ways of doing things. What new interpretations or perspectives could be garnered from a fresh perspective? 3. What new story could be told of the future if a new approach could be developed? 4. Determine how the new perspective delivers the results needed for today and enables the success both parties want for the future.	
REVIEW IT	1. How well do you feel the perspectives were identified and explored for potential reframing possibilities? What were they? 2. What options exist now that did not exist before this process? 3. What possibilities do you think might still exist that were not identified, and what will your next steps be? 4. Was the G.R.A.C.E. model evident and in balance during this process?	

BLOCK 5: CATALYST FOR CHANGE		CONSIDERATIONS
KNOW IT	1. Creating opportunities by making offers, declarations and requests. 2. Creating stretch goals. 3. Finding motivators, and the path, for getting from Point A to Point B. 4. Developing actionable performance objectives.	• Be sure to identify the assumptions and expectations embedded in the desired change, as they will serve as the criteria by which people will judge themselves, each other and the results.
PREPARE IT	1. Prioritize what is really important vs what's nice to have. 2. Identify people/resources to help implement the change. 3. Think through a change management plan for all parties, including actionable performance objectives and accountabilities. 4. Know the G.R.A.C.E. model and understanding how exercising intentional goodwill, being authentic, seeking genuine connection and enabling empowerment will help Create the Catalyst for Change.	• Understand that leaders have often been working through their vision and their plan and emotionally are already operating with the assumption that the change has already been made. • People in organizations need their own time and space to deal with change.
DO IT	1. Have all parties declare desired results, conditions for satisfaction, upside expectations, perceived risks and competing claims to priorities or goals. 2. Identify key milestones, and supporters and potential resistors who are critical to the success of the change. Describe the leverage or threat each plays in the change. 3. Develop key messages that can be used to communicate important points, foster support for and commitment to the change, and address items of concern or resistance. 4. Identify or create opportunities for people to ask questions, engage in discussions or otherwise become engaged in the new approach.	• Be sure to help people understand and identify the "What's In It For Me." • Know what you want and ask for it. **5**
REVIEW IT	1. How well do you feel about the resulting goals, action plan and commitments that have been generated? 2. What new possibilities does this open up for you if you're successful with this action? 3. How did this interaction strengthen your relationship with the others involved? What was the impact on the goodwill in these relationships? 4. Was the G.R.A.C.E. model evident and in balance during this process?	

Prepare, Prepare, Prepare!

Using these building blocks of Relationship Architecture requires some careful thought, consideration of possible ways conversation can go and discussion items can be interpreted, and is enhanced through some serious preparation. It is assumed at this point that you really are interested in building stronger more productive relationships and will be willing to put this into the "worthy of investment" category. This investment you make in preparation time and energy for these conversations will pay off huge dividends for you and for the others in your relationships. Those huge dividends translate into playing a bigger space, and realizing bigger results.

The first century Roman philosopher Seneca said *"Luck is what happens when preparation meets opportunity."* Nothing has changed in two thousand years. We're not after luck, however, with these conversations. We are after bigger results. Being prepared for these conversations, even before you can or intend to have them, will get you closer to your goals. Go back and look at the "Prepare It" sections of each of the tables presented here. There are concrete steps shown in each building block that will help you get the most out of your discussions. They are outlined again here with the thought that you will do some research and constructive preparation. Look at the steps that say "Know..." or "Consider..." and work through those areas in your mind, and even deeper at the heart, passion and purpose level. Other steps may require some paper and pencil to jot down important thoughts as groundwork for productive conversation. These building blocks of Relationship Architecture are designed to work hand-in-hand with the guidelines of the previous chapter on G.R.A.C.E. in Conversation.

◇

"Luck is what happens when preparation meets opportunity."

—Seneca

Block 1: Managing the Context
PREPARATION STEPS

1. Know the benefit of understanding the other person's context and sharing your own.

2. Develop some questions you can ask that would help you better understand the other person's context.

3. Consider what challenges might arise in this process and how you will handle those challenges.

4. Know the G.R.A.C.E. model and how exercising intentional goodwill, being authentic, seeking genuine connection and enabling empowerment will help you and the other person better Manage the Context.

Block 2: Point CounterPoint (PCP)
PREPARATION STEPS

1. Identify how this process can help both parties gain clarity on their stance or options.

2. Know where you are coming from.

3. Know ahead od time the kinds of situations where you can use PCP.

4. Consider what challenges might arise in this process and how you will handle those challenges.

Block 3: Standing in the Issues
PREPARATION STEPS

1. Determine to be an advocate for the other person and their important issues.

2. Know how to ask the right questions and listen for the reality behind surface responses. Create a list of questions to help you "dig deeper."

3. Identify what you want the other person to know about what's important to you.

4. Understand how to balance advocacy and inquiry, and what that looks like in practical application.

Block 4: Looking for Possibilities
PREPARATION STEPS

1. Identify what breakthrough you'd like to accomplish for yourself and the other person.

2. Describe what you would now like to embrace and what you would like to "let go of."

3. Identify "outside the box" possibilities to look at for inspiration or alternative ways of doing things.

4. Identify what challenges each of you will have in creating a commitment to moving forward.

Block 5: Catalyst for Change
PREPARATION STEPS

1. Prioritize what is really important vs what's nice to have.

2. Identify people/resources to help implement the change.

3. Think through a change management plan for all parties, including actionable performance objectives and accountabilities.

4. Know the *G.R.A.C.E. at Work* model and understanding how exercising intentional goodwill, being authentic, seeking genuine connection and enabling empowerment will help Create the Catalyst for Change.

Remember to Review
You may think that review of these kinds of conversations is a redundant and unnecessary piece of this process. However, constructive review is always helpful to correct wrong turns, prepare for the next conversation, and generally bolster your commitment to the relationship. Just take a few moments to go through these questions after you have completed a powerful conversation that employed these building blocks of Relationship Architecture:

1. What was the general context of this conversation, and the issue(s) being discussed?

2. How were the five components of the *G.R.A.C.E. at Work* model implemented during this conversation? Briefly note what you saw working well, and what might have been missing or misapplied. Was this model in balance, during the process?

3. What were the "DO it" steps for this Building Block conversation *(refer to tables on previous pages)*, and your observations regarding the success/ outcome of each step?

4. What were your general observations about this conversation? Did you achieve your intended and desired outcomes?

5. How can your next conversation be improved, using these building blocks and processes?

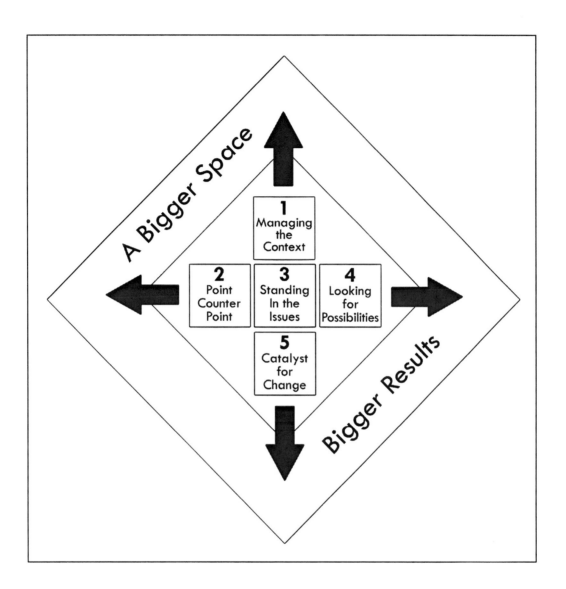

Growing the Space through Relationship Architecture

Chapter 10

Making G.R.A.C.E. Happen

Assessments and Application

"The first step to becoming is to will it."

– *Mother Teresa*

Making G.R.A.C.E. Happen

LIKE everything worthwhile, making G.R.A.C.E. happen in our lives requires some practice and effort. This chapter offers the starting place and exercises to give G.R.A.C.E. a real workout to enable you to feel more comfortable and more adept at employing the components and attributes of *G.R.A.C.E. at Work* in all your relationships.

Part 1: G.R.A.C.E. at Work Assessments

There are four different types of assessments available to measure performance in the *G.R.A.C.E. at Work* model. These are found at the *Playing In A Bigger Space* website (*www.playinginabiggerspace.com*) and through online

...give G.R.A.C.E. a real workout...

booksellers as a separate companion workbook to this book. To make the most of your desire to practice G.R.A.C.E., you are encouraged to obtain these assessments for self, targeted individuals, teams, and full 360 feedback (*available also as a fully administered online service*).

G.R.A.C.E. at Work **SELF Assessment**

This assessment measures your current overall general application of the *G.R.A.C.E. at Work* model. It contains seven statements (regarding the attributes of a component) for each of the five G.R.A.C.E. components, for a total of 35 statements.

G.R.A.C.E. at Work **TARGETED Assessment**

This assessment measures your current application of the *G.R.A.C.E. at Work* model, *as it concerns a specific (targeted) individual*, a person with whom you may have difficulty. It will often show how our behavior can change toward certain individuals when we might score higher on a general, non-targeted basis. After you have completed the Self Assessment, it is a very interesting and eye-opening exercise to do this Targeted Assessment (*the language for these statements is slightly different than that for the Self Assessment, allowing you to answer for a specific individual*). Our responses may change when we put a particular person into the picture. Choose a person with whom you may be experiencing some difficulties in relationship, whether on an organizational, professional or even personal basis. We may be perfectly willing to extend Goodwill to most people in general, but perhaps we withhold that in certain individual cases. This Targeted Assessment is designed specifically for you to improve problematic relationships *(we all have them!)*. Once we are aware of these differing responses, we are much better able to recognize and amend certain behaviors. If you are really serious about employing transforming components of G.R.A.C.E. *at Work*, consider doing this particular assessment for each important person in your life, whether at work or at home. Re-taking this assessment after you have incorporated G.R.A.C.E. is very helpful to measure progress.

G.R.A.C.E. *at Work* **TEAM Assessment (Dual)**
This assessment measures the general application of the G.R.A.C.E. *at Work model for teams, and* differs from the others in that it is a "dual" assessment, designed to measure both your behavior, and that of your entire team *(as a whole)*. There are two columns for your responses. One is your own personal set of ratings intended to rate *your behavior in the team environment* (how you respond *in reality in this particular team* or group environment). As with the Targeted Assessment, you may find some discrepancies from your Self Assessment responses. The other column is marked "Team Rating." You also rate these statements, but instead of *your* behavior, you will consider your *team's behavior as a whole*. For example, while you may have a positive attitude and manner, and all your actions may be driven by positive intent, this may not be true for your entire team. You may begin to see gaps between your responses and those for your team. You will want to consider how you can close those gaps. Your team should be involved as well.

G.R.A.C.E. *at Work* **360 FEEDBACK**
This assessment measures your performance in the general application of the G.R.A.C.E. *at Work* model *by specific individuals around you*. It is designed for full 360 feedback. The people around us will observe and interpret our behavior differently than we do. A 360 assessment measures our own rating against the ratings of others. The resulting differences reveal where our blind spots (which are weaknesses or challenges) and our hidden strengths (areas we may not think are strong for us) lie. Once known, a development plan

can be devised to strengthen our leadership skills and behaviors. The language of the 360 assessment of *G.R.A.C.E. at Work* has been adapted for others who will rate you, instead of that used for self assessments.

The *G.R.A.C.E. at Work* 360 Assessment is also available as a fully administered broad spectrum online tool, providing results in full color bar graph reports. If you are interested in using this service, please visit **www.playinginabiggerspace.com** for more information.

Part 2: Exercising G.R.A.C.E.

THE *G.R.A.C.E. at Work* concept resonates with us because of its emphasis on relationships and creating a mutual win for both parties in the relationship. But how do you really go about creating GR.A.C.E. in your relationships? Like most everything else worthwhile in life, it requires preparation, practice, and commitment. If you are really interested in improving the relationships in your personal and professional lives, there are five practice plans here to achieve G.R.A.C.E. There is a plan for each of the five components of the *G.R.A.C.E. at Work* model. Each plan contains 10 steps toward making G.R.A.C.E. happen. Carefully consider the statements found at the beginning of each worksheet, and make any comments that will help you actually do the things listed there. Make copies of these lists and keep them somewhere you will see them daily. We *can* teach old dogs new tricks, but sometimes we need reminders that we are in training to transform our behavior, or we fall back to what we've always done. Develop creative ways to keep your intentions at the forefront of your behaviors.

Goodwill Exercises

GROW your capacity for gratitude,
then practice the attributes of goodwill.

	TO DO LIST	COMMENTS
1	Remember all the people who have had a positive influence on your life, and reflect what they did to contribute to your success.	
2	Consider how fortunate you are to have had the opportunity to interact with and learn from these people. Develop a grateful attitude.	
3	If it's still possible, consider contacting them to thank them for their influence in your life.	
4	Identify the things you learned that you can replicate with others to show goodwill.	
5	Reflect (often) on what goodwill really means (assume positive intent, give without condition, forgive, etc.)	
6	Consider why goodwill is important in relationships.	
7	Think about how you can be in a "goodwill mode" all the time. Overcome internal roadblocks to goodwill.	
8	Daily consider all the good things in your life, actively be thankful, and look for opportunities to share your resources.	
9	Think about individuals with whom you have difficulty practicing goodwill and identify the issues that prevent this. Resolve these issues that are hurdles to goodwill with others.	
10	Consider your agenda for today, and actively plan how you can show goodwill to others.	

Steps to G.R.A.C.E. through GOODWILL

In general, what *intentional* steps can you take to *make G.R.A.C.E. happen*, regarding the GOODWILL component? (*Be specific, name names, dates, detailed steps, etc.*) What is your commitment to doing these things and taking these steps?

1.

2.

3.

4.

5.

6.

7.

Comments:

Results Exercises

Identify and summarize goals, articulate compelling vision and results, know responsibilities.

	TO DO LIST	COMMENTS
1	Become a master "results oriented" thinker. Consider current projects and relationships. Can you quickly summarize the REASONS for the project/relationship? Practice this skill often and learn how to keep the RESULTS-REASONS-RELATIONSHIP analysis as the foundation for your projects.	
2	Consider how others might perceive intended goals and results. Is everyone clear?	
3	Practice being goal-oriented in your meetings and discussions.	
4	Learn the process of successful visioning – developing a compelling vision based in reality, complete with purposeful process. This is an art that requires practice!	
5	Communicate your vision and goals with clarity, describing all the components of the RESULTS-REASONS-RELATIONSHIP.	
6	Completely explore the responsibilities and accountabilities that are needed to achieve goals and vision. Who is responsible for what? What accountabilities are in place?	
7	Communicate roles and responsibilities, and expected accountabilities. Question for clarity, understanding and commitment. This process should be repeated throughout the course of the project.	
8	Establish markers that will reveal progress. Evaluate completely, and readjust action plans, responsibilities, and team understanding when necessary.	
9	Daily evaluate your agenda, identify your goals and desired results, and hold yourself accountable FIRST.	
10	Develop all action plans in terms of RESULTS.	

Steps to G.R.A.C.E. through RESULTS

In general, what *intentional* steps can you take to *make G.R.A.C.E. happen*, regarding the RESULTS component? *(Be specific, name names, dates, detailed steps, etc.)* What is your commitment to doing these things and taking these steps?

1.

2.

3.

4.

5.

6.

7.

Comments:

Authenticity Exercises

Know yourself, know others, be transparent, and provide a safe space for others to do the same.

	TO DO LIST	COMMENTS
1	KNOW YOURSELF! Spend some serious time discovering your authentic self, what makes you that way, and who is the REAL you.	
2	Understand what being authentic means (includes vulnerability, accountability, ownership, etc.)	
3	Make choice, a deliberate decision and commitment, to being authentic and transparent always, in every relationship.	
4	Identify what is most important to you, and what is non-negotiable (unwilling to compromise) and assess how your actions support your priorities.	
5	Take and declare an open stand on your issues, without "attitude."	
6	Hold yourself accountable for your actions and words to support your authentic self, and take responsibility for those actions and words.	
7	KNOW OTHERS! Take time to get to really know the people with whom you have relationships (working or otherwise) What makes them tick? What are their values and beliefs?	
8	Create a safe space where others can also be open, authentic, transparent, accepting and willing to share without fear of judgment, reprisal, non-acceptance, etc.	
9	Daily evaluate your agenda, identify your goals and desired results, and hold yourself accountable FIRST.	
10	Get honest feedback from others. Honestly evaluate your authenticity often.	

Steps to G.R.A.C.E. through AUTHENTICITY

In general, what *intentional* steps can you take to *make G.R.A.C.E. happen,* regarding the AUTHENTICITY component? (*Be specific, name names, dates, detailed steps, etc.*) What is your commitment to doing these things and taking these steps?

1.

2.

3.

4.

5.

6.

7.

Comments:

Connectivity Exercises

Think and seek connections, co-create value, and jointly pursue mutual goals.

	TO DO LIST	COMMENTS
1	HUMANS MUST INTERACT, and connect. Train yourself to look for connections, to actively "think "connections" so that wherever you are, whomever you are with, you are aware of either existing or potential connections.	
2	Connectivity means finding ways to identify with, affirm and encourage others, understanding how they feel, what is important to them, identifying and realizing differences, strengths and weaknesses, and cultivating a genuine desire to associate with and relate to others. Train yourself to consistently approach others in this way.	
3	Learn how to empathize with others, and find ways to engage them.	
4	Seek opportunities to co-create vision and goals for mutual benefit.	
5	Know what is important to others. Discover shared vision, and what might become shared goals.	
6	Think beyond the obvious. Connections can exist in places never before intended, designed, or considered.	
7	Understand how your words and actions impact others. Evaluate whether or not gaps exist between intention and impact, and work to bridge those gaps.	
8	Clearly communicate connection points, expectations, responsibilities and accountabilities.	
9	Learn to network effectively and continually build connections.	
10	Remember that connections require maintenance. Know what that means for each connection, and be sure to "service" regularly.	

Steps to G.R.A.C.E. through CONNECTIVITY

In general, what *intentional* steps can you take to *make G.R.A.C.E. happen*, regarding the CONNECTIVITY component? *(Be specific, name names, dates, detailed steps, etc.)* What is your commitment to doing these things and taking these steps?

1.

2.

3.

4.

5.

6.

7.

Comments:

Empowerment Exercises

See potential, and create a "nutrient-rich" environment for free, unfettered growth.

	TO DO LIST	COMMENTS
1	POTENTIAL IS EVERYWHERE, IN EVERYONE. Learn how to spot it, seeing beyond the obstacles. Practice this everywhere, with everyone.	
2	Understand the true meaning of empowerment. It does not mean YOU do it, it means you create the environment for others to achieve success.	
3	Like everything else, empowerment requires very stable balance. Discover the balances required between challenge and support. For each relationship, this balance may look different. Know how to motivate without pressuring, how to guide without hindering personal expression. There are many such balances (advocacy and inquiry, task and relationship – the Dynamic Tensions). Know them, and observe them.	
4	Create a safe space for others to grow. This involves building an environment of trust and openness without judgment.	
5	Embrace this: "It's not about me." When we empower others, it should not be for personal advancement. It is about enabling others to advance, to grow and succeed. While mutual goals may be pursued, empowerment sets self aside so that others may have the spotlight.	
6	Mutually define boundaries for empowerment, learning and responsibility. If necessary, guide yourself and others to reframe how you think about things. This is a powerful form of empowerment.	
7	Define and communicate understanding of expectations, and mutual commitments to goals, roles, and consequences.	
8	Learn how to leverage all people and all resources to empower results in joint (team) ventures.	
9	Be realistic. Empowerment is often done one step at a time. Expectations must match reality.	
10	Allow time for growth, learning and achievement of potential.	

Steps to G.R.A.C.E. through EMPOWERMENT

In general, what *intentional* steps can you take to *make G.R.A.C.E. happen*, regarding the EMPOWERMENT component? *(Be specific, name names, dates, detailed steps, etc.)* What is your commitment to doing these things and taking these steps?

1.

2.

3.

4.

5.

6.

7.

Comments:

Making G.R.A.C.E. Happen: Summary

Summarize your intentional steps *(from each of the previous exercises)* to develop a plan for growth of G.R.A.C.E. in your relationships. If you are serious about making G.R.A.C.E. happen, also develop a way to hold yourself accountable for these actions.

	INTENTIONAL STEPS TO MAKE G.R.A.C.E. HAPPEN	ACCOUNTABILITIES FOR THESE STEPS
Goodwill		
Results		
Authenticity		
Connectivity		
Empowerment		

Part 3: Mapping Relationships for Success

THIS book is only the beginning of learning about *G.R.A.C.E. at Work* and the first steps to application. The following worksheets are intended for you to use as often as you desire in personal and professional diagnostics and application. *You may copy these sheets if necessary for additional use.* Are you serious about building and maintaining productive and powerful relationships? If so, some of those may require, or benefit greatly by, a little extra effort, questioning and commitment. Follow the instructions on these worksheets. Use them in especially important, challenged, or critical relationships where both parties want to make the extra effort required to strengthen existing relationships, or build powerful new ones.

1. MAPPING THE RELATIONSHIP FOR SUCCESS

Whether you are in a new relationship, or continuing one already established, it is helpful to define the expectations in each of the 5 areas of GRACE: Goodwill, Results, Authenticity, Connectivity and Empowerment. Write brief descriptions of your expectations, both for your own behavior and that of the one in relationship with you (in the spaces below). For example: GOODWILL: How will you show or extend goodwill to this person? How do you expect him or her to do the same? Provide specific details so that expectations and roles are clear. For a more complete understanding, ask the other person to do the same exercise. Compare your notes in conversation together. This tool can serve as a helpful visual aid for powerful and/or difficult conversations. *Keep in mind the 7 attributes of each of the components of the GRACE model, and consider them in your listing. These attributes are provided in a summary format on the first model of this worksheet. A blank worksheet follows for more space to write.*

Make copies of the blank worksheet provided, one for each person in the relationship. They are for targeted, specific relationships. For best results, each person should complete the worksheet. Make as many copies of this form as you need, one for each person, and perhaps more for later comparisons.

RESULTS

1. Know why we are doing what we are doing.
2. Know intended results, have ownership.
3. Create/improve value, future, for all parties.
4. Know what other parties believe to be true.
5. Contribute, committed, to relationship in mutual parts.
6. Strategy (action plans) to accomplish desired outcomes.
7. Measure performance against action plans, make changes.

GOODWILL

1. Positive attitude/manner, actions driven by positive intent.
2. Refrain from judgments.
3. Genuinely desire well-being of others, no hidden motives.
4. Generous spirit, freely give without condition.
5. Excuse offense without payment, no hard feelings.
6. At peace with "what is," harmony in relationships.
7. Thankful, express gratitude to, and for, others.

AUTHENTICITY

1. Truthful about feelings, thoughts, desires.
2. Unpretentious, modest, not given to pride or arrogance.
3. Accountable, answerable, reliable, responsible.
4. Reveal real me, no pretense, accessible, visible, clear.
5. Consistently authentic principles, actions, behavior.
6. Confident of self/others, faith all will act appropriately.
7. Leverage strengths of self/ others, manage weaknesses

CONNECTIVITY

1. Awake, conscious of self/others, alert to possibilities.
2. Affirm others, express approval/ validity, confirm value.
3. Recognize, sensitive to feelings/ thoughts/experiences of others.
4. Savvy with people, know-how of human dynamics.
5. Collaborator, genuine desire to "co-labor," align with others to produce greater results.
6. Innovatively connect with others to achieve goals.
7. Repair, recreate/restore "disconnects, "openness, no hidden agendas.

EMPOWERMENT

1. Take first step(s) necessary to make something better.
2. Knowledge of entire system, understand impacts of actions/processes on others.
3. Careful, efficient, tactful handling resources, always seek maximization.
4. Enhance/encourage growth, maturity of employees through development opportunities.
5. Test/experiment (with attitude of positive gain) to discover better means to achieve desired outcomes.
6. View things/people from different perspectives, viewpoints, perceptions; openness, no hidden agendas.
7. Observe, appreciate, acknowledge good work with appropriate affirmation.

MAPPING THE PLAN

The 5 Components and 7 Attributes of G.R.A.C.E.

Diagram center labels: R Results, G Goodwill, A Authenticity, C Connectivity, E Empowerment

As you "map" the plan for this relationship, consider how you will accomplish, in tangible ways, the 7 attributes for each of the 5 components of G.R.A.C.E. at Work model, as summarized above. Jot your ideas on the worksheet on the next page, or construct your own larger worksheet.

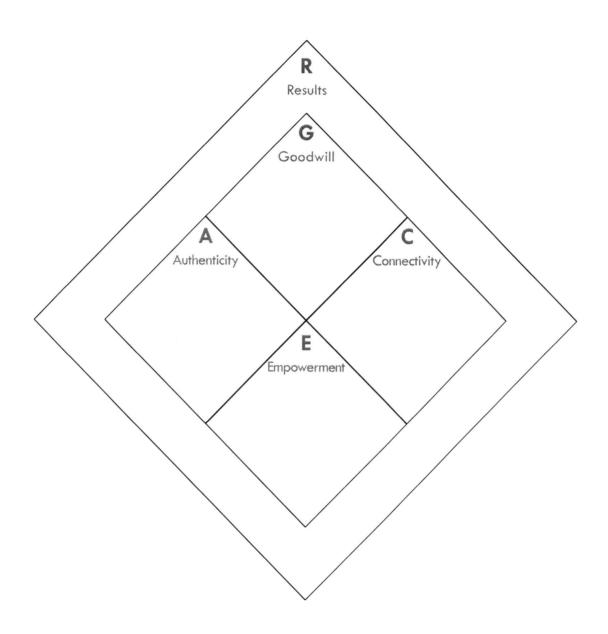

Exactly HOW will I employ the 7 attributes of the
5 G.R.A.C.E. Components in this relationship?

2. RELATIONSHIP DIAGNOSTIC TOOL

This worksheet is designed to allow you to compare the answers each person provides on the previous worksheet (Mapping the Relationships for Success). This allows both people to see gaps, misunderstandings, and opportunities for greater G.R.A.C.E. Sit down together to evaluate personal comments on the previous worksheet. *Combine* the responses of each party on this master diagnostic worksheet. *Compare* the responses. How do they differ? How do they compare? What gaps exist? How do these gaps need to be filled?

INDIVIDUAL A	G.R.A.C.E COMPONENT AND ATTRIBUTES	INDIVIDUAL B
	GOODWILL	
	1. Positive attitude/manner, actions driven by positive intent.	
	2. Refrain from judgments.	
	3. Genuinely desire well-being of others, no hidden motives.	
	4. Generous spirit, freely give without condition.	
	5. Excuse offense without payment, no hard feelings.	
	6. At peace with "what is," harmony in relationships.	
	7. Thankful, express gratitude to, and for, others.	
	RESULTS	
	1. Know why we are doing what we are doing.	
	2. Know intended results, have ownership.	
	3. Create/improve value, future, for all parties.	
	4. Know what other parties believe to be true.	
	5. Contribute, committed, to relationship in mutual parts.	
	6. Strategy (action plans) to accomplish desired outcomes.	
	7. Measure performance against action plans, make changes.	

INDIVIDUAL A	G.R.A.C.E COMPONENT AND ATTRIBUTES	INDIVIDUAL B
	AUTHENTICITY	
	1. Truthful about feelings, thoughts, desires.	
	2. Unpretentious, modest, not given to pride or arrogance.	
	3. Accountable, answerable, reliable, responsible.	
	4. Reveal real me, no pretense, accessible, visible, clear.	
	5. Consistently authentic principles, actions, behavior.	
	6. Confident of self/others, faith all will act appropriately.	
	7. Leverage strengths of self/others, manage weaknesses.	
	CONNECTIVITY	
	1. Awake, conscious of self/others, alert to possibilities.	
	2. Affirm others, express approval/ validity, confirm value.	
	3. Recognize, sensitive to feelings/ thoughts/experiences of others.	
	4. Savvy with people, know-how of human dynamics.	
	5. Collaborator, desire to "co-labor," align to produce greater results.	
	6. Innovatively connect with others to achieve goals.	
	7. Repair, recreate "disconnects," openness, no hidden agendas.	
	EMPOWERMENT	
	1. Take first step(s) necessary to make something better.	
	2. Knowledge of system, understand impacts of actions/processes.	
	3. Careful, efficient handling of resources, always maximizing.	
	4. Encourage growth of employees through development opportunities.	
	5. Experiment to discover better means to achieve desired outcomes.	
	6. View things/people from different perspectives, openness.	
	7. Observe, appreciate, acknowledge good work with affirmation.	

3. RELATIONSHIP ACTION PLAN

This worksheet allows both parties to create a mutually agreeable action plan, a development plan for the relationship, which identifies and states specific actions for both, particularly as they relate to the 7 attributes of the G.R.A.C.E. components. Make a plan to bring this relationship into alignment and balance. In each individual's column, list the behaviors and actions for which each is responsible in this plan. Be brief, but specific.

INDIVIDUAL A	G.R.A.C.E COMPONENT AND ATTRIBUTES	INDIVIDUAL B
	GOODWILL	
	1. Positive attitude/manner, actions driven by positive intent.	
	2. Refrain from judgments.	
	3. Genuinely desire well-being of others, no hidden motives.	
	4. Generous spirit, freely give without condition.	
	5. Excuse offense without payment, no hard feelings.	
	6. At peace with "what is," harmony in relationships.	
	7. Thankful, express gratitude to, and for, others.	
	RESULTS	
	1. Know why we are doing what we are doing.	
	2. Know intended results, have ownership.	
	3. Create/improve value, future, for all parties.	
	4. Know what other parties believe to be true.	
	5. Contribute, committed, to relationship in mutual parts.	
	6. Strategy (action plans) to accomplish desired outcomes.	
	7. Measure performance against action plans, make changes.	

INDIVIDUAL A	G.R.A.C.E COMPONENT AND ATTRIBUTES	INDIVIDUAL B
	AUTHENTICITY	
	1. Truthful about feelings, thoughts, desires.	
	2. Unpretentious, modest, not given to pride or arrogance.	
	3. Accountable, answerable, reliable, responsible.	
	4. Reveal real me, no pretense, accessible, visible, clear.	
	5. Consistently authentic principles, actions, behavior.	
	6. Confident of self/others, faith all will act appropriately.	
	7. Leverage strengths of self/others, manage weaknesses.	
	CONNECTIVITY	
	1. Awake, conscious of self/others, alert to possibilities.	
	2. Affirm others, express approval/ validity, confirm value.	
	3. Recognize, sensitive to feelings/ thoughts/experiences of others.	
	4. Savvy with people, know-how of human dynamics.	
	5. Collaborator, desire to "co-labor," align to produce greater results.	
	6. Innovatively connect with others to achieve goals.	
	7. Repair, recreate "disconnects," openness, no hidden agendas.	
	EMPOWERMENT	
	1. Take first step(s) necessary to make something better.	
	2. Knowledge of system, understand impacts of actions/processes.	
	3. Careful, efficient handling of resources, always maximizing.	
	4. Encourage growth of employees through development opportunities.	
	5. Experiment to discover better means to achieve desired outcomes.	
	6. View things/people from different perspectives, openness.	
	7. Observe, appreciate, acknowledge good work with affirmation.	

Profiles in G.R.A.C.E.

Real People Practicing G.R.A.C.E. at Work

Setting an example is not the main means
of influencing another, it is the only means.
— Albert Einstein

THROUGHOUT *my leadership journey I have been privileged and honored to know and work with a number of people who are great practitioners of the G.R.A.C.E. at Work model. I have watched them put this model to work, and I have been gratified to observe the results. Some have used the model purposely, changing their leadership behaviors to adapt to G.R.A.C.E. in the workplace. Some inherently are gifted in these areas. All have benefited, and all are growing. These are real people in real companies, experiencing real results from G.R.A.C.E. I want to share these people (and one organization) with you, in part to offer "living proof" of the veracity of G.R.A.C.E. at Work, but also in part to serve as my personal thanks to these people who have also enabled me to play in a bigger space.*

Larry Small
Pfizer Pharmaceuticals (formerly Wyeth)
Senior Vice President

LARRY SMALL knows all about playing in a bigger space. I coached Larry for two years, through one of the biggest transformations of his career, using the *G.R.A.C.E. at Work* model. His company was purchased by Pfizer Pharmaceuticals, and this former "science and research" guy had to redesign himself as he moved into an entirely new position. Because of his science background, and relative comfort zone in that area, Larry previously focused only on what was happening in science and research. Tucked away in their relative "niches" sometimes different functions don't always understand what the other one is all about. In his new position, however, Larry knew that if he was going to be successful, if his entire group was going to be successful, he had to redefine who he was personally, and what his group could do to add value to the organization. Larry was instrumental in, and pleased to see that all of his team members were also promoted and assigned important roles in the new organization. Together, however, they needed go from having identities as scientists, to developing business savvy, and understanding consumer wants and needs. In essence, they would be managing their own "franchise" of sorts. Larry wasn't just a scientist now, he was a leader of scientists. He had to grow personally, and authentically.

"I began to see myself as an ambassador for my R&D function within the organization. I didn't spend as much time focused narrowly on the science. I had to see myself as the chief sales and marketing office of my area, much like an entrepreneur. I talked, I listened a lot, and I waited. I was building relationships while we were refining our strategy. Nothing happens without these relationships in place. A senior team member reminded us wisely that we have to believe in who we are, what we want to do (both as individuals and as a team) in order to achieve success. We have to be authentic, empower others to be authentic, and build authentic relationships."

Much of Pfizer's work is done in partnership with other organizations across the globe. Trust and shared purpose enabled Larry's team to build an environment where others were empowered. He had to build an ongoing dialogue with customers, encourage the rise in his group's ability to produce, and keep his clients engaged. There were many players on this team, spread out across the world, and all of them had to be engaged, empowered and integrally involved. Larry became a broker of ideas, keeping himself open to new possibilities, fresh and current with outside dialogue between all groups. He not only brokered ideas, he brokered relationships. Larry was undergoing a huge metamorphosis, utilizing and realizing the power of G.R.A.C.E. at Work. He began to fully understand the difference between transactional as opposed to transformational relationships, and the difference between compliance driven and commitment driven partnerships.

As Larry grew into this "bigger space," others saw the shift in him and his group and they provided more opportunities to initiate things and deliver. He actively worked at building a vital network of connections around the world, all achieved through relationships that empower and have trust and shared purpose.

Larry remembers one of the most impactful moments of his leadership, when he realized that one of the roles in his team was going to be eliminated. However, this colleague was offered another position, but she wasn't very happy about it, and did not fully understand the ramifications of its possibilities. Larry empowered her to understand the scope and the potential of this new role, and she became very engaged. This leader spoke several different languages, and was proficient in managing a conversation that has technical, regulatory and medical considerations – very vital and valued skills in a global marketplace. With Larry's help, she began to see the impact she could have, and the exciting challenges she would face. When Larry saw the change in this former teammate, he began to really get excited about the concept of leadership. Helping people reframe how they see themselves and the way in which they interact in the world is key to playing in a bigger space, and Larry loved this part of leadership.

> Helping people reframe how they see themselves and the way in which they intereact in the world is key to playing in a bigger space, and Larry loved this part of leadership.

Larry Small has since retired. His greatest realization was that he was more than just a research pharmacist who made some scientific contribution. He became a leader. He sees his greatest accomplishments, however, more in the advancement of his team members, and in the building of solid connections that advanced his organization into the bigger future they saw together. He fostered the kind of collaboration and empowerment his people and his organization needed to play in a much bigger space. He retired knowing he was truly a leader, not just a chemist, and that his leadership would live on in his people, and in his organization.

It was a wonderful experience to watch Larry incorporate the sound practices of *G.R.A.C.E. at Work* to enable himself, his team and his organization to play in a much bigger space. Larry is one of those people I have worked with that I can proudly point to and say, *"It works!"*

Earl Devaney
Inspector General, US Department of the Interior
Overseer, American Recovery and Reinvestment Act

I FIRST MET Earl Devaney at Georgetown University. He came through the coaching program when I was Co-Program Director. I taught a class he was in, and came to know this remarkable guy. If I had to name one person who had an unwavering eye on desired results, and incorporated every facet and concept of *G.R.A.C.E. at Work* in order to achieve them, it would be Earl.

Earl didn't really have to go back to school. He graduated many years before from college and immediately entered the Secret Service under the Nixon administration. At the time of his retirement from the Secret Service in 1991, Devaney was Special Agent-in-Charge of the Fraud Division and was recognized as an international expert in white collar crime. Since that time Earl Devaney has become a veteran public official dedicated to accountability and transparency in government. President Clinton appointed Devaney as the Inspector General of the Department of the Interior in 1999. During his tenure at the Office of Inspector General (OIG), he oversaw the public corruption investigations that led to the convictions of Washington lobbyist Jack Abramoff and Interior Deputy Secretary Steven Griles. He also presided over the oil and gas investigations that engulfed the Minerals Management Service from 2007 to 2009. Before this appointment, Devaney spent eight years as the Director of the Office of Criminal Enforcement, Forensics and Training for the Environmental Protection Agency. In that job, he supervised all of EPA's criminal investigators, the agency's forensics laboratory, and its enforcement training institute. In 1998, he received the Meritorious Presidential Rank Award for outstanding government service.

> If I had to name one person who had an unwavering eye on desired results... it would be Earl.

Most recently, Earl E. Devaney was appointed by President Obama to serve as overseer of the American Recovery and Reinvestment Act of 2009, which is charged with overseeing spending under the $787 billion recovery (stimulus) program. Twelve Inspectors General from various federal agencies serve with Chairman Devaney. This Board issues reports to the President and Congress, and also maintains the website (Recovery.gov) so the American people can see how Recovery money is being distributed by federal agencies and how the funds are being used by the recipients. Earl has been dubbed the "Stimulus Watchdog."

The reason Earl was back in the classroom at Georgetown is because he has an enormous commitment to leadership – his own. This is a man who takes leadership development, both his own and that of those he leads, to heart. He constantly searches for ways to improve his own game, and provide better leadership for others. Earl doggedly and consistently pushes out the boundaries to achieve greater and greater results.

As the Inspector General at the Department of Interior and earlier in his career in other federal jobs, he had continually raised concerns about the lack of transparency and accountability in government. Now, he is part of an historic exercise in transparency and accountability. Devaney was focused on results, but knew he needed the right connections, and a way to empower everyone to reach those authentic results. *"I borrowed people from across the government ... I ended up with a lot of good people. I'm told it normally takes two years to get an agency going. ...we created an open process and turned it into a 32 day process."* Earl Devaney knew he could do the job, but he also knew it would require great relationships and unwavering focus on results to get where they wanted, and *needed*, to be.

Coming out of the Secret Service, which by its very nature promotes a suspicious, critical eye and lack of trust in people and life in general, surprisingly Devaney is a man of huge goodwill. He knew the Georgetown program would help him, and smooth out any remaining rough edges in leadership. His role as the so-called "Stimulus Watchdog" is a high risk venture. He knew if "he pushed the button and something didn't happen," he, and his team, would have been deep in the proverbial doo-doo. Earl brought organization, integrity and results to this historic venture.

One thing I know about Earl is that he is going to pull out all the stops to make something happen. In his words, *"Once they gave me the wherewithal to go ahead, I went full bore. My goal was the best obtainable version of the truth."* Earl never took his eyes off the desired results, and they became bigger, because Devaney practices, in earnest, *G.R.A.C.E at Work*. Earl is man who achieves big results.

Christine M. Wahl

Founder
Georgetown University Leadership Coaching Certificate Program

IT IS APPARENT that Chris Wahl was born to coach. With over 20 years of experience, she has coached long before coaching became a viable and credible discipline in organization development. Her coaching practice spans numerous industries and is focused on coaching leaders and their teams. She is dedicated to helping leaders and executives develop a way of being and acting that motivates, inspires, and gets results.

Prior to Wahl's current position at Georgetown, she directed the GU Organization Development Certificate Program. She holds a B.A. in Psychology and an M.A.Ed. in Counseling. Wahl has a string of coaching certifications (including MCC, from the International Coach Federation, ICF), has authored a number of books and is a frequent contributor to journals and speaks regularly at coaching and leadership conferences. If anyone has ever been qualified to be a coach, it's Chris. Perhaps the greatest single competency that truly identifies Chris as a coach, however, is her amazing ability to *empower others to play in a bigger space*. In her role as coach, she "holds the space for people" as she says. She sees where potential can lead, and empowers others to achieve that bigger space. She plants this process on a firm foundation of goodwill, taking the most positive approach, free of judgment, and open to emerging possibilities.

> Perhaps the greatest single competency... is her amazing ability to empower others to play in a bigger space.

I have been a personal recipient of Chris' goodwill, and incredible connectivity and empowerment. She gave me an opportunity to shepherd people through the Georgetown program for three years, and then appointed me as the Co-Program Director. Chris had me in the roles of learning circle advisor, instructor and then co-program director, so I would have every opportunity to learn and grow, playing in a much bigger space each time. I recently had the privilege of being a contributing author in her latest book (*On Becoming A Leadership Coach: A Holistic Approach to Coaching Excellence*). She doesn't just help people grow into and play in *their* bigger spaces, she shares her own.

Chris has an innate way of understanding where people are, what challenges would help them grow, and how she can empower them. She is enormously loaded with goodwill. Throughout her long academic career, Chris Wahl has found great success, and has greatly influenced both students and staff to reach higher and play in a bigger space. Much of Chris' success is due to the fact that she actively and consistently practices the concepts of *G.R.A.C.E. at Work*. The other part of it is her intuitive and insightful sense about people. People feel empowered, and step onto higher planes and into bigger spaces when Chris is around.

Marty (Martha) Wilson
Vice President IT, Capital One

E MPOWERMENT is a really big deal for Martha Wilson. Marty says that her leadership journey actually began at a young age playing sports. Highly competitive, Wilson is also very much a team player, and is a great cheerleader for all her teammates. She remembers playing on teams where she was sometimes the weakest and sometimes the strongest player – the bench warmer or the team captain. Marty says she realized early on that regardless of her position or skills, she could add the most value by understanding her unique role and celebrating it, as well as the roles of others, hence empowering everyone into achieving better results. She believes that her sporting experiences helped her become an effective leader today, managing teams in a business environment.

I coached with Marty for almost two years, and was privileged to see her in action, and to experience firsthand how her desire to play in a bigger space was not just for herself, but for everyone around her. When she was in the Director role, she found herself leading a very diverse team of people, all of them older than herself and some by as many as 30 years. She built trust among this group by relying on their unique knowledge and skills, and developing empowering relationships with each of them. This wasn't always easy, and in fact involved having to be very authentic and honest in the termination of one gentleman who had been in his role for 20 years. Even in this difficult and sad situation, the employee actually thanked Marty for being honest, forthcoming, and approaching even the hardest tasks with goodwill. Her most difficult role, Wilson acknowledges that this is where she learned the most about leadership and about herself. *"I had to operate from a stance of goodwill to be able to exercise the demands of my role while building credibility and trust for the future."*

> She might be fiercely competitive, but this leader is also the poster child for G.R.A.C.E.

Marty was promoted to Vice President of End User Services at Capital One Financial. She saw this as a great opportunity to help her team and Capital One associates "play in a bigger space," and realize greater results. Her team provides IT solutions to help people get the most out of their technology. *"I believe that if I can empower my team they can empower their customers."* She has a penchant for giving people room to grow and perform.

I have often wondered how being competitive can couple with empowerment in an authentic way that yields results. Martha Wilson embodies this concept. I believe it is her desire to play in a bigger and bigger space, and bring her entire team along with her, that enables her to effectively empower others to achieve as well, despite her competitive nature. Marty has a great heart for people, is full of genuine goodwill, and is an interesting and successful blend of empowerment, results and authenticity. She continues to grow her leadership competencies, but she is a natural and easy practitioner of every component of the *G.R.A.C.E. at Work* model. She might be fiercely competitive, but this leader is also the poster child for G.R.A.C.E.

Transportation Insight, LLC

I WAS INTRODUCED to this unique company by one of its former Vice Presidents, a friend and colleague. Transportation Insight, LLC is a private company that uses analytical mathematical models to help figure out how to best optimize shipping in the trucking industry. It was founded in 1995 as a small consulting company but rapid growth has skyrocketed them to a position as a nationwide lead logistics provider with multiple accolades and accomplishments. They were recognized as one of the Grant Thornton North Carolina Top 100 Private Companies, and have been recognized for four years in a row in *Inc. Magazine's* 2011 Exclusive List of America's Fastest-Growing Private Companies. Today, Transportation Insight has 42 branch offices throughout the U. S., and two headquarter facilities in Hickory, NC.

When we observe companies like this one, companies that begin small and morph quickly into "bigger spaces," it begs the questions of *why* and *how*. Every entrepreneur, every business owner and every leader would like to know the answers and reasons behind to the success of Transportation Insight, LLC. For this humble group, the answer is simple—a strong belief in shared mutual purpose, and shared mutual results. Everyone wins. The principals of this company consider themselves stewards of all their resources, and create unique opportunities of value for both customers and employees. They have created an interesting and inviting territory of equally "shared space."

Dr. Paul Thompson, CEO, says the company has a commitment to excellence. This isn't just a marketing piece or a nice tagline. He says the heart of their success is the simple fact that *people do business with people*. They understand that growth depends on powerful and productive relationships that have mutually shared interest and purpose, and are based in trust. This company develops trust and kinship in the marketplace, cultivating relationships that lead everyone into those bigger spaces. The founders and employees of this rapidly growing company know the best way to do this, to keep playing in bigger spaces, is through goodwill, focus on results, authenticity, connectivity and mutual empowerment to achieve mutual results.

People do business with people is one of the greatest arguments for practicing the concepts of *G.R.A.C.E. at Work*, the model for powerful and productive relationships. Wherever there are people, there are relationships. And when people want powerful results, they need powerful relationships. It really is very simple, yet so many people and businesses fail to see this critical ingredient to success and growth.

This company also believes and practices a concept seemingly in opposition to standard business practice. Whether you wish to label it *"you reap what you sow,"* or *"what goes around comes around,"* Transportation Insight strongly believes in giving back to the community, and empowers their employees to do humanitarian projects, and make foreign mission trips. While these will have lasting benefit to those who receive from such endeavors, the firm believes that their employees also experience profound leadership development, learn how to keep things in proper perspective and remember the bigger picture. I'm not sure if Transportation Insight has even heard of the *G.R.A.C.E. at Work* model, but from what I have seen, they certainly practice it. Perhaps that is because this model captures the essence of human dynamics, the way people relate and work best together to achieve the greatest results, in the largest "space" possible.

It is tremendously gratifying to observe a company such as this that so obviously employs what G.R.A.C.E. contains, to achieve such success. If they continue these practices, I have no doubt they will continue to grow into bigger and bigger spaces.

Concluding Thoughts...

IT IS MY HOPE and desire that you are able to employ the *G.R.A.C.E. at Work* model, as all these leaders have done, and realize and celebrate the results that follow. Wherever you are in relationship, whatever the nature of that relationship, this model will allow you to play in a much bigger space. It works every time. If you honestly employ the model, you will honestly achieve more productive relationships which will ensure greater results. There isn't too much in life that carries a guarantee of satisfaction, but I believe this model will bring that, and more, to the authentic practitioner of *G.R.A.C.E. at Work*.

Some might think that all the assessments and exercises — this kind of effort —is not necessary, or even somewhat elementary and a waste of time. It is a guarantee, however, that if both parties put the effort into doing the exercises and assessments and then advance into meaningful and productive dialogue regarding the results, the relationship can only be strengthened, and sometimes in ways that are surprising, and amazing.

As you continue to work on embracing the *G.R.A.C.E. at Work* concepts, components and attributes, you will experience amazing transformations both in yourself, and in those with whom you work or are in relationship. These principles apply to every relationship, not just those in the work or business environment. I encourage you to make the same application to home relationships, or various other groups with whom you associate or work. As you experience these transformations, I would very much like to hear your stories and your personal and professional experiences with *G.R.A.C.E. at Work*. Please feel free to contact me with questions, comments and definitely your triumphs as a result of application of this model.

Dr. Eric deNijs
Executive Coach
eric@ericdenijs.com

Acknowledgements

The People Behind G.R.A.C.E. at Work

"Sometimes our light goes out but is blown into flame by another human being. Each of us owes deepest thanks to those who have rekindled this light."
— *Albert Schweitzer*

MY DEEPEST THANKS go to my family. First and foremost thank you and love go to my wife Nancy, who has now supported me and survived two big projects, and whose love has enabled me to play in my bigger space. She is the consummate mate and I have been extremely blessed to have her as my wife. To Paul, Melissa, and Danny de Nijs who have been extremely supportive even though their patience for the G.R.A.C.E. project has necessitated summoning a load of goodwill to see us all through the end of it.

Thanks to my Dad and Mom, Paul and Joan de Nijs, who came to this country after surviving the horrors of World War II in both theaters, so they could play in a bigger space. Their sacrifice and their encouragement to take advantage of what this country had to offer and really realize its full potential has been a great example of *G.R.A.C.E at Work*. Although my dad came here with only two suitcases and $40 to pursue his dream, his goodwill and optimism was sufficient to overcome a lot of obstacles. I can still hear him saying, *"Keep moving forward. No matter what, keep moving forward."* Many thanks also to my other Dad and Mom, Dale and Ruth Penning, whose love and support reinforces my belief that I have the best in-laws in the whole wide world. Thanks to my brothers Kurt (and Allison) and Roger (and Sheri) and my sister Kim (and Chris) who have always been there when I needed them.

Much appreciation to my colleagues from the Georgetown University Leadership Coaching Program, Chris Wahl, Frank Ball Neil Stroul, Randy Chittum, LeeAnn Wurster-Naefe, Sheryl Philips, Sue McLeod, Karen Gravenstine, Kate Ebner, Pat Mathews, Julie Shows, Jennifer Sinek, Hany Malik, Roz Kay and Jennifer Whitcomb. Their friendship and coaching presence has served as a great collective role model and a source of encouragement along the way. Chris Wahl offered me the opportunity to be a part of the Georgetown faculty at a time while I was still growing as a coach and has challenged and supported me in ways that are magnificently G.R.A.C.E.-ful. Thank you so very much!

To my friends Jim Quigg, Gray Oliver, Dan Erhard, Wayne Hast, Ken Young, Andrew Lohr, Peter Murchie, Christian Kubista, Alan DeCerff,

Doug and Amy Byl, and Dan and Julie Post, thanks for always sharing your kindness and support in ways and times that are and were inspiring.

To Kathy Heywood, whose friendship, coaching, editing, and unbelievable patience with me and the project made this a reality. Her perseverance and "Kathy Dust" is unequaled. Her commitment and dedication has helped me play in my bigger space.

Finally, I'd like to acknowledge one of the greatest examples of helping others play in bigger space. Out on the rough sea, in the middle of the night, Peter called out to Christ, who had demonstrated the art and possibility of walking on water. Attending to the voices of both victory and retreat, Peter sought an invitation from Christ to step out of the boat and to come join him on the water. Playing in a bigger space meant stepping outside of his comfort zone in the realm of possibilities. The possibilities? He might walk or he might sink, but until he put his total trust and confidence in Christ, in the relationship that had grown over the months, he would not step out of the boat. Trusting in the goodwill of his friend, he stepped out of the boat and even though he slipped beneath the waves at one point when he took his eyes off Jesus, he ended up walking on water because of the love and goodwill of Christ. G.R.A.C.E. *at Work* is about building powerful relationships based on goodwill and trust, thereby helping ourselves and others to step outside our individual boats.

With my deepest gratitude to all who made this book possible,
Eric de Nijs

About the Author

"I love being a writer.
What I can't stand is the paperwork."

—*Peter De Vries (a fellow Calvin College alumni)*

DR. ERIC DE NIJS is an Executive Coach specializing in leadership development and helping leaders improve their leadership effectiveness, leadership presence, and ability to engage their life passion. His specialties include coaching and training for individuals and teams, improved organizational performance, strategic planning, communicating with confidence and creating greater stakeholder engagement, leadership presence, new leader assimilation, high performance teams, influence without authority, and transformational relationships to achieve greater results.

> Great leadership is not about having all the answers. Great leadership is about helping others increase their capacity to contribute and add value.

Eric believes that strong alliances, powerful conversations and learning are at the heart of great leadership. Great leadership is not about having all the answers. Great leadership is about helping others increase their capacity to contribute and add value. His approach to coaching centers on assisting his clients to create catalyst for personal transformation that equips them to engage their passion, leverage their strengths, and overcome the obstacles that stand in the way of their greater success. He positions the coaching relationship as a learning space for clients to think out loud, to see themselves from a different perspective, and to learn new things away from the grind of the regular work routine. Eric encourages his clients to commit to self-reflection and the practice of new skills and perspectives that will create the breakthrough required for today's results and the capacity for tomorrow's success. *G.R.A.C.E. at Work* was developed as a result of many years of corporate experience, internal and external coaching and showing leaders and organizations how to "play in a bigger space."

Over the past 25 years Eric has worked with executives in organizational effectiveness, continuous improvement, and management development in diverse kinds of businesses including financial services, marketing, manufacturing, healthcare, food processing, food and beverage distribution, defense contractors, heavy construction, fund raising, and not-for-profit organizations. His clients include Capital One, Wyeth Pharmaceutical, The

E-Groupe *(engineering consulting)*, the Office of the Inspector General for the United States Department of the Interior, Recovery and Transparency Board, Arlington County Government, the FDIC, Fortune 200 Company, and a national health care provider. He has served as an examiner for the quality award programs of both the State of Michigan and the State of Virginia, and President of the Board of Directors for the Inner City Christian Federation, a housing ministry for low income families.

Dr. de Nijs is also a Co-Program Director and instructor for the Georgetown University Leadership Program, helping prepare the next generation of leaders and coaches, and a contributing author to *On Becoming a Leadership Coach* (Palgrave, August 2008). He holds a doctorate in Human Resources Development, Master's Degrees both in Counseling and in Higher Education, a Bachelor's Degree in Psychology, and certifications in coaching from both Georgetown University and the International Coaching Federation. Eric is also certified in a variety of assessment tools, including the DISC profile and the Leadership Circle 360 instrument.

Eric and his wife Nancy make their home in Richmond, Virginia. They have three children and enjoy camping, hiking and traveling – and along the way, showing the keys to "playing in a bigger" space at work, at home and anywhere in between.

"Lists really get to the heart of what it is we need to do to get through another day on this planet."

— *Sociologist Scott Schaffer*

Illustrations, Charts, Graphics, Worksheets

CPSIA information can be obtained at www.ICGtesting.com
Printed in the USA
LVOW11s1934031113

359807LV00007B/234/P